Baedeker

Vienna

www.baedeker.com

Verlag Karl Baedeker

SIGHTSEEING HIGHLIGHTS ✶ ✶

Vienna is not only »Sisi« and Wiener Schnitzel. It is true that both are inseparably associated with the city, but there is a lot more to be discovered in this capital on the Danube. We have put together a list of the best sights that shouldn't be missed.

Artistically crafted cameos
like the Gemma Augustea can be found in the Kunsthistorisches Museum

✶ ✶ Hofburg
»Sisi« was not the only one to live in this palace, which is comprised of a total of 18 buildings. ▶ page 198

✶ ✶ Silberkammer (Imperial Silver Collection)
See how the ruling family set their dining table. ▶ page 202

✶ ✶ Albertina
The world's largest graphic collection can be found in the newly re-opened Albertina. The Habsburg state rooms are really worth seeing. ▶ page 159

✶ ✶ Kaiserappartements (Imperial Apartments)
See the opulent chambers of Elizabeth and her husband. ▶ page 203

✶ ✶ Belvedere
The copy of the Palace of Versailles is a crowd pleaser. ▶ page 170

Magnificent residences
like the Belvedere recall Vienna's glorious past

Rich in detail
After elaborate reconstruction, the Albertina has been restored to its original splendour of 1822

Artistic Pride
Anton Pilgrim immortalized himself not once, but twice. The portrait on the organ's base bears the date and a monogram.

✶✶ Schatzkammer (Treasury)
Objects of inestimable value are on display in the Hofburg. ► page 203

✶✶ Spanische Reitschule (Spanish Riding School)
Watch the world famous Lipizzaner stallions perform. ► page 206

✶✶ Österreichische Nationalbibliothek (Austrian National Library)
One of the world's most important libraries with collections dating back to the 14th century ► page 208

✶✶ Karlsplatz
The square is dominated by the Karls-kirche, Fischer von Erlach's Baroque masterpiece. ► page 223

✶✶ Kunsthistorisches Museum (Museum of Art History)
Works by Raphael and Titian have found a home here. ► page 232

✶✶ Museum Quarter
You will find innumerable museums covering a diversity of subjects here. ► page 259

✶✶ Naturhistorisches Museum (Natural History Museum)
If you ever wanted to know what a bouquet of 2,102 gems looks like, stop by and take a look in this museum. ► page 263

✶✶ Schloss Schönbrunn
A place that breathes history like few others in Europe. ► page 274

✶✶ Staatsoper (State Opera)
Only the best in the world are asked to appear here. ► page 287

✶✶ Stephansdom (St Stephen's Cathedral)
The »Steffl«, with its 137m/450ft high tower, is Austria's best-known symbol. ► page 290

Heroes
Archduke Karl succeeded in defeating Napoleon at the Battle of Aspern. In gratitude he was honoured with a statue on Heldenplatz

BAEDEKER'S BEST TIPS

Knowing a city's highlights is important for a successful visit, and discovering a little more is always fun: Baedeker's best tips for Vienna will get you ahead of the pack.

🔲 Fuchs Museum in the Wagner Villa
You can kill two birds with one stone when you visit the former private villa of the pioneer of modern architecture.
► page 50

🔲 Vienna, City of Jazz
There is a city in the southern USA that remains ahead, but Vienna is catching up fast! ► page 57

🔲 Musical Shrine
Where did Beethoven actually write some of his symphonies? Read about it on
► page 59

🔲 Vienna nights
The city's nights are long. Find out what's going on in Otto Wagner's Stadtbahnbögen at the Gürtel on ► page 69

🔲 Baby Breakfast
Entrust your children into the care of experienced childminders and relax.
► page 83

🔲 Sociable Campus
Why can't the students withstand the temptations of the former general hospital? We give the answer on ► page 92

🔲 Hot and Good
Never mind what the tasty sausages are called where you come from, in Vienna they are called Frankfurters. Where it is worth buying some, you'll find out on
► page 161

🔲 Literature for Free
German-language authors in a marathon reading of their own works in the Burgtheater ► page 180

Vienna is musically way ahead,
and not just in classical music

Endless Variety:
There are many ways to prepare a cup of coffee, but the accompanying glass of water is obligatory

Sweet Temptation
Who can resist a piece of Sacher Torte?

A Night on the Town
Vienna's »Bermuda Triangle« isn't the only place where the nights are long

Jeans or Black Tie
No matter what you put on, there is no lack of a chance to party

Artistic Upheaval at the beginning of the last century: Klimt's portrait of Emilie Flöge
► page 34

BACKGROUND

The Wiener Werkstätte made it their goal to produce ceramics that everyone could afford
► page 47

PRACTICALITIES

Otto Wagner's Kirche am Steinhof made him one of the pioneers of modern architecture
► page 230

Devotional objects belonging to Empress Elizabeth, alias »Sisi«, can be found in the Hofburg
► page 62

The styles of every era are represented in the architecture of the Ringstrasse: the State Opera is historically inspired by the Renaissance
► page 288

A magnificent garden connects the Upper and Lower Belvedere
► page 170

Background

THE CITY ON THE DANUBE
LOOKS BACK ON OVER 2,000
YEARS OF HISTORY, BUT IT WAS
A LONG AND TURBULENT JOURNEY
FROM THE ROMANS AND THE HABSBURG
EMPERORS TO THE DEMOCRACY OF TODAY.

LOOKING BACK TO THE FUTURE

Vienna, the European capital that immediately brings to mind Mozart, hand kissing and opera balls is supposed to be a city changing with the times. Hard to imagine with a nation that cannot conceal its sense of etiquette, that likes to make a show of noncommittal courtesy and that prides itself on a history during which it was the focal point of an empire for centuries.

But tradition is only one facet of the Danube metropolis, progress is another. For example, the modern staging of plays at the Burgtheater (National Theatre) is either euphorically accepted or torn apart by the public. The buildings of the internationally recognized architect Hans Hollein unleash long-lasting discussions about contemporary

architecture, and Austrian literature was not only significant during the *Fin de Siècle*, but can also demonstrate success today. Elfriede Jelinek won the Nobel Prize for Literature in 2004. Since the fall of the Iron Curtain, Vienna has also become a popular travel destination for Eastern European countries, giving the city a more cosmopolitan atmosphere.

Myths surrounding Empress Elizabeth who, as »Sisi«, mirrored the Habsburg monarchy at the *Fin de Siècle*, and for whom a special Sisi museum was established in the Hofburg in time for her 150th wedding anniversary, contribute to the popular

Always in a good mood: *ticket sellers in front of the Stephansdom*

appeal of the city on the Danube, and Vienna's substantial art collections are also a strong incentive for the visitor. The Kunsthistorisches Museum (Art History Museum) established by Gottfried Semper at the end of the 19th century, during the construction of the Ringstrasse, holds one of the most important art collections in the world. No doubt the thieves who stole Benvenuto Cellini's golden salt-cellar in a cloak-and-dagger operation in 2003 – once a highlight of the Sculpture and Decorative Arts collection – thought so too.

The Liechtenstein Collection has returned after its exile in Vaduz, and Rubens, Raphael, Rembrandt und others compete side-by-side for the favour of the visitor in the freshly renovated Liechtenstein Palace. A new cultural complex has also been created with the conversion of the Baroque imperial stables into the Museum Quarter,

Relaxation
First for a simple meal accompanied by refreshing wine are the Heurigen taverns and their gardens

Climb aboard
Fiacres offer tours, and not only tourists with tired legs take advantage of their service

Empire
Many monumental buildings recall the former Austro-Hungarian Empire. The sphinx in the garden gazes with a knowing look

To top it all
Towers and domes characterize the imperial city

Entertainment
There is much to see and experience in Vienna. Alongside traditional concerts, operas and musicals, the street life is also enticing

Democracy
Pallas Athena, the Goddess of Wisdom, ensures that it is upheld, standing in front of parliament

which not only houses the first class art collections of the Leopold Museum, the MUMOK and the Kunsthalle, but is also a favourite meeting place for the cultural scene. The Albertina has become one of Vienna's most popular museums after its almost ten-year renovation, where not only the exhibits attract, but also the palatial Habsburg state rooms, that are open to the public for the first time. The *Prunkräume* (prunk = splendour in German) certainly live up to their name. Meanwhile, at the Museum für Angewandte Kunst (Museum for Applied Arts) – MAK for short – contemporary artists have created a successful symbiosis of Viennese Historicism and contemporary art in their designs for the exhibition halls.

Vienna's calling card, however, remains the Ringstrasse, one of the most magnificent boulevards created in Europe since the middle of the 19th century. It is an architectural eulogy to the past: the opera house recalls an era that had already come to an end with the completion of the Ringstrasse; Classical Antiquity complemented by elements of the Italian Andrea Palladio provided the architectural framework for parliament; and just as the temple frontage of the parliament building is meant to recall the world's first democracy, so the town hall recalls the great bourgeois tradition of Flemish medieval architecture. Finally, the university built by Heinrich Ferstel takes up Italian Renaissance designs, while also paying homage to the Louvre, which had been recently completed.

How about food and drink? Well, the tradition is the same as ever: the most popular place to meet is the coffee house. Today the famous old addresses are augmented by espresso bars and minimalist clubs decked out in polished wood and glass, but modern tastes have not changed the essential experience, which is to find a place where the everyday can be left behind, where you can meet friends or just go to read a book.

Equestrian statue of Joseph II at the Hofburg: *he is popularly called the emperor of the people*

Facts

Here you will find background information on Vienna. Current information on politics, economy and transportation will help you get to know this beautiful Baroque city, and the insider knowledge provided will ensure your visit will be an unforgettable experience.

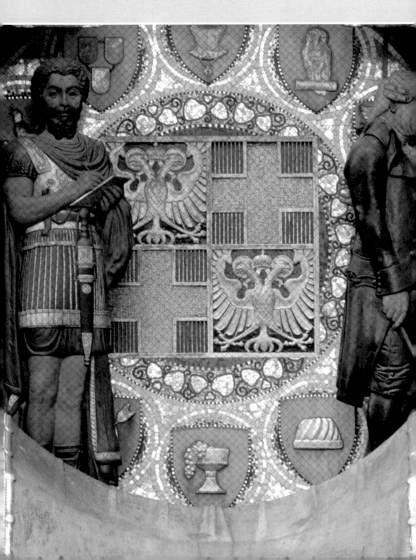

Population · Politics · Economy

Capital and Federal State

Vienna is both the capital city of Austria and one of the country's nine federal states. It is the seat of the federal presidency, the federal government, and the highest organs of the federal administration. It is also home to the state government of Vienna, the supreme judicial court and a Catholic archbishop. It is the smallest federal state in area, yet the most densely populated and most intensely industrialized. Thus the Danube metropolis is the political, economic, intellectual and cultural centre of the nation, despite being surrounded by the state of Lower Austria and its peripheral location geographically.

Administrative Structure

A municipality and federal state at the same time, Vienna's administrative structures serve a **double function**. The municipal council, elected for five years, consists of 100 members and is also the provincial (state) parliament. The **mayor**, whom the municipal council elects from its midst, concurrently holds the office of provincial governor. Michael Häupl of the SPÖ (Social Democratic Party of Austria) has been exercising both these offices since 1994. When he was re-elected in 2006, Häupl had already held the office for 12 years. The governing city senate is composed of the mayor, two deputy mayors and nine to 15 executive city councillors. Because of the decentralized administration, the **23 districts** are presided over by district councils, who elect the district chairpersons from their midst.

City Districts

The city is divided into 23 numbered districts: 1. Innere Stadt (city centre), 2. Leopoldstadt, 3. Landstrasse, 4. Wieden, 5. Margareten, 6. Mariahilf, 7. Neubau, 8. Josefstadt, 9. Alsergrund, 10. Favoriten, 11. Simmering, 12. Meidling, 13. Hietzing, 14. Penzing, 15. Rudolfsheim-Fünfhaus, 16. Ottakring, 17. Hernals, 18. Währing, 19. Döbling, 20. Brigittenau, 21. Floridsdorf, 22. Donaustadt and 23. Liesing. District number one, the city centre, corresponds to the historic centre. Districts 2 – 9, that developed out of the former suburbs are called the »inner districts«, and the »outer districts« of 10 – 20 are those beyond the former ramparts, now a ring road named the Gürtel. Of course these also developed from former suburbs and in a broader sense, the outer fringe districts are numbers 21 – 23. The smallest district (Josefstadt) encompasses about 2 sq km /1 sq mi, the largest (Donaustadt) is 102 sq km /63 sq mi. With only 18,000 inhabitants, the Innere Stadt is the least populated district; the most populated is Favoriten, with 148,000 inhabitants. Each district has its own characteristics. Part of the 3rd district (Landstrasse) is consid-

← *Typical Art Nouveau: Franz von Matsch has famous personages parading hourly »am Hof«, Haydn is followed by Marcus Aurelius.*

The Districts of Vienna

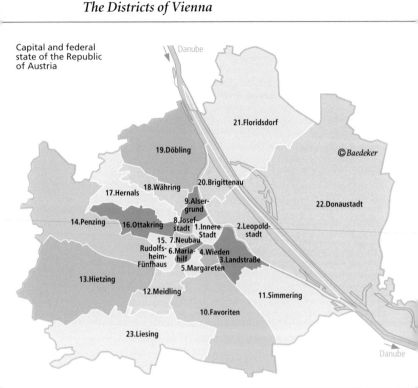

Capital and federal
state of the Republic
of Austria

Danube

21.Floridsdorf

19.Döbling

©*Baedeker*

20.Brigittenau

18.Währing

17.Hernals

9.Alser-
grund

22.Donaustadt

14.Penzing   16.Ottakring   8.Josef-
stadt   1.Innere   2.Leopold-
Stadt   stadt

15. 7.Neubau
Rudolfs-   6.Maria-   4.Wieden
heim-   hilf   3.Landstraße
Fünfhaus   5.Margareten

13.Hietzing

12.Meidling   11.Simmering

10.Favoriten

23.Liesing

Danube

ered the diplomatic quarter; the 4th (Wieden), together with the city
centre, are the most exclusive. The 5th (Margareten), 6th (Mariahilf)
and 7th (Neubau) districts bear witness to the rise of the middle
class; trade and commerce also gained a foothold here, and factories
and workers' housing was erected next to bourgeois buildings. Today,
Vienna's largest shopping boulevard goes through Mariahilf. In the
7th district, the charming but pretty much run-down Spittelberg
Quarter was redeveloped in the course of urban renewal. The quiet
8th district (Josefstadt) has always been a favourite of civil servants.
The 9th (Alsergrund) is Vienna's academic quarter with a multitude
of doctor's surgeries, hospitals and sanatoriums. The 10th (Favorit-
en), 11th (Simmering), 12th (Meidling) and 15th (Rudolfsheim-
Fünfhaus) districts are the most densely populated, and are home to
the working class, retirees with modest pensions, and residents of
tenement blocks. The 16th (Ottakring) and 17th (Hernals) districts
closing in on the Vienna Woods, are similar to the neighbouring
areas and, like Ottakring, are also being renewed. The 18th

(Währing) is popular as a residential area and one of Vienna's most beautiful parks, the Türkenschanz Park, belongs to it. With its outskirts, Gersthof and Pötzleinsdorf, it reaches up to the wooded hills of the city boundaries. The 13th (Hietzing) and the 19th (Döbling) compete for the title of Vienna's most beautiful suburb. In Hietzing, the area surrounding Schönbrunn Palace is characterized by elegant villas, and even the municipal buildings radiate a certain dignity. Döbling, in contrast, has combined old wine villages with wine restaurants and has attracted the newly rich. The 23rd district (Liesing), bordering on Hietzing, is a merger of sleepy villages in the middle of gently rolling hills. Rodaun is one of them, famous for being the one-time residence of Hugo von Hofmannsthal.

Beyond the Danube Canal lies the 2nd district (Leopoldstadt), once the home of Balkan merchants, Turks and Jews from the Levant and Poland. Today it is the district where the Prater, the fair grounds, the national sports stadium and the harness horse racing track is to be found. Many high-rises of corporate head offices tower above the left bank of the Danube Canal. Next to it, in the 20th district (Brigittenau), the view is defined by dreary tenement blocks and fortress-like municipal buildings. In the area beyond the Danube –somewhat disparagingly called »Transdanubia« – follow the 21st district (Floridsdorf) and the 22th district (Donaustadt), where garden allotments are tended beneath factory smoke stacks. A modern skyline has emerged in the latter, dominated by UN City and Donau City.

Population

In the Middle Ages, Vienna, with its 20,000 residents, was already one of the largest cities in the German-speaking world. It experienced its greatest influx during the »Gründerzeit« (Founding Era), a time of rapid industrialization after the founding of the Prussian-lead German Empire towards the end of the 19th century. Between 1880 and 1905, the population rose from 592,000 to two million. The newcomers came from all parts of the multi-national nation – primarily from Bohemia, Moravia, Hungary and Galicia. By 1900, with more than 60% of the immigrants speaking a foreign language, Vienna was considered a gigantic **melting pot of ethnic and religious groups**.

Following the Second World War, political refugees, mostly from Hungary and Czechoslovakia, came to Vienna, and most have been given Austrian citizenship by now. Between 1963 and 1989, it was predominantly guest workers from Yugoslavia and Turkey who sought to settle in Vienna. Since the fall of the Iron Curtain in 1989, Vienna has become the gateway to the »Golden West« for people from southern Poland, the Czech Republic, Slovakia and Hungary. There has also been substantial immigration from the countries of former Yugoslavia stricken with economic adversity, civil war and displacement. Nevertheless, the population has been continuously declining again since 1994 to at least 1.7 million today.

Facts and Figures Vienna

© Baedeker

Vienna

Location
► 48° 14' northern latitude
16° 21' eastern longitude

Area
► 415 sq km/160 sq mi
► Land: 393 sq km/152 sq mi (95%)
Water: 19 sq km/7 sq mi (5%)
(Danube and Vienna)
► Highest point: 542m/1.778ft
(Hermannskogel)
► Lowest point: 151m/495ft (Lobau)

Population
► 1.7 mil, approx.
17,000 in the 1st district
► Population density:
4050 per sq km/0.4mi

Comparisons
► New York City 8.2 mil
► London 7.5 mil
► Austria 8.3 mil

Government
► Capital of Austria and also a
federal state
► 23 Municipal districts
► City government: mayor
(who is also Provincial Governor)
► Seat of OPEC, the International Atomic
Agency and 4th UN city
(next to New York, Geneva and Nairobi)
► City centre is a UNESCO World Heritage
Site

Economy
► Traffic: c23%
► Trade: c22%
► Service sector: c20%
► Industry: c8%
► Tourism: c6%
► Other: c21%
► Unemployment: 8.5%

Tourism
► About 10 mil overnight stays per
annum
► Average length of stay: 2.5 days

Traffic
► TrafficAirport: Wien-Schwechat,
c13.5 mil passengers per annum
► Road network Vienna: 2710km/1694mi
► Public transport network: over 900km/
562mi

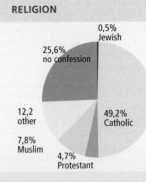

RELIGION

0,5% Jewish
25,6% no confession
49,2% Catholic
12,2 other
7,8% Muslim
4,7% Protestant

At present there are around 30,000 foreigners registered in Vienna without Austrian citizenship, including primarily citizens of former Yugoslavia, Turkey, Germany, Poland, Hungary, Slovakia, the Czech Republic and Rumania.

Foreign Residents

Hub between East and West Europe

Austria's transformation to a small republic after the fall of the monarchy in 1918, as well as its peripheral location on the fringes of the East-West conflict after 1945, meant Vienna lost its position of power in global economics. Since 1989, however, Vienna is once again at the hub of **East-West trade in Europe**, because of its special position at the crossroads between Eastern and Western Europe. Numerous foreign businesses, banks and commercial trading companies now maintain branches in the city. Domestic businesses also make use of the advantages. The capital is the seat of the central offices of most of Austria's large corporations and all of the major Austrian banks.

Global Economic Site

> **? DID YOU KNOW …?**
>
> ■ …that Vienna earns around € 65 billion, almost 30% of Austria's GDP, and that its economic growth lies above the national average?

Vienna is the administrative, commercial, industrial and financial centre of the Austrian nation. Although the smallest federal state in area, the city has the largest share of employment opportunities in Austria. A fourth of all the jobs in the country are in Vienna.

Economic centre

The most important sectors of the Viennese economy are commerce and services. Almost half of all employees work in them and the jobs in these sectors are concentrated in the 1st district and the inner districts (2 – 9, 20). Because of this concentration on services and small to medium sized companies, the labour market has remained relatively stable in economically difficult times. Among Vienna's distinctive features are the so-called **cottage industries**, that work in the production of fashion accessories, lace, petit point embroidery, luxurious leather goods, gold and silver articles, and handicraft products. Because of the high rents and minimal possibility of expansion, however, many of the cottage industries formerly found in the city's back courtyards have migrated to the northern, eastern and southern outskirts, where a commercial and industrial belt has developed. The Viennese tourist board has recorded more than 10 million overnight stays annually in the last couple of years, 8.4 million of them by foreign tourists. The majority are from Germany, followed by visitors from Austria and Italy.

Economic sectors

◀ Tourism

History of the City

The foundations for a city that is today one of the most beautiful and most visited places in Europe were laid with the first settlements in the Vienna basin. However, dark chapters, like the story of the First World War, are also part of Vienna's heritage.

The Beginnings of the City

4,000 years ago	First Indo-Germanic settlements
around 15 BC	The Romans found »Vindobona« camp
AD 487	End of Roman domination
AD 955	The Ostmark (Eastern March) again set up as boundary
AD 1137	First mention of Vienna as a city

The settlement of the Vienna basin can be traced back to the Neolithic period, with traces of Indo-Germanic settlements around 2000 BC in the north-western wooded hills. The Illyrian population of the early Iron Age (from 800 BC) was displaced by the Celts in the late Iron Age, around 400 BC, and Leopoldsberg was probably crowned by a Celtic citadel.

Prehistoric settlements

Around 15 BC the Romans established the **fortified military outpost of Vindobona** (from the Celtic *Vedunia* meaning *forest stream*) with 6,000 men on the Danube frontier to protect against the Germanic tribes living to the north. After the first century AD, a Roman civilian frontier city with close to 20,000 inhabitants developed around it, on the slopes of the Belvedere. The Belvedere, settled since the Bronze Age, was the junction of the Danube River Valley with the trade routes running along the western, flood-free right bank above the Danube, whose major arm roughly corresponds with today's Danube Canal. At first, the camp belonged to the province of Noricum and, after 103 AD, to the province of Pannonia Superior. The settlement was destroyed around 170 AD, during the Marcomannic Wars, but was rebuilt afterwards under Emperor **Marcus Aurelius**, who is presumed to have died here in 180 AD. In 213 AD, Vindobona was granted a town charter (municipium), and in 280 AD, the first vineyards were planted.

Roman Period

Early during the Great Migration, about 400 AD, the civilian city was destroyed by the Goths, and the Romans evacuated the Danube region completely in 487 AD. In all probability, the sheltered settlement site on the Danube, conveniently situated near major trading routes, continued to exist, however, and the Frankish king Charlemagne is said to have founded St Peter's Church there in 792 AD. Vienna was mentioned as Wenia in the Salzburg Annals of 881 AD and, thanks to its river harbour, Vienna had developed from a village into a merchant town defended by a castle by the 11th century.

Early Middle Ages

← *Anything but modest – the dome of the Hofburg. The federal president officiates where kings and emperors once resided*

Rule of the Babenbergs

Upswing Following Emperor Otto I's victory over the Hungarians, the Ostmark (Ostarrichi, Austria) was again established as the frontier march of the realm in 955 and the Babenbergs, presumably from Franconia, were named the margraves of the Ostmark in 976, who were elevated to dukes in the 12th century. The first documented mention of Vienna as a city (civitas), in 1137, followed the transfer of the ducal residence from Klosterneuburg to Vienna under Duke Henry II »Jasomirgott«. At the same time, merchants from the upper Danube region and the Rhineland, as well as Flemish cloth makers, settled there. In 1192, the English king, **Richard the Lionhearted** was imprisoned while returning from the Crusades for publicly insulting the duke. The ransom money was used to improve Vienna's fortification walls. Under Duke Leopold VI (1198 – 1204), the Glorious, Vienna experienced an **economic and cultural upswing**. The Teutonic Knights were summoned to Vienna, and famous minstrels, like Walther von der Vogelweide, socialized at the court. The city expanded and gained a new ring wall with the construction of the ducal seat on the site of today's Stallburg. Through the granting of a **city charter with trading privileges** in 1221, the city blossomed as an important hub of eastern and southern trade, and was granted Imperial Immediacy. This expired, though, with the death of the last Babenberg, Duke Frederick II, the Quarrelsome, in 1246. Under the rule of the Bohemian king Ottokar Pemysl II (1251 – 1278), Vienna's economic position was maintained, but it lost its political importance in favour of Prague.

Habsburg Rule

1273	Rudolph I becomes first Habsburg king
1365	Founding of the university
1485 – 1490	Hungary occupies Vienna
1529	The city is besieged by the Turks
1679	The plague claims 30,000 lives
1683	Second siege by the Turks

Reforms After the election of **Rudolph I** of Habsburg to German king in 1273, Ottokar Pemysl II refused to recognize him and died in the decisive battle on the Marchfeld in 1278. Rudolf I entrusted the ruling of Austria to his two sons. By 1320, Vienna had a population of around 40,000 and a self-confident middle class of merchants, craftsmen and farming burghers, whose number was later greatly reduced through **plagues and disastrous fires**. An upswing in the city was seen in

Emperor Maximilian I drove out the Hungarians

1365 when the **university was founded**, the second after Prague in the German language area at the time. The mayoral and council election regulation of 1396 provided the merchants and tradesmen with a voice in the town council. In 1421, a horrific pogrom (Viennese Geserah) decimated the Jewish community in the ghetto around Judenplatz that had existed since the start of the 13th century. When Duke Frederick V (1440 to 1493) ascended to the throne of the Holy Roman Empire in 1452 as **Frederick III**, Vienna was **transformed into an imperial capital**, and ordinary citizens were gradually displaced by aristocratic imperial officials. While the Hofburg was being enlarged to serve as the imperial residence, St Stephen's Cathedral was elevated to the status of a bishop's church in 1469. Between 1485 and 1490, the Hungarian king, **Matthias Corvinus** occupied Vienna. But Emperor **Maximilian I** (ruled 1493 to 1519) drove the Hungarians out of the city again and extended his authority through politically favourable marriages with Spain, Bohemia and Hungary. The double marriage between the children of the Bohemian king Vladislav and Maximilian I's grandchildren in 1515 laid the cornerstone for the future Austro-Hungarian Empire.

Siege of the city by the Turks

Vienna became a bastion of **Humanism and the Reformation** at the beginning of the Renaissance, in the early 16th century. During the religious dissention, Vienna joined the Protestant faith. The crushed revolt of the Estates against Ferdinand III ended with the »**bloody assizes held in Viennese Neustadt**« (1522), during which the mayor, Martin Siebenbürger, and his followers were sentenced to death. In 1525 a **fire in the city** destroyed over 400 houses and, a year later, a new city order did away with civil self-government. Fate dealt Vienna another blow with the **siege by the Turks** in 1529; although successfully repulsed, the outlying districts that had recently been built were reduced to rubble. Through the advance of the Turks into the Danube region, Vienna lost its value as a centre of long-distance trade, and its middle class became impoverished. The nobility, who had gathered around the residence of the mighty Hapsburgs, now also became a determining factor in the city, and the court element consisting of the aristocracy and officials gained the upper hand over middle class merchants. The inner city, especially in the vicinity of the imperial residence, became the residential area of the nobility. The middle class moved to the outlying towns that grew up around the monasteries that were founded during the course of the Counter Reformation. The Counter Reformation gained significance following the advent of the Jesuits in 1551, although three quarters of Vienna's population at first belonged to the Protestant faith. This finally caused Emperor Maximilian II to grant religious freedom in 1571, though it was repealed again in 1577. Furthermore, the danger posed by the Turks led to the building up and extending of a massive **ring of defence**. Beginning in 1583, Prague temporarily became the capital under Emperor Rudolph II, until Emperor Matthias returned to Vienna in 1612.

In 1590, a **severe earthquake** shook the area between the Hungarian lowland plains and Württemberg, Slovenia and Saxony, damaging seven of Vienna's 17 churches at the time, including the southern tower of St Stephen's Cathedral. Because the Viennese had been warned by two minor tremors and had made their way out into the open as a precaution, only nine lives were lost by a collapsing guest house. Only a few years later, the Counter Reformation propagated

The Viennese also successfully withstood the second Turkish Siege in 1683

the »**monastery offensive**« with the construction of numerous monasteries and churches of monastic orders (Franciscans, Dominicans, Capuchins, Barnabites, Carmelites, and Servite Friars). A **Jewish ghetto** was once again established in Leopoldstadt between 1625 and 1670. The city passed through the **Thirty Years War** (1618–1648) without destruction. Instead, in 1679, Vienna was once again struck by the **plague** that claimed 30,000 victims within a short time. In 1683, Grand Vizier Kara Mustafa stood with 200,000 men at Vienna's gates. Barely 20,000 Viennese under the leadership of Count Rüdiger von Starhemberg stood defence against the superior numbers of the Turks, who were finally routed by the imperial relief army (60,000 men) and the cavalry (approx. 20,000) of the Polish king, Jan III Sobieski.

Rise to a Metropolis

1740	Maria Theresa ascends the throne
1783	Appointment of an independent magistrate
1814–1815	Congress of Vienna

After fending off the second great siege by the Turks, the Habsburg Empire began to stretch out to the south-east and at the same time Vienna rose to become the magnificent capital of a great European empire. The city was now structured into three distinct areas: the court, aristocracy and clergy inhabited the historic city centre within the ramparts; the middle class resided in the surrounding suburbs embraced by a secondary fortification completed in 1704, which is today the Gürtel ring road; and a third distinct area was made up by the rural towns to the south and west, where the summer palaces of the nobility and ruling house (Schönbrunn Palace) were also located. Vienna became the starting point for a network of commercial roads that radiated into the whole empire, along which factories for hand-crafted goods and commercial branch offices were established. The enormous need for goods and finances in the imperial capital made Vienna a **site of wholesale trade and finances** of European importance and led to a **building boom**, the likes of which had never been seen before, with monumental buildings in high Baroque style. About 160,000 people lived within the Linienwall when Maria Theresa ascended the throne in 1740. As ruler alongside her husband, Emperor Franz I, Maria Theresa improved the foundation of the education system by introducing **universal compulsory education** and tightening the central administration. According to the first census in 1754, Vienna had 175,000 inhabitants. Joseph II reformed vast areas of public life according to Enlightened Absolutism between

Epoch of Absolutism

1780 and 1790. He issued a **tolerance edict** that also allowed Jews more room to develop, abolished serfdom, torture, compulsory guild membership and prepared Vienna for the Industrial Age. Moreover, the city administration was freed from the imposition of the will of the ruler by the installation of an independent magistrate in 1783, when the city had a population of 231,000. The **general hospital**, founded in 1784, became the centre of the Viennese school of medicine.

Napoleon, Congress of Viena

The process of disassociation from the German Empire was so advanced at the end of the 18th century, that the Holy Roman Emperor, Franz II, proclaimed his own Austrian Empire encompassing all of the hereditary lands in 1804, which he ruled as Emperor Franz I. After the founding of the Confederation of the Rhine, he finally gave in to the pressure from Napoleon and, in 1806, renounced the title of Holy Roman Emperor. Vienna was forced to submit to **Napoleonic invasion** twice – he lodged at the Schönbrunn Palace. The costs of the occupations were considerable and it ruined the financial budget. In spite of that, the **Congress of Vienna**, held from 1814 to 1815, under the chairmanship of the Austrian chancellor, Prince Metternich, was magnificent. It was here that Europe's statesmen, including Czar Alexander I, the Prussian Hardenberg, and France's foreign minister Talleyrand, decided on the realignment of Europe after the fall of Napoleon. In Vienna, the past glory of the nobility was restored, censorship of the press tightened and spying as an institution introduced. Liberal bourgeois progress gave way to a frightened retreat into private life and an apolitical stance, generally known as the **Biedermeier Period** – an ironic neologism taken from Joseph Victor von Scheffel's small-minded and pedestrian literary characters, Biedermann and Bummelmeier.

Industrialization

| 1848 | Franz Joseph I ascends to the throne |
| 1873 | World Exhibition in Vienna |

Revolution

Vienna's population had risen to 318,000 by 1829. The **Vienna Philharmonic** was founded in 1842. A year later, technical progress arrived in the city with the introduction of gas lighting. Major railway stations were built along the Linienwall for the most important railway lines in the empire. The textile industry, the food sector and machine construction drew increasing numbers of workers which caused the suburbs to become more and more crowded, increasing social conflicts. Incited by the February Revolution in Paris, the citizens of Vienna also took to the streets demanding more freedom and

The revolution of 1848 led to the fall of Metternich

participation in lawmaking and administration, which escalated into the **March Revolution of 1848** against the regime of Prince Metternich. Although the revolution was crushed by the Prince of Windisch-Graetz, it led to **Metternich's resignation** and finally, in December, to the **Abdication of Emperor Ferdinand I**.

Only 18-years old and militaristic, Franz Joseph I ascended the imperial throne at the end of 1848, and performed a political balancing act between conservative national inertia and economic-industrial farsightedness. Under his rule, Vienna developed from a city with half a million inhabitants to a modern metropolis with 2 million inhabitants by 1905. As capital of one of Europe's major nations and its economic centre in a time of stormy industrialization, Vienna became the destination of immigrants from all corners of the empire, but most of all from Bohemia, Moravia and Galicia. These immigrants increased ethnic, linguistic and religious diversity but, for the most part, they were quickly assimilated. With the development of tenement blocks as cheap accommodation to cope with the population explosion, many Baroque buildings were lost.

The Era of Franz Joseph I (1848–1916)

! Baedeker TIP

Life at Court

Those especially fascinated by Emperor Franz Joseph and his legendary wife Elizabeth (Sisi), should visit the imperial apartments in the Hofburg and the Prunkräume (state rooms) in the Schönbrunn Palace. Both residences provide insight into the lifestyle of this famous ruling couple. The Hofburg has even installed a separate Sisi Museum (see p.203).

A uniform grid of **blocks of four to five-storey tenement houses** began to spread over the west and south of the city and up to the slopes of the Vienna Woods. To better organize the city administration, nearby towns were incorporated in 1850, and the outlying areas after 1890. A **division of the city into districts** took place, which remains essentially the same today. In place of the glacis and the city wall that had been razed in 1856, a broad ring road was laid out around the medieval heart of the city. It was not only flanked by representative administrative and cultural buildings such as the Parliament, city hall, opera, Burgtheater, museums and the university, but also designed to include residences for the aristocracy and upper classes. Just like the historic centre, however, it was also interspersed with coffee houses, hotels, businesses and offices. The liberal mayor Cajetan Felder was able to proudly present the magnificent imperial city of Vienna to an international public in 1873, during the **World's Fair**. The city has the »municipal socialism« of the Christian Socialist Karl Lueger, mayor from 1897 to 1910, to thank for its **development of infrastructure**. For example, its drinking water system supplied by the Styrian and Lower Austrian limestone Alps, the »urban railway«, schools and hospitals were constructed during his time, as well as the parks, and a belt of woods and grassy areas.

First and Second World War

1918	Proclamation of the Republic
1927	Unrest and general strike
1938	German forces invade
1945	The Red Army captures Vienna

Federal capital of the First Republic

The First World War ended in 1918 with the collapse of the Austro-Hungarian Empire and the **abdication of the last Austrian emperor, Karl I**, who had reigned since 1916. On November 12 1918, the First Republic was proclaimed with **Vienna as the federal capital**, in which 2.3 million people lived. Overnight, the capital city of an empire with twelve nationalities and 50 million subjects became the capital of a small country with only 6.6 million inhabitants. This shrinking process was accompanied by major domestic problems that the socialist city government elected in 1919 had to solve. For most of its existence, »Red Vienna« was administered by Karl Seitz, who governed the city from 1923 to 1934. Unemployment spread and housing shortages increased because private tenement block construction came to a standstill. The city administration attempted to cope with the misery be establishing social housing in the form of monumental workers' tenement blocks, like **Karl Marx Hof** and **En-**

gelshof, which filled vacant spaces in the suburbs. During the civil war of 1934, they even served as fortresses for the workers. In 1922, Vienna's status as Austrian federal capital was augmented by being designated a federal state as well. In this way, the municipal council also became the Viennese provincial parliament. However, the development of a functioning civil community was constantly made more difficult by the polarization in political life between the social democrats and clerical conservatives which led, among other things, to civil war-like unrest, including a general strike in 1927.

In 1933, the domestic conflicts once again came to a head when Engelbert Dollfuss, as federal chancellor, eliminated the parliamentary constitution with a **coup d'état** and the social democrats called for armed resistance against him. Massive deployment of the army ruthlessly crushed the revolt and strengthened Dollfuss' authoritarian fascist regime, which transformed the republic into a state of estates and banned the Social Democratic Party, as well as the trade unions. After Dollfuss' assassination in 1934, Kurt Schuschnigg (Christian Social Party) took over the government and came increasingly under pressure from the National Socialists (Nazis). After unrest and an ultimatum, Schuschnigg resigned, paving the way for the invasion of

Austro-Fascism and the Second World War

The conflicts were intensifying and Vienna faced hard times – martial law was declared in 1934

the **German army** on March 12, 1938, and the union (»Anschluss«) of Austria with Hitler's Germany. With the incorporation of 97 neighbouring communities, Vienna was made »Reichsgau Greater Vienna« and capital of the »Ostmark«. The Nazi take-over was followed by the systematic expulsion, imprisonment and murder of countless political opponents and Jewish citizens of Vienna. The Second World War claimed the lives of more than 200,000 Viennese; over 40,000 Viennese Jews were victims of the Holocaust in Nazi concentration camps. Vienna became the **target of heavy air raids** early in the autumn of 1944. After 52 bombing raids and 10 days of fighting within the city, more than 21,000 houses were destroyed, close to 86,000 flats rendered uninhabitable, 120 bridges blown up and almost 3,700 gas and water mains interrupted. Mid-April 1945, the city was taken by the Red Army.

Second Republic ► Vienna was divided into four occupied zones under the Allies USSR, USA, Great Britain and France. Although the occupation administration in the inner city rotated monthly, the city administration under Mayor Theodor Körner (1945–1951) remained intact as a whole. Karl Renner emerged from the general elections in November 1945 as federal president and Leopold Figl as federal chancellor; both offices have their seat in Vienna. With the help of Marshall Plan funds, reconstruction was accelerated after 1947, and the city was able to improve its image, nationally and internationally, under Mayor Franz Jonas (1951–1965), who was also federal president from 1965 to 1974.

Reconstruction

1955	Austria regains its sovereignty
1969	Construction of the Underground begins
1989	Zita von Habsburg laid to rest
2001	The inner-city declared a Cultural World Heritage Site

With the ratification of the Austrian State Treaty between Austria and the victorious powers on 15 May 1955 in the Belvedere, Austria regained its **complete sovereignty** and after the last Allied forces had withdrawn from Vienna, Parliament passed the constitutional law on **permanent neutrality** on 26 October 1955.

In 1956, the seat of the International Atomic Energy Agency was established in Vienna. In 1961, the summit meeting between the U.S. President John F. Kennedy and the chairman of the Council of Ministers of the Soviet Union, Nikita Khrushchev, took place in Vienna. In 1967, Vienna became the seat of the United Nations Industrial Development Organization (UNIDO). A new era of transportation

? DID YOU KNOW …?

■ …that Vienna now has a museum that deals exclusively and extensively with the subject of »The Third Man« (see Baedeker Special, p.270), Carol Reed's classic film on the dreary post-war years in the Danube metropolis? (Pressgasse 25, opening times: Sat 2-6pm; info at www.3mpc.net).

started when construction of the Underground began in 1969. Ten years later, with the opening of **UN City**, Vienna became the UN's third headquarters. In 1984, the Viennese elected Helmut Zilk the new mayor of their city. The new artistic directors of the major theatres of the Danube metropolis, Peter Weck, Otto Schenk, Claus Helmut Drese and Claus Peymann (from Germany), revived Vienna's cultural life. With the opening of the »Austria Centre Vienna« in 1987, Vienna's conference capacity was increased by almost 20%. **Former Empress Zita von Habsburg**, who was the last Empress of Austria and Queen of Hungary, died in 1989 at the age of 96, and was laid to rest in the Imperial Crypt with huge public participation. With the opening of the Iron Curtain in 1990, Vienna was once again at the heart of Europe, which brought economic, cultural and political revival and renewed contact with East European states. In a plebiscite in May 1991, the Viennese surprisingly decided against holding the EXPO 1995.

A **major fire** in November 1992 destroyed the Redouten Halls (assembly halls) in the Hofburg, which were restored by the mid-1990s. In 1994, construction began on the grounds of the planned Donau City which, together with the adjacent UN City, is planned to develop into a second, highly modern city centre for Vienna.

At the end of the millennium, the Viennese celebrated Austria's 1000 Year Jubilee (1996), the 100th anniversary of the death of Empress Elizabeth (1998) and the Strauss Year (1999). In 2001 the historic centre of Vienna was declared a Cultural World Heritage Site by UNESCO. The Museum Quarter was opened in the same year, after three years of construction, and a price tag of around € 2 billion.

In the city council elections of 2005 the Social Democratic Party (SPÖ) got the most votes, just like in 2001. Dr. Michael Häupl (SPÖ) has been both mayor and landeshauptmann (provincial governor) since 1994. During the soccer European cup in 2008 in Switzerland and Austria, Vienna was one of the playing sites. In May 2008 the extension of subway line U2 to the Ernst Happel Stadium was opened.

Arts and Culture

Baroque architecture and Art Nouveau painters, the musical genius of Mozart, as well as Schubert, Strauss and others come to mind when thinking of art and culture in Vienna. The city itself is one gigantic work of art with its Baroque secular buildings and Art Nouveau facades. Even the Underground stations are works of art here.

Art History

The Vienna Museum Karlsplatz provides a graphic overview of the city's history. Hilltop settlements have been documented on this strategically important site for trade routes dating back to about 2000 BC, which then lost their significance in the Bronze Age. Indo-European people settled in the south of today's city, around Rennweg. Settlements have been substantiated in this area up to Roman times. The Celts penetrated from the West into the Vienna basin in the middle of the 4th century and established their settlement of Vedunia on the site of today's Hohen Markt. A **large treasure trove** of gold coins with images of Celtic kings provides evidence of this period.

◄ Romans

Prehistory

Following the Roman policy of expansion and also to secure the empire's frontier, Augustus peacefully integrated the eastern alpine countries and the Vienna basin into his empire in 15 BC. Large **fortifications were built along the Danube** to provide protection against imminent raids by the Germanic tribes: first Carnuntum, on the plains in the east that had no natural defence; and a little later, Vindobona was built, which was originally constructed in wood and then replaced by massive stonework. Today, excavated sections of the camp's main canal (Am Hof 9) and the remains of two officers' houses (Hoher Markt 3) can be viewed.

Romanesque

The first documented mention of Vienna was in 881 as Wenia. Following the gradual urban development begun in the 12th century, Vienna experienced a **cultural blossoming** in the Romanesque period. **St Stephen's Cathedral** was begun as a major building project in the first half of the 12th century. Of the Romanesque triple nave basilica with transept, sanctuary square and apses, the west wall, Roman towers and large round-arch portal still survive. Christ is enthroned as judge of the world in the middle of the semi-circular area in the Mandorla above the rainbow. The twelve Apostles appear to the side as half figures with the two Evangelists, Luke and Mark. The columns and architraves are covered with bands of ornamentation and floral themes, and above the flower bud capital is a narrow section of bas-reliefs. In the left area, the world of demons represented by fantastic chimeras, a monkey and a horned animal is shown; in the right area, the world of evil is represented by humans abandoned to animals, dragons and devils. The **Ruprechtskirche** was built on top of an earlier structure between 1130 and 1170. Attached to the imposing west tower with paired round-arched windows, is a simple church with a Gothic choir that was later restored. Two decorative

← *Klimt painted a portrait of his companion Emilie Flöge in 1902.*
  She didn't like it, so he sold it to what is today the Vienna Museum.

The oldest portrait in German art depicts Rudolf IV

features date from the 12th century. Vienna's only Romanesque stained glass window panes can be seen in the centre choir window, displaying a crucifixion group and an enthroned Mother of God. Pillar plinths and half columns and transverse arches dating back to the first building period are inside the **Schottenkirche** (construction began c1160), a triple nave basilica with a west building and transept, a tower in the crossing, and originally three apses. Hidden behind the Classical west facade and the High Baroque projecting portal, the Michaelerkirche announces the transition to Gothic. Late Romanesque capitals, circular arches, dentil friezes, and arcades that are already tending toward pointed arches document the initial building phase in the first half of the 13th century. Among the **secular buildings** of this period are the remains of a tower on the house in the Griechengasse 7 and the oldest section of the Hofburg – the **Schweizerhof**, mentioned for the first time in 1279. Originally a square structure enclosing an inner courtyard with square towers and a structureless facade, its medieval appearance was greatly altered in numerous remodellings in the following centuries. The structure owes its name to the Swiss Guard, which was housed here.

Gothic

Architecture In 1304, the **Gothic rebuilding of St Stephen's Cathedral** began with the spacious nave under a uniform, high ceiling with colourfully glazed bricks and the southern tower, now a symbol of the city, with a chapel incorporated at its base. Filigree tracery adorns the gables of the nave and the tower. The structure is given a secular character with its representation of the church sponsors, Rudolf IV and Katherine of Bohemia, and also through the custom observed up to the end of the Gothic Period of honouring the majority of rulers along with their wives with statues on the exterior of the building. The choir, built between 1304 and 1340, is fashioned as a triple nave hall, each ending in a polygon, whose austere impression results from the smooth surfaces of the wall around the windows with simple, profiled embrasures, and the buttresses. The walls of the nave were raised after 1359. In 1446, the last of the vaulting was completed. Other Gothic sacred buildings are the **Augustinerkirche** (built 1330 to 1339) with a long narrow nave ending in a heptagonal shape and additional windows; the **Minoritenkirche**, whose three-part tympanum bas-relief on the main portal built in 1350 exhibits signs of French influence; and the **Maria am Gestade Church** (built 1330 – 1414) with a filigree stone helmet crowning its steeple.

The **oldest portrait in German art** is in Vienna: the portrait of Duke Rudolf IV, which is in the Cathedral and Diocesan Museum. Rudolf not only supported the enlargement of St Stephen's Cathedral but, in 1365, founded the university in Vienna to counter the one in Prague. The duke is portrayed in three-quarter profile in a half-figure portrait against a dark background with a Carolingian crown. There is a noticeable discrepancy existing between the two-dimensionality of the crown and the garments and the sophisticated detail in the physiognomy, which displays individual traits with the slightly opened mouth and the beard. The unknown artist can be traced through his style to Bohemia. **Panel painting** began in Vienna early in the 15th century with disembodied heads on a gold background. Southern German influences become noticeable by the mid-century and the individuals depicted are rendered full-bodied in native surroundings. A further step in development can be seen on the panels of the high altar (1469) of the in Vienna. The **panels on the life of Mary** are by an older painter and are kept in heavy, subdued colours, whereas the Passion pictures were fashioned with gently and thinly applied colours and betray a Dutch influence (Rogier van der Weyden and Dirk Bouts), which is noticeable after the 1460s in Viennese panel painting. Panel painting came to be increasingly preferred over wall-painting. The Church and the wealthy middle class were important patrons, who either donated altars for churches and chapels, or commissioned panel paintings for domestic use. Landscapes had just been deemed worthy of painting in the 1500s, and the **artists of the Danube School** melded figures that they kept intentionally small with evocatively illuminated landscapes that were often captured in all their topographical detail. **Albrecht Altdorfer and Wolf Huber** should be mentioned here as important exponents. An illumination workshop that primarily supplied the royal court was established at the end of the 14th century in Vienna. There are three important examples from the field of **Gothic sculpture** that should be introduced. The stonemason **Anton Pilgram** immortalized himself twice in his work in St Stephen's Cathedral. On the base of the organ (1513) – the

Painting

? DID YOU KNOW ...?

- ... that the oldest view of Vienna can be seen in the painting collection of the Schottenstift (Benedictine Abbey of Our Dear Lady to the Scots) on the Freyung? It forms the background of a high altar panel with the theme of the »Flight to Egypt« and in topographical terms conveys almost exactly how the city looked in the 15th century.

instrument itself has been in a different place since 1720 – he appears to bear the whole weight of the pipes; meanwhile, on the pulpit (1515), he is looking out of a window holding a compass in his right hand. Both self-portraits are very animated, exhibiting individual facial features that the delicate treatment of the surface of the stone imbues with psychological nuances. **Nicolaus Gerhaert von Leyden** gave particular attention to the imperial protocol required by his patron, Frederick III (1415–1493) during the construction of his crypt in St Stephen. Frederick, surrounded by coats of arms, wears the coronation regalia and the emperor's crown while holding the sceptre and the imperial orb in his hands.

Renaissance

Architecture Building activity in this period was modest. The type of palace and castle building, such as in Italian cities, did not develop here, and influences from the strongholds of the Renaissance were hardly assimilated. The ground-plan of the medieval castle (1543–1557) was retained during its remodelling, the towers were demolished, the façade made uniform, the courtyard, and the portals and the gatehouse were sculpturally decorated, giving the castle the appearance of a palace. The **Stallburg** (imperial stables built 1558–1564), with its magnificent arcaded courtyard, and the **Amalienburg** (1575 to 1611) with its plain facades, were built as a four-winged complex with an inner courtyard. From this it can be seen that the Hofburg was not conceived as a single, uniform building complex but is composed of various individual structures. Work was begun on a new building in 1569 in the south-west of Vienna, for Maximilian II, where a **belvedere** was built in the middle of a great garden with geometrical, decorative areas bordered by flowers, and with a chapel, observation tower and an underground grotto. Maximilian had artists brought in from various places where art was flourishing. For example, he contracted the Dutch artist Bartholomeus Spranger, the sculptor Hans Mont and the Italian Licinio Prodenone.

Painting In the 16th century, under the influence of Italian Renaissance painting, **Jakob Seisenegger** created full length official portraits intended to enhance the prestige of the subject, and **Johann Bocksberger** created frescoes in the time around 1540. Bocksberger was particularly good at figural compositions and decorative tasks. Around the middle of the century, artists such as **Giuseppe Arcimboldo** were called to the Viennese court, undoubtedly popular because of his bizarre and peculiar imagery. Also employed were **the Fontana brothers** and **Francesco Terzio**; as well as **Lucas Valckenborch** from the Netherlands, who was responsible for landscapes and portraits. Renaissance painter **Bartholomeus Spranger** was known for his elegance and the refinement of his draughtsmanship for themes including mythology. Around 1600, the influence of Venetian

The gold in the Belvedere's Baroque gable reflects the sun

painting increased, which was regarded as the most modern in terms of formal aesthetic considerations.

One of the most important tasks for sculptors in the 16th century Sculpture was the fashioning of memorial plaques. The divisions of a winged altar were often adapted for the design of a memorial plaque, an example of which is the **memorial plaque for Jobst Truchsess** of Wetzhausen (1524) by Loy Hering that hangs in the Deutschordenskirche (Church of the Teutonic Order). Elaborately decorated sarcophagi were one of the ways to satisfy the growing desire for fame and recognition. In the Michaelerkirche, a **funerary monument for Baron Johann Trautson** was built in 1590 and in the Votivkirche stands the **sarcophagus of Nicholas, Count of Salm**, also by Loy Hering. The deceased kneels before the cross on the tomb cover; the flat reliefs recall the battles against the Turks that Salm led as city commandant.

Baroque · Rococo

After the period of the Turkish sieges (1529–1683), during which Architecture the city had had to concentrate exclusively on maintaining its fortifications, the populace was gripped by a feeling of elation encouraging rapid reconstruction. But it was above all the clergy and the emperor who initiated a tremendous **building boom**, supported by the high nobility, who had winter palaces constructed in the city, and summer palaces in the suburbs. Among the most important buildings of this period were the **Schönbrunn Palace**, the **Karlskirche**, the **Reichskanz-**

lei of the Hofburg (Imperial Chancellery), the **Spanish Riding School**, the **Upper and the Lower Belvedere**, the **Hof and Staatskanzlei** (court and state chancellery) and the **palaces Schwarzenberg and Trautson**.

Under the aegis of **Johann Bernhard Fischer von Erlach** and **Lukas von Hildebrandt** two significantly different styles of architecture determined Vienna's appearance in this period. Fischer's work was greatly influenced by his studies under Bernini in Rome. The original appearance of **Schönbrunn** Palace as a colossal complex on a ground plan laid out at right-angles was obscured through subsequent alterations. Among Fischer's later works is the **Hofbibliothek** (Imperial Library built 1723–1735), which displays the austere forms of early French Classicism. Fischer's architecture is distinctive through its geometrical structuring; the individual components are massive and designed to be noticed. This is seen clearly in a later work, the **Karlskirche** (built 1716–1739). It was designed and sited with an optimal architectural view in relation to the Hofburg in mind. Behind

Schönbrunn Palace lies in the midst of a fabulous garden

the wide frontage incorporating a portico, pediment and the two triumphal columns, the building with its elevated cupola stretches out in front of the chancel.

The designs of his rival, Hildebrandt, who began working in Vienna in 1700, were completely different. His architecture lives from a wealth of building ornaments that cover the walls and seeks to optically break up the building through a play of light and shadow. He also adopted French ideas during the construction of the **Upper Belvedere** (1721 – 1722). The architectural prospect conceived for viewing from a distance consists of interconnecting pavilions stacked toward the centre creating a large, broad effect. The conformity between the interior and exterior is achieved through the carrying over of the systems and themes from the inside onto the exterior walls. Following French horticulture, a **Vienna garden style** developed in **garden design** between 1690 and 1740, with its own characteristics, as well as Italian elements. The important clients were the emperor, the nobility and wealthy citizens. The **gardens of Schönbrunn Palace**, designed by Fischer and carried out by Jean Trehet, follow the

great example of Versailles, adopting its solar symbolism and making use of the Hercules theme for imaginative garden sculptures. Hildebrandt grouped two lush decorative borders around the base of a fountain and two smaller ornamented lawn borders in the **garden of Schönborn Palace** (1706 – 1711). The **Liechtenstein Palace garden** (1691 to 1711) presents an artistically elaborate park. Between the belvedere and the palace, four completely identical parterres are laid out with central fountains along a central axis flanked by avenues which provide an exquisite panorama. An abundance of ornamentation and a large number of garden statuary give the parterre its character.

Vienna's most famous garden was created between 1716 and 1721 between the prestigious palatial buildings of the Upper Belvedere on the hill and the residential palace in the valley, and drew heavily on French models. The garden section of the **Upper Belvedere** is structured by lawns and decorative flowerbeds with permanent ornamental patterns and an area of hedges; the lower section with the orangery is divided more sombrely, with four borders clearly demarcated. The iconographic design for the sculptural decoration is meant to be a symbolic representation of princely power. Not only exotic plants were cultivated in this garden; a **collection of animals**, unsurpassed at the time in its abundance of species, were kept in vivariums. For a long time the park was considered one of the most extravagant in the world.

Painting **Daniel Gran's** commission in 1724 to paint the interior of the **Schwarzenberg Summer Palace** broke the dominance of Italian artists in Vienna. In the **Kuppelsaal** (Dome Hall) which no longer exists, he created a triumphant composition of light and colour. In 1730, Gran began decorating the **Imperial Library**, for which a comprehensive program was worked out to glorify Charles VI as patron of the arts and sciences. The sharply contoured figures seem to float down in front of a very sparse background. Other fresco painters like **Johann Michael Rottmayr** and **Anton Franz Maulbertsch** continued this tradition, further developing the illusionist character of architectural features only painted in perspective, and attempted to widen the optical illusion of space in that way.

Austria offered no native models of panel painting that could be fallen back on. **Peter Strudel** came to Vienna in 1686, where he founded a private academy six years later. His colleagues were hesitant in support because it was mostly the nobility who granted commissions, and they wanted genre paintings, portraits, landscapes and still life paintings. Portrait painting was primarily dominated by **Martin Meytens**, who was very much celebrated in aristocratic circles, but who was better at brilliantly capturing superficial likenesses than producing pronounced character studies.

Sculpture The desire for more three-dimensional decoration in Baroque architecture resulted in many commissions for decorative architectural sculpture. **Christoph Mader** was entrusted with the reliefs on the columns in the Karlskirche, **Giovanni Stanetti** with the pediment bas-reliefs, **Franz Caspar** with the angels in front of the church and **Lorenzo Mattielli** with the figure on the gable, the figures on the fascia and the high altar and its angel statues. There is more concentration on movement and silhouette effect in these figures than on fine detail. Secular architecture and gardens and landscaping offered a wide field of activities for sculptures. Many city squares were decorated with fountains. In 1679 Leopold I vowed to erect the **Pestsäule** (Plague Column) to commemorate the end of the plague. Important artists like Matthias Rauchmiller, Fischer von Erlach, Paul von Strudel and Johann Frühwirth were involved in the conception of the plague column. Above the plinth dedicated to the Holy Trinity rises a pyramidal cloud of angel figures bearing the symbols of power and rulership. The column gives a homogenous impression although construction was constantly delayed and the artists changed.

Classicism

Once again, new trends, this time Classicism, were primarily determined by foreign artists. Louis Montoyer built a magnificent **palace** for the Russian ambassador, **Rasumofsky** (1805 – 1811). The structure gains a formal note through organizing decorative elements like columns, pilasters, coffered ceilings and walls of cultured marble with symbolic bas-reliefs. Although parts of the palace were damaged in a fire in 1814, it is one of Vienna's most magnificent Classical buildings. The stylistic characteristics of Classicism are less apparent in **Palais Pálffy** and the **Austrian Hungarian Bank**. Occasionally they are found in the remodelling and extension of buildings such as Schönbrunn Palace, Jesuitenkirche and the outer Burgtor (castle gate). Among the outstanding sculptural works of Classicism is the **memorial to Marie Christine of Austria** (1798–1805) in the Augustinerkirche, which was designed by **Antonio Canova**. It was fashioned as a wall pyramid. A funeral procession with the allegorical figures of Virtue and Charity pass through an illusory gate. A guardian spirit with a lion is placed to the right, above is Felicity with a portrait medallion of the duchess. The **Vienna Academy** was given a boost through the naming of Heinrich Friedrich Füger as director in 1795, who was distinguished by intellectually-guided art and a return to Classic models and ideals. Mythological depictions were part of the ideals of the period. A small group of ar-

The end of the plague was commemorated with a column in 1681

tists rebelled against simply copying Classical Antiquity and, in 1809, formed the **Lucasbund** school in Vienna. Some artists remained devoted to mythological themes, others championed the religious and moral duties of art.

Historicism

Vienna's major building project in the 19th century was the 4km/ 2.5mi **Ringstrasse**, which was officially opened with a ceremony in 1865. Numerous architects were called upon for the buildings that were to be designed in historical style as **Ludwig Forster** had envisioned in his overall concept. The ring grounds were divided into four zones for different uses. Along with culture and administration, there was also to be space for commerce, finance, individual branches of industry, and an exclusive residential area.

»Doormen« in front of Palais Pálffy

Viennese Historicism started with the neoGothic twin-towered **Votivkirche** by **Heinrich Ferstel** (1879) and the **Staatsoper** (state opera) in neoRenaissance style by **August von Siccardsburg** and **Eduard van der Nüll**. Important building complexes in historicized form followed between 1872 and 1883: the **Rathaus** (town hall), the **Parlament** (parliament), the **university**, the **Burgtheater** (National Theatre), both **museums** and the **stock exchange**. The **extension of the Hofburg** was the final building project. Three features of the Ringstrasse stand out. The most important monumental buildings are detached and most of them are surrounded by gardens. The buildings were designed to be viewed from a distance and are meant to radiate greatness and power. Historical styles were deliberately chosen: neoClassical Greek forms were used for the parliament to recall the origins of democracy in Antiquity, and the medieval glory of the city was reflected in the neoGothic Rathaus. Even during his lifetime, **Hans Makart** was given exuberant tribute for his allegorical paintings that displayed a great variety of forms with a decorative tenor. He took over the special school for historical painting in 1878 that tended toward operatically staged compositions. He also designed the procession for the silver wedding anniversary of the Austrian imperial couple in 1879 with a series of floats, which consciously incorporated the buildings on the Ringstrasse in the staging of the parade. He received his greatest commission in 1881 to **decorate the stairs in the Kunsthistorisches Museum** (Art History Museum).

Jugendstil (German Art Nouveau)

Architecture The **Vienna Secession** was a movement that split from the traditional art market, carried by the idea of giving art its freedom again and breaking new ground. The group of artists not only published its own magazine »Ver Sacrum«, but also supported the architect **Joseph Maria Olbrich** in the building of the exhibition building for the Vienna Secession. The building, made up of white cubes with the distinctive principal motif of a metal dome composed of 3000 gilded laurel leaves, was constructed between 1897and 1898. An impression of purity, grandeur and solemn dignity was intended. Another pioneering architect working in Vienna was **Otto Wagner**. His buildings from around 1900 with their decorative elements belong to Jugendstil. The **Stadtbahn (light railway) pavilions on Karlsplatz**, with their marble and gold plating, were built in 1901; between 1904 and 1906, he built the **Postsparkassenamt (post office)**, a building with granite and marble plate facing and a counter hall of glass and steel almost devoid of ornamentation. The **St Leopold Church on Steinhof** (1905 – 1907) is characterized by clear geometric forms that are faced with marble plates and covered by a dome raised on pillars. **Josef Hoffmann** designed for the **»Wiener Werkstätten«** (Vienna Workshops) craftwork luxury items consisting of geometric objects given a simple decoration. He also planned some important buildings in Vienna, such as the **Purkersdorf Sanatorium** (1903 – 1905), the **Siedlung Wien Kaasgraben** (suburban development, 1913), and houses for the International Werkbund Exhibition of 1932 (Association of Architects, Designers and Industrialists), as well as several private homes.

Adolf Loos wanted to break away from Historicism and the representatives of the Secession with his essay »Ornament and Crime« (1907). In his business on Michaelerplatz (1910/1911), the Werkbund residential estate (1932) and the Villas, he was guided by the compactness of the cube as a structural shell.

Gustav Klimt was an active founding member of the Secession and was its president until 1905. He gained official recognition with his early commissioned works in the 1880s, as well as with the decorating of the staircase in the Vienna Burgtheater and, in 1891, with his work for the Kunsthistorisches Museum (Art History Museum). He created the **»Beethoven frieze«** in 1902 in the Secession's pavilion for the exhibition of Max Klinger's statue »Beethoven«; further commissions followed. Klimt's style of painting is characterized by a decorative and symbolic ornamentation of picture and figure, often based on a connection of delicately coloured, naturalistic, erotic pictures of bodies and ornamentally designed areas. Klimt was friends with **Egon Schiele**, who expressed his themes of the tragic or fateful transience of human beauty in a completely different manner. Fragility, people in extreme situations and fleeting moods are expressively given form in an angular and agitated style. **Oskar Kokoschka**, who completed his education in Vienna, was influenced by the Secessionists. His subject matter was portraits which, in later works, developed into character portrayals of particular depth. He also painted land-

Painting

A NEW DEPARTURE IN ART

1897 was the founding year of the artists' association that became known as the Secessionists, which broke away from the established art world at the time. This movement not only incorporated traditional arts, but also all applied arts – and that was a new departure.

Vienna in 1897: a circle of young artists around the painter **Gustav Klimt** resigned from the established artists' association and founded their own interest group – as it would be called today – entitled »The Association of Fine Artists Secession«. Fearing for its position of influence and power, the establishment was outraged, interpreting the breakaway as a declaration of war. The Secessionists, meanwhile, who wanted to put an end to the stuffy Viennese politics of culture and open the way for modern European art movements, were full of idealistic enthusiasm.

Today we have come to know these trends under the collective term of **Jugendstil** or **Art Nouveau**, which encompassed almost all spheres of classical art forms and also – what was new at the time – all applied arts, such as crafts, industrial design and graphics. Following the proposition that all spheres of daily life ought to live up

to aesthetic ideals, the applied arts, which high art had always considered its poor relation, gained a completely new significance. It was therefore not surprising that among the founding members of the Secessionists, there were not only painters such as Klimt and architects such as **Josef Hoffmann** and **Joseph Maria Olbrich**, but also craftsmen like **Koloman Moser**.

A Rejection of Historicism

In March 1898, the **Secession** made its Viennese debut with its first exhibition, which not only introduced art of the European avant-garde, but also work by the Secessionists, and it enjoyed great interest among the Viennese public. A rejection of the excessive decoration of late Historicism was also signified by the exhibition building of the Secession inaugurated in the same year: a mighty cube with a dome of gilded bay leaves that earned itself the nickname *Kraut-*

The ceramics of the Viennese Workshops was supposed to be affordable.

Ode to Art Nouveau: The Stadtbahnpavillon by Otto Wagner is decorated with gold and marble elements.

kopf (cabbage head) from the Viennese. The design for the Secession building was by Joseph Maria Olbrich, who also immediately bade farewell to Vienna with this project, being called to the artists' colony in Darmstadt by the Archduke Ernst Ludwig. Olbrich learnt his trade from **Otto Wagner** who, as academic teacher of the Secessionist generation of artists, had lasting influence. His most famous contribution to Austrian Art Nouveau is the **Viennese post office building**, built between 1904 and 1906. Construction components of this building, such as the metal rivets holding the granite and marble panels, or the warm air ventilation shafts, were no longer covered behind cladding, but incorporated into the decorative design elements of the interior. Just as with most of his colleagues, Otto Wagner designed the functional interior himself – the building and interior melded into one unified artistic creation. Collaboration with craftsmen was required in order to realise this kind of project, but few workshops declared themselves willing.

Craftwork for the Masses

In other centres of European Art Nouveau – whose work the Viennese public was able to see for the first time during the eighth **Secession Exhibition** held in November 1900 – the problem was solved by establishing specialist workshops. Thus the architect and professor at the School of Applied Arts Josef Hoffmann founded the **»Viennese Workshop«** in 1903, in association with Koloman Moser and the industrialist **Fritz Wärmdorfer**. The business already employed one hundred master craftsmen two years later and, in a show of egalitarianism, each item carried the mark of the artist who designed it as well as the craftsman who actually made it.

After just a few years, however, a gulf opened between aspiration and reality. The original ideal of providing high quality crafted utilitarian goods for the general public soon had to give way to the laws of the market place. The price for survival – the Viennese Workshop existed until 1932 – was the **exclusivity of the products** which, due to their high production costs, were only affordable for a small section of society. A stylistic change also took place among the craftsmen, towards a more decorative and playful treatment of forms.

Inevitably, the romantic return to the production methods and conditions of a pre-industrial era was therefore temporary, though its impact on design history was both interesting and extremely fruitful.

scapes and visionary content that took on anti-fascist expression, especially during the Spanish Civil War. Strong radiant colours, whose emotional effects were known to the artist, identify his Expressionist roots.

Art from 1919 to 1945

The **construction of social housing** played a central role after the First World War. Franz Schuster and Oskar Strand created quite a few buildings as part of the urban settlement and garden city movement. **Karl Ehn**, an exponent of Expressionism, influenced municipal housing development with tenement blocks like the **Karl Marx Hof** (1927 – 1930). **Clemens Holzmeister**, professor at the Vienna Academy from 1924, gradually divorced himself from historical forms of style and designed churches, hotels and residential buildings in the more restrained forms of Modernism. In painting, Albin Egger-Lienz, with his popular monumental style, and Albert Paris Gütersloh, with his expressively fantastic compositions, stood in contrast to each other.

Art since 1945

Architecture

After the Second World War, all efforts had to be concentrated on reconstruction of the, in part, heavily damaged city. There were no spectacular projects in the area of housing development, and the 1960s estates on the north-eastern and southern outskirts of the city are similar to contemporary projects in other large European cities at the time. Roland Rainer built the extremely functional municipal hall from 1952 to 1958, whose main structure is dynamically directed upwards with a wide window front supported by thin concrete pillars. The Kirche Zur Heiligen Dreifaltigkeit (1965 – 1976) by **Fritz Wotruba** is composed of unfinished, elongated rectangular concrete structures sculpturally fitted into one another. It was not until the 1970s and 80s that buildings by internationally renowned architects were erected in Vienna. **Hans Hollein** received commissions to remodel the **Retti candle store** in post modern style in 1964/1965, and the **Schullin jewellery store** in 1974; and he also created the **Haas House** in 1990, a business and office building with restaurants opposite St Stephen's Cathedral. The round curve of its gradually stepped facade ends in a glass bay front. Inside, the striking five-storey atrium and terraces are attractive. The architectural group **Coop Himmelb(l)au**, who specialize in creating more flexible living spaces, built the **Roter Engel** (Red Angel) in Vienna in 1980/1981 as a combination of wine bar and music theatre, where interiors are distinguished from one another by walls made of various materials, such as corrugated iron, asphalt, concrete and wood. Among the most important deconstructionist projects with which the architects wanted to repress perfectionism and soulless architecture is the remodelling of the **Ronacher Theatre**, which, being a 19th century structure, had to be updated for the technical demands of the 21st century. Next to the existing fabric of the building, the new façade appears rather plain; however, the roof was opened up and a new rooftop extension was inserted. The architect **Gustav Peichl**, a member of the teaching staff of the Academy of Fine Arts since 1973, has proved himself a pragmatist with a positive relationship to technology, who combines functional and economical construction with cool technical elegance. Between 1966 and 1968, he built the Rehabilitation Centre in Vienna Meidling, a star-shaped complex with everything spatially closely connected and ingenious terraces that at any time of day provide sunny or shady areas. The painter and graphic artist **Friedensreich Hundertwasser** had the residential and commercial building on the corner of Kegelgasse and Löwengasse (1983 to 1985) and the **Kunst Haus Wien** (art museum) fashioned in a continuation of Viennese Jugendstil forms, where ornamental spiral lines and small onion towers in brilliant colours complement rounded or curved building structures. An imposing high-rise landscape developed along the **Wagramer Strasse** in a mixed use of Classicism with a striking trio of towers in which Coop Himmelb(l)au, NFOG (Peter

The image of KunstHausWien is off-beat, colourful and playful

Nigst, Franco Fonatti, Marco Ostertag, Horst Gaisrucker) and Peichl/Weber were architecturally involved. The architectural remodelling of **Brigittenau** in the 20th district is impressive, with Europe's third highest office building, the Millennium Tower (202m / 663ft; 1999) on an octagonal foundation in Handelskai by Gustav Peichl, Boris Podrecca and Rudolf Weber.

Ottakring in the 16th district has gained new importance as a residential area through the U-3 terminal station, where old and new buildings mix. The architects include the architectural firm of Nehrer + Medek and Partner.

The so-called revitalized large areas such as the four **historic gasometers** (1896–1899) in Simmering, which were converted by Coop

Baedeker TIP

Fuchs Museum in the Wagner Villa

The painter Ernst Fuchs lives in the villa that Otto Wagner, a pioneer of modern architecture, had built for himself in neoRenaissance style around 1887. A large part of the spectacularly furnished interior rooms is open as a private museum for tours by small groups. Mon – Fri 10am to 4pm; more detailed information at www.ernstfuchs-zentrum.com.

Himmelb(l)au, Wilhelm Holzbauer, Jean Nouvel und Manfred Wehdorn for residential and commercial purposes, is controversial. Not one of the architects was able to create a convincing solution and no one really wants to live there. Standing out among the industrial structures are the elegant **Fernwärmewerk Wien Süd** (South Vienna district heating plant, 1996) by Martin Kohlbauer, the **U-6 station Erlaaerstrasse** (1995) of crinkled aluminium trapezium sheet metal by Johann Georg Gsteu and the **U-6 station Handelskai** (1996) in lattice girder framework with the maintenance walkways on the exterior, by the U-Bahn architectural group (Wilhelm Holzbauer, Heinz Marschalek, Georg Ladstätter, Bernd Gantar).

The most spectacular project, Danube City, is presently in construction. A second city, a **»global village«**, is emerging between UN City and the Danube to ease the strain on the city centre by providing residential and office space, shops, hotels and recreational and cultural facilities. Neumann and Krischanitz designed a plan that divides the whole area in three-dimensional parcels that are to be successively built and used without having established particular, detailed buildings at the outset. Hans Hollein was entrusted with the construction of the **primary school** and the **day nursery** and Wilhelm Holzbauer with the **»Tech Gate Vienna«** office building and the oval **Andromeda Tower**.

Painting   The so-called **Viennese School of Fantastic Realism** developed in Vienna after 1945 in dissociation from abstract art and in exploration of French Surrealism. Its most important exponents are **Ernst Fuchs, Rudolph Hausner and Erich Brauer**. After the experience of fascism, they critically reflected upon the subjects of war and peace, nature and culture, as well as the philosophical, ethical and psychological issues of modern civilization. **Maria Lassnig** began with expressive figurative painting, became involved with the Avant-garde and, in the early 1950s, turned to informal art, but soon returned to new, free figuration. Lassnig is a proponent of strongly self-centred painting that expresses emotions as physical experiences in symbolic body shapes and in psychologically meaningful colours. **Arnulf Rainer** began with expressive paintings in fantastic realistic style, which he then extended to an exhibitionistic psychological dialog with his own body. Whereas his early works were executed in very dark tones, he has brightened up his colour palette in the last couple of years. Among Austria's most significant **sculptors** of the 20th century are Fritz Wotruba and his student **Alfred Hrdlicka**. Wotruba's early works were figures and torsos in rigorously closed forms, which the artist began to reduce and make more abstract after the war. Although he does not choose very large formats, his works appear somewhat monumental. Hrdlicka assumes contemplation of nature as a basis for artistic expression that must be conveyed through the senses. He suggests the flesh as the »embodiment of generators of new ideas«. Thus his sculptures worked

The Memorial Against War and Fascism

directly out of stone possess graphic creative expression and formal complexity. They often have problems of violence as their subject. From 1988 to 1991, Hrdlicka created the four-part **Memorial against War and Fascism** on Albertinaplatz that was at first very controversial. **Hermann Nitsch** has been causing a stir in Vienna since 1957 with his symbolic blood offerings in his **»Orgien-Mysterien-Theater«** (Theatre of Orgies and Mysteries) and later with actionist »splatter paintings«. The resulting **Vienna Actionism** art trend developed around 1960, parallel to Flux and Happenings. The Viennese artists – next to Nitsch, **Otto Muehl, Günter Brus and Rudolf Schwarzkogler** – broke cultural taboos and propagated the release of anarchic creativity. Their ideas led in the 1970s to the founding of the socially utopian »Analytical Action Organization for Consciously Living Life«.

Franz West creates furniture sculptures, combining art work and articles of daily use, as in his peculiar seating in the Documenta X halls in Kassel, Germany. **Gerwald Rockenschaub** relied on the dialog between art's interior space and the exterior space of the city in his stagings of Austria's Venice Biennale pavilions in 1993, and in Linz in 1995. **Heimo Zobernig** works out concepts of social and artistic interaction with paintings, sculptures, videos and performances.

Music

Court and Church Around the middle of the 12th century, when Vienna became the residence of the Babenbergs, the court and church continually ensured the patronage and production of music. Furthermore, there was broad scope for the performance of liturgical music, not only in the churches of St Stephen's – probably Vienna's central parish church after 1147, the Schottenstift, St Ruprecht and St Peter, but also in the monasteries founded in the 13th century. The music was performed in less strictly religious settings when it found its way into the organizational structure of a brotherhood, like that of the **Brotherhood of the Body of Christ** which existed in the 15th and 16th centuries at St Stephen's. Folk music was referred to as early as the 13th century, in verdicts of the Vienna municipal judiciary against itinerant minstrels. These musicians also enjoyed social acceptance, however, and **Eberhard** and **Wolfker** were mentioned in court records in 1215. The Babenberg rulers also encouraged the composition of courtly love songs. It was primarily **Reinmar von Hagenau** († before 1210) and his apprentice, **Walther von der Vogelweide** (1170 – 1230), who practiced this art at the Viennese court, an era that ended with the acclaimed work of **Hugo von Montfort** (1357 – 1423). **Heinrich von Meissen** († 1318) made the transition bridge to the art and music of the Meistersingers.

The Imperial Chapel Viennese musical life was given a boost through the **founding of the university** in 1365, and by theory and musical practice becoming more systematized in the school at St Stephen's. An important factor for the future was the **Imperial Chapel**, an institution of the Habsburg court. There had already been such a Chapel Royal since 1308 under Albrecht II, and the Imperial Chapel became more important under Maximilian I, who turned it into a centre of European music. It was the focus of Viennese musical life from Maximilian I's reign onwards. The initial dominance of the Dutch gave way early in the **17th century** to the influence of Italian musicians, who followed Ferdinand I from Graz. With masters like **Johann Heinrich Schmelzer** (1623 – 1680) and **Pietro Antonio Ziani** (1630 to 1711), the Italian-orientated tradition led to a brilliant development of ensemble music, a process that culminated in a golden age of Austrian Baroque with **Johann Josef Fux** (1660 – 1741) and **Georg Muffat** (1653 – 1704). **Heinrich Ignaz Franz von Biber** (1644 – 1704) marked an important stage of development in this process for the composition of sonatas for solo violin, without which later achievements, such as the solo sonatas of Johann Sebastian Bach, would be unthinkable.

The musical genre that outshone them all at this time, however, was **opera**. Ferdinand III brought Italian opera to the Viennese court and, from then on, it provided the background that shaped the style for development in opera that spanned over three generations. Opera experienced its golden age in Vienna under Leopold I (1658 – 1705). In competition with the French court and Pietro Francesco Cavalli who was active there, the Vienna court was able to secure the serv-ices of **Marc Antonio Cesti** from 1666 to 1669, an outstanding expo-nent of the Italian opera tradition. Cesti provided the most brilliant opera event in Vienna of the 17th century with his celebratory opera **»Il pomo d'oro«** (»The Golden Ap-ple«, 1666), the highlight of the wedding celebrations of Leopold I with Margarita of Spain. The Vien-na court thus had a part in the very important effect Venetian op-era had in the overall development of opera. Whereas around 1600 an uninterrupted vocal line continued to be favoured almost to the exclu-sion of instrumental music in the musical dramas of composers like **Jacopo Peri** and **Giulio Caccini**, a permanent musical form in the sense of a unification of dramatic plot and musical happenings would later evolve.

The death of Johann Josef Fux in the middle of the **18th century** marked not only the end of the golden age of Baroque, but also the end of the Imperial Chapel as a site of musical innovation. Composers now gained prominence without being closely associated with the Imperial Chapel. These included **Christoph Willibald Gluck** (1714 – 1787) and **Wolfgang Ama-deus Mozart** (1756-1791). The op-era reform associated with the name Gluck took place for the

Now as before, someone is always playing first fiddle

most part in Vienna. Working together with the Italian librettist **Ra-nieri de Calzabigi**, Gluck reshaped the Italian »opera seria« and the French »tragédie lyrique« into a complete musical dramatization of opera in which the compositional means were orientated toward a »musical truth«, a dramatic plot and its individual character roles. Of Gluck's many operas, the ones having the most far-reaching influence were *Orpheus und Euridike* (1762, Vienna), *Paris und Helena* (1770, Vienna), *Iphigenie in Aulis* (1774, Paris) and *Iphigenie auf Tauris* (1779, Paris).

Even though Gluck's work in musical drama did not prevail beyond the 18th century, the development of instrumental music continued in the wider German-speaking world and ultimately became concentrated in Vienna in the period after 1740. The acclaimed **triumvirate of Haydn, Mozart and Beethoven** set a level of standards that early on earned this period the name **»Classic Viennese«**. These musical giants overshadowed for the most part their forerunners like Georg Christoph Wagenseil (1715–1777) and Matthias Georg Monn (1717–1750), whose Symphony in D-Dur, composed in 1740, is one of the earliest in the new instrumental style. **Franz**

The Schubert memorial in the Stadtpark

Schubert (1797–1828) combined classical music with the most diverse musical genres. For example, the genre of the *Lied* (song) makes up a significant part of his work. His compositions were not only directed at the general public, but also at a close circle of friends that served as an audience in informal gatherings, or **»Schubertiaden«**, for his wonderful music. Musical life in Vienna changed in a decisive way in the mid-18th century, with the emergence of **public concerts**. In 1771, **Florian Leopold Gaßmann** organized the *Tonkünstler-Sozietät* (musicians' society), whose members were professional musicians.

19th Century In 1812, the **»Imperial Austrian Society of the Friends of Music«** was founded, and in 1817 the Conservatorium was opened. In 1842, Otto Nicolai, the conductor of the court opera at the time, started **philharmonic concerts**.

The 19th century, moreover, forms the chronological framework for the rise of those genres, which like few others embody the phenomenon of »Viennese music«: the operetta, the dance, and especially **the waltz**. The triumphant rise to success of the waltz, from **Joseph Lanner to Johann Strauss, and to his son, alsoJohann Strauss**, achieved one of the great refinements of popular light music by raising it to »musical art«. A development culminating in the operetta had its origins in the field of regional theatre, which was very important in Vienna, with exponents like **Josef Anton Stranitzky** (1676 – 1726). The direct forerunner was the Viennese folk play of the 19th century, shaped first and foremost by **Johann Nestroy** and Ferdinand Raimund. The operetta reached its high point with **Franz von Suppé, Franz Lehár, Johann Strauss (son), Karl Millöcker** and **Carl Zeller**, before, in a »silver era«, operettas from the likes of **Oskar Nedbal** (*Polenblut*, 1913) and **Emmerich Kálmán** (*Die Chárdásfürstin*, 1915) announced the demise of this genre. The death blow was dealt by American influences like jazz and musicals.

From the 1860s and 70s, Vienna was once again the chosen home of outstanding composers like **Johannes Brahms** and **Anton Bruckner**. Their work was central to a heated debate on basic issues of musical aesthetic. In reaction to the expressive aesthetic of the Romantic, the music critic Eduard Hanslick (*The Beautiful in Music*, 1854), a fierce advocate of aesthetic formalism, became the focus of a passionate argument that split the Viennese music world into »**Brucknerians**« and »**Brahmsians**«. A special feature of Vienna's world of music is **Schrammelmusik**. The name goes back to the **brothers Josef and Johann Schrammel**, who were very successful with their Schrammel Quartet of **two violins, a guitar and a clarinets** from 1884 to 1893. The music, often accompanied by folk singers, yodellers and whistling, was played for relaxation in a comfortable place. The Schrammel brothers left behind more than 250 dances, marches and songs.

Shortly after the musical dispute on symphonic writing, **Gustav Mahler** advanced Viennese opera to Central Europe's leading institution for the art under his direction (1897 – 1907). As composer, he became the centre of attraction for a young generation of composers who were interested in a fundamental departure from the late-Romantic process of development in music. As a result, music composition theory developed in the following decades around the composers **Arnold Schönberg, Alban Berg and Anton von Webern**, collectively known as the »**Second Viennese School**«. Their rejection of tonal harmony relationships in favour of the harmonic equality of each half-tone step (twelve-note composition or dodecaphony) marked one of the most important turning points in music history. The reopening of the Vienna City Opera in November 1955, destroyed in 1945, marked the start of a musical revitalization, and many other musical institutions were developed. At the vanguard were the **Vienna Philharmonic**, the **Vienna Symphonic**, the **Radio Wien Orchestra** (ORF), the **Vienna State**

20th Century

! Baedeker TIP

From Rock to Jazz
A landmark in the Viennese music scene is the Metropol (17, Hernalser Hauptstr. 55, tel. 40 77 74 02). With a history that reaches back to 1865, the music performed here ranges from rock and ballads to jazz. Herbert Grönemeyer, Konstantin Wecker and Georg Danzer have all played here to enthusiastic audiences.

Opera and the **Volksoper** (People's Opera). Many music festivals, along with a large number of church venues provide excellent scope for the continued cultivation of classical and church music.

Part of the **more recent Viennese music scene**, including the works of Hanns Jelinek (1901 – 1969), reflects a commitment to tradition. Vienna has many musical institutions of rank, including the Musikverein, inaugurated by Emperor Franz Joseph in 1870, the Konzerthaus, and the Vienna State Opera, which counts among the leading opera houses of the world. Complementing this tradition are the **Liedermacher (song-writers)**, who give a typical Viennese accent to their music. Among the most well-known interpreters are Wolfgang Ambros, who became known for ironic, melancholy pieces like *Es lebe der Zentralfriedhof (Long Live the Central Cemetery)*; Georg Danzer who wote about contemporary issues; Reinhard Fendrich, who is popular for his humorous songs; and Ludwig Hirsch, who is known for his quiet chansons about outsiders and the degenerate side of Vienna. The star of **Viennese rock** was »Ostbahn-Kurti«, a character that had been floating around the scene for years. With his band »Die Chefpartie«, he brought new and old rock and blues to

The figures in the Golden Hall of the Musikverein listen to the very best concerts

the stage with texts about the world of the average person in Vienna (*Favoriten-Blues, I foahr erster Klass*). In the recent past, however, only one artist has gained international attention, Johann Hans Hölzel alias »Falco« (1957 – 1998), with hits like *Der Kommissar* and *Rock me Amadeus* (► Famous People).

Vienna has established itself as a **musical city** with wide public appeal. Musicals like »Cats«, »Elizabeth« and »The Fearless Vampire Killers« are box-office hits at the Theater an der Wien and at the Raimundtheater, while colourful revues and variety shows are celebrating a major comeback in the resurrected Ronacher.

! *Baedeker* TIP

Jazz City Vienna

The local jazz scene is becoming ever busier and easily stands up to comparison with the world's capitals of jazz. In addition to traditional places like »Jazzland« and »Porgy & Bess«, the star keyboard artist and born Viennese, Joe Zawinul, opened Birdland in 2004, in the basement of the Hotel Hilton – another venue for exceptional international gigs (► p.88).

Famous People

Mozart, Freud, »Sisi« and Beethoven. The names read like a »Who's Who« of the 18th and 19th centuries, but not all the famous and important people were from back then. Elfriede Jelinek and Johann Hans Hölzel, better known as »Falco«, also already have their place in history.

Ludwig van Beethoven (1770 – 1827)

Born in Bonn, Beethoven came to Vienna as a 22-year-old and stayed until his death. He was considered difficult, closed himself off from the world and never really became Viennese, although he found patrons and made friends like Archduke Rudolf and the princes Lichnowsky, Lobkowitz and Kinsky. His **inner unrest** is reflected in the number of times he moved house. In 1802 in Heiligenstadt, while becoming increasingly deaf, Beethoven composed the »Heiligenstadt Testament«, a document assumed to be a letter to his brother. Beethoven's only opera, »Fidelio«, had its premier in 1805, at the Theater an der Wien. He stood at the pinnacle of his fame around 1810; afterwards, his hearing became continually worse until eventually, by 1819, he was completely **deaf**. The composer was buried eight years later in Währing cemetery and his remains were transferred to the Zentralfriedhof (Central Cemetery) in 1888.

He came and stayed

> **!** ***Baedeker* TIP**
>
> **Musical Shrine**
>
> A must for Beethoven lovers is the Pasqualati-haus (1, Mölkerbastei 8; Tue – Sun 9am to 12.15pm, 1pm – 4.30pm). The composer intermittently lived here and composed important works over the years, including the 4th, 5th and 6th symphonies, and »Fidelio«.

The major part of his work was composed in Vienna; all **nine symphonies** were first performed here. He created instrumental music to express deep emotion. The increasing greatness of his work is demonstrated by the exciting »Eroica« symphony, the sublime 6th symphony, the »Pastorale«, the exuberant 7th symphony, and the immortal **9th symphony** which first rang out in 1824, in the Kärntnertor Theatre.

Conveying emotion with instrumental music

Johann Hans Hölzel »Falco« (1957 – 1998)

Johann Hölzel was born on 19th February 1957, in Vienna. He broke off his studies at the Vienna Jazz Conservatory after three semesters and, in 1977, took the stage name of **Falco**. The East German ski jumper Falko Weißpflog had greatly impressed Hölzel with his achievements at the time. In 1981, Falco had his breakthrough with the single ***Der Kommissar***, which climbed to number one in almost all European countries. He even earned »Gold« for the single in Canada. In 1986, he succeeded in doing what every artist dreams of – his single ***Rock me Amadeus*** held the top position on the American Billboard charts for three weeks. Because this success was so fantastic, it weighed heavily on the singer. He was perfectly aware that he would never be able to repeat this success, but would always be measured

Pop star

← *The popular actor Fritz Muliar (1919-2009) in his signature role as »Good Soldier Švejk«*

by it. In the time that followed, interest in him and his music diminished until in 1995, he again landed a hit with *Mutter, der Mann mit dem Koks ist da*, under the pseudonym »T>>MA«. He emigrated to the Dominican Republic in 1996, where he was killed in an automobile accident shortly before his 41st birthday in 1998. His pallbearers were the rockers who had appeared 13 years previously in the video version of *Rock me Amadeus*. After his death, his album, *Out of the Dark*, was a great success.

Johann Bernhard Fischer von Erlach (1656 – 1723)

Baroque architect Austria's most important architect and master builder of Baroque began his career as a sculptor. Born in Graz, Fischer von Erlach lived for several years in Rome and worked there in Bernini's circle before he began work as a master builder in 1686, primarily in Salzburg and Vienna. Fischer von Erlach combined the form elements of Italian high Baroque with early French Classicism and late Antiquity. He achieved a synthesis of south European exuberance and Viennese elegance. His religious buildings often merge narrow, rectangular buildings with the central structure on an elliptic groundplan. His major work was a commission given by Karl VI to fulfil his vow to erect the **Karlskirche** in Vienna. Fischer von Erlach created a church that combines elements of Antiquity, Roman Baroque and early Classicism. First place among Vienna's secular buildings, the **Hofbibliothek** was completed by his son. He was also in charge of the first phase of construction of the **Schönbrunn Palace**, Prince Eugene's winter palace, as well as the building of the **Trautson Palace** and sections of the Schwarzenberg Palace.

Sigmund Freud (1856 – 1939)

Born in Freiberg in northern Moravia (today Príbor), Freud spent his youth in Vienna where he later also studied medicine. After the

first semester, Freud concentrated on the field of mental illnesses without known organic causes and their treatment. Freud worked in the city as a lecturer in neuropathology from 1885, and as professor and neurologist after 1902. His Jewish parentage finally forced him to emigrate to London in 1938, where he lived until his death. Freud is regarded as the **»father of psychoanalysis«**. He analyzed abnormal human behaviour and dreams and developed a psychotherapeutic method of treatment for mental disorders that focused on overcoming suppressed traumatic experiences. He saw all psychological activity as being determined by the force of drives. He believed subconscious drives, above all those of a sexual nature, seek gratification, while at the same time the psychological organism seeks to achieve a balance between these inner forces and external stimuli. According to Freud, suppressed traumatic experiences – above all in childhood – are the causes that bring on psychological disorders. Freud presented the sex drive as a determinant of human behaviour in *Beyond the Pleasure Principle* (1920), and counter-balanced it with the death drive. He traced cultural achievements back to an adaptation and redirection of the sex drive. A museum has been installed in Freud's flat at Berggasse no.19.

Hugo von Hofmannsthal (1874 – 1929)

Hugo von Hofmannsthal was a true son of the multinational nation of Austria. His Jewish ancestors came from Bohemia and Milan. Even his first poem, published when he was 17 years old, under the pseudonym »Loris«, was considered a literary sensation. His lyric poetry and dramas made him one of the most successful exponents of literary Impressionism and Symbolism. His work, **Der Schwierige**, (The Difficult Man) remains a part of Viennese theatre repertoire to this day. With his unconventional opera librettos for Richard Strauss, the poet created a new form of musical theatre and promoted the concept of theatre festivals with plays like **Jedermann** (Everyman), which is still brilliantly performed annually in Salzburg. Hofmannsthal formulated an important contribution to modern Austrian literature and philosophy of language with the publication of the **Chandos Brief** (A Letter) in 1902, which explored the role of speaking and remaining silent in human relationships.

Exponent of literary symbolism

Friedensreich Hundertwasser (1928 – 2000)

The tradition of Austrian Jugendstil lives on in the colourful, imaginative works of the native Viennese Friedrich Stowasser, who adopted the name Friedensreich Hundertwasser in 1949. Among the works of the artist who became known as the »painter of spirals« in 1953, are paintings, drawings, designs for postage stamps and telephone cards and various architectural projects. As early as the 1950s, the environmentally engaged artist appeared in public with happenings and manifestos, including the 1958 »Verschimmelungsmanifest gegen den Rationalismus in der Architektur« (Mould Manifesto against rationalism in architecture). Hundertwasser championed the preservation of nature and people-friendly construction. For example, a brightly coloured, low-income apartment block was built in Vienna between 1983 and 1985 with uneven, undulating floors. The design for the **KunstHausWien** museum, opened in 1991, is also his. He was given a permanent exhibit there, with over 300 pieces. Following his death, he was laid to rest on his property in New Zealand.

Political artist-architect

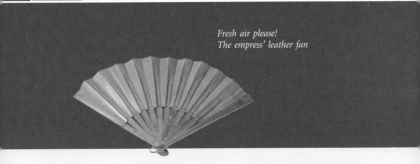

Fresh air please!
The empress' leather fan

ENFANT TERRIBLE OF THE HOFBURG

Arguably Europe's most admired woman, Empress Elizabeth of Austria led a life that paid no heed to public opinion, conventions or political calculation. The Empress, who oscillated between unrestrained self glorification and nerve-shredding depression held a fin-de-siècle mirror up to the Danube monarchy.

Elizabeth – who early on received the pet name of **Sisi** in her family – was born in Munich on Christmas Eve 1837, the second daughter of the Duke Max of Bavaria, who was not a member of the royal house of Wittelsbach. Consequently, the family was mostly relieved of ceremonial life at court and able to enjoy a private life. Elizabeth and her seven siblings experienced a **childhood without worries,** living at the Munich Max Palace and spending summers at the rustic country seat of the Possenhofen Palace on Lake Starnberg.

Happy Childhood

Since she was not deemed a suitable candidate for any royal court – unlike her sister Helene – systematic learning was peripheral, and Sisi's carefree disposition was delighted with games, sport and pranks. But it was to turn out differently. When Elizabeth accompanied her sister Helene to her engagement in Bad Ischl with the 23-year-old **Emperor Franz Joseph I of Austria** in August 1853, Franz Joseph immediately fell in love with Elizabeth and only wanted to marry the little cousin and no one else. You don't turn down an emperor, and thus Sisi gave herself up to her fate, somewhat embarrassed, insecure and intimidated by her royal relation. The country child from Bavaria had to be re-educated into an emperor's bride at top speed, with lessons in foreign languages, court etiquette and conversation. The sixteen-year-old bride's somewhat stressful journey to Vienna began in 1854, with receptions and honours at every stop. Elizabeth von Wittelsbach, the duchess from Bavaria, and Emperor Franz Joseph I were married at the Augustinerkirche in Vienna, 24 April 1854. The exhausting **eight-day wedding festivities,** the utterly unfamiliar court protocol, the strict mother-in-law Aunt Sophie, all produced culture shock for Sisi.

»I have awoken in a prison, and my hands are tied, and my longing grows for freedom that has left me!« wrote the freshly installed empress only two weeks after her wedding.

The empress in a ball gown on a portrait by Franz Xaver Winterhalter in the Hofburg

Escape from the Imperial City

At first she dedicated herself to the role of a pliant and quick to learn wife, if somewhat melancholy, whose main purpose was bringing imperial offspring into the world – a responsibility she pursued without delay. The hoped-for successor to the crown, **Crown Prince Rudolf**, was born in 1858, after the daughters Sophie (1855-1857) and Gisela (1856-1932). Since the youthful and inexperienced mother was not considered suitable for bringing her children up to be good Habsburgers, the supervision of the nursery was taken over by the mother-in-law, Archduchess Sophie. Initially, Franz Joseph's genuine affection mitigated Sisi's antagonism towards the Viennese Court and her depressive phases but, when rumours of her husband's affairs circulated, the 22-year-old empress and mother of two children, ran away from Vienna with her small entourage, and began two years of **exile** in Madeira, Venice and Corfu. Her outrageous behaviour was explained at Court as being due to life-threatening Tuberculosis.

During her long absence from the Viennese Court, a girlish, frightened, neurotic Sisi became transformed into a self-confident – even egocentric – Empress Elizabeth, who realised that her much-admired beauty and her rediscovered powers of self-assertion could be used as a weapon. Franz Joseph still admired her beauty and held her in an almost **submissive honour.** Thus, threatening to abandon Vienna once more if her wishes were not fulfilled, she successfully agreed with him that Crown Prince Rudolf's heartless militaristic upbringing would be replaced by an intellectual education and also established far-reaching liberties for herself at Court, including the installation of a fitness room at the Hofburg, complete with machines. Elizabeth held physical work-out sessions at every day.

Beauty and Egocentricity

By her mid-twenties, the delicate figure of the 50kg, 1.72m/5ft 8in Elizabeth, with artistically made up chestnut hair and dressed in rustling dresses and sparkling diamonds, was a magical appearance that evoked unrestrained enthusiasm throughout Europe. Huge efforts were necessary to maintain her beauty throughout her life, which increasingly led the empress to an almost full-time occupation with herself. Her narcissism caused her to hide **symptoms of aging** on her face behind veils, to become humanly distant and, eventually, to prohibit any paintings or photographs that showed her older than forty. Her opposition to the Viennese Court expressed itself in a love of Hungary. She learnt the Hungarian language and drew Hungarians into her inner circle of confidantes. During the war with Prussia in 1866, she sought safety for herself and her children in Hungary, where she made the acquaintance of the politician Gyula Andrassy, who became a life-long friend. Together with him, she persuaded Franz Joseph to establish the **Hungarian Compromise** which granted special rights and freedoms and was against the political wishes of Sophie (the emperor's mother) who wanted to promote Bohemia.

Georg Raab portrayed Elizabeth as Hungarian Queen in 1867

Queen of Hungary

Budapest and Vienna became capitals of equal status and the coronation of Franz Joseph and Elizabeth to **King and Queen of Hungary** in Budapest in 1867, was the highest political achievement of the empress. Ten months later Marie Valerie was born (1868-1924), the 'Hungarian child' who was entrusted to Elizabeth's care. In Hungary she was more or less at liberty to pursue her expensive **passion for horse-riding**, which included everything from circus dressage to hunting, and which took her on several journeys to England and Ireland in the 1870s.

»1000 brush strokes every day...«

Her representative duties in Vienna were only met reluctantly. Neither the jubilee festivities for Franz Joseph's

She would not allow pictures of her published, which showed her older than 40 years.

25th year in power in 1873, nor the imperial couple's **silver wedding** in 1879, were an occasion for her to spend longer periods in Vienna or even to appear in public. Elizabeth became increasingly shy of contact, concerned herself almost obsessively with her fading beauty with sessions lasting several hours, tortured her body with excessive sport and dieting and, every now and then, shocked the Imperial Court with her **republican ideas**. She read the books and poems of Heinrich Heine with great enthusiasm and was inspired to write her own verse, which she recorded in her secret diary that she left to the Swiss Republic for posterity. Elizabeth rarely saw her children and relations with them were extremely restrained, with the exception of Marie Valerie. Crown Prince Rudolf's love for his mother – with whom she shared many behaviour traits and convictions – was not returned. His unhappy marriage with Stephanie of Belgium sent the already delicate Crown Prince into ever

deeper depressions. Only **Rudolf's suicide** in 1889 drew Elizabeth out of her self-obsession and, at the same time, awoke such **strong feelings of guilt** that the empress spent the rest of her life bitter, lonely and suffering from nervous exhaustion. She travelled obsessively through Europe, dressed in black and incognito, at once plagued by rheumatism, suicidal feelings and sorrow at the world's misery.

Death in Geneva

She was finally relieved of the pointlessness of her existence by the fatal stabbing with a pointed file by the anarchist **Luigi Lucheni**, in Geneva. Her last words were: »What has really happened to me?« She died on 10 September 1898, at the **age of sixty**. The perpetrator was immediately arrested and shortly afterwards condemned to life in prison. In fact, he had wanted to murder the Duke of Orléans, but when he had been unable to find him, he killed the empress instead, whom he met by chance on the shores of Lake Geneva. At first he was proud of his deed, but then Lucheni committed suicide in his cell in 1910. Shortly after the crime, the empress' body was transferred to Vienna, where it was interred in the imperial vault with all the world's eyes on her once more.

Gustav Klimt (1862 – 1918)

Vienna's **leading exponent of Jugendstil** was born in Baumgarten as the son of an engraver. Klimt graduated from the Kunstgewerbe-

Animal-loving artist

schule (School of Applied Arts) in Vienna where, between 1897 and 1905 he headed up the »Secession« he had helped to found, an avant-garde association of artists inspired by European Art Nouveau. From 1886 to 1888, together with his brother Ernst Klimt and Franz Matsch, Klimt created the mural decorations on the side staircases of the Vienna Burgtheater. In addition, he decorated the Kunsthistorisches Museum (Art History Museum). It was not until the end of the 1890s that Klimt found the style that was to be typical of him, when he discovered French Impressionism and Symbolism, as well as the art of the Pre-Raphaelites and German Jugendstil. The works that followed were characterized by a fusion of flat linear figurative and ornamental elements. Nudes and portraits of women were portrayed in masterful drawings and delicately coloured paintings, whose decorative effect is often enhanced by the application of gold colour. In 1902, Klimt created the monumental **»Beethoven Frieze«** for the Vienna Secessionist exhibition.

Karl Kraus (1874 – 1936)

Writer and Journalist

Karl Kraus' life story can be read in the magazine he founded in 1899, *Die Fackel* (The Torch), which was published periodically over 37 years before Kraus ceased publishing in 1936, powerless against the brutal attacks by the Nazis. The sharp-tongued journalist created a forum for his malicious and witty commentaries with the *Fackel*. At the same time, he critically assessed his times and fought against corruption, thoughtlessness and hypocrisy of all kinds using satire, essays, aphorisms and poems with unsparing, unerring accuracy. Kraus was able to sit in a coffee house and discuss a single passage of text for hours, and even the empty spaces in his magazine during the war years were often more eloquent than words. In his major dramatic work, *Die letzten Tage der Menschheit* (The Last Days of

Mankind), the confirmed pacifist documented the apocalypse of the First World War and exposed its causes in the »armoured commercial world«.

Maria Theresa (1717 – 1780)

Maria Theresa was the daughter of Emperor Charles VI, who, lacking a male child, had the right of succession conferred on his daughter through the Pragmatic Sanction of 1713. When he died in 1740, she succeeded him in the Hapsburg countries. She became Archduchess of Austria and Queen of Hungary and Bohemia. After her husband, Duke Francis Stephen of Lorraine was elected emperor as Franz I in 1745, she was popularly referred to as empress, though this was technically incorrect. The woman »with the heart of a king« was forced to defend her country against France, Prussia, Saxony and Bavaria. Despite strenuously waged wars, she eventually lost Silesia, the best developed province of the Habsburg Empire, to the Prussian king, Frederick the Great. Domestically, Maria Theresa introduced **comprehensive civil reforms**, including a **new penal code** and mandatory education (»School Edict«, 1774), the abolition of torture and the amelioration of serfdom, which the nobility successfully prevented from being abolished. Despite being deeply pious, she took a strong position against the Catholic Church. The monarch combined power with a maternal disposition. She bore 16 children, including **Marie Antoinette**, the wife of King Louis XVI, who was executed during the French Revolution.

Habsburg Ruler

Wolfgang Amadeus Mozart (1756 – 1791)

The composer born in Salzburg demonstrated an unusual musical talent at an early age. As a 6-year-old »child prodigy«, he gave piano concerts in Munich and Vienna, which were followed by further appearances in Europe. As concert master in Salzburg for the archbishop, he travelled several times to Italy, which left its mark on his music. In 1781, a break with the archbishop led to his moving to Vienna, where he married Konstanze Weber in 1782, and worked as a freelance musician from then on. In 1782, the opera *Die Entführung aus dem Serail* (The Abduction from the Seraglio) had its premiere, in 1786 the opera *Figaros Hochzeit* (The Wedding of Figaro), and in 1791 *Die Zauberflöte* (The Magic Flute). But Mozart also experienced disappointments in Vienna, mostly of a financial nature, that adversely affected his health. Nine weeks after the premiere of The Magic Flute, he suffered an attack of severe miliary fever. He was buried in an unmarked communal grave in St Marx cemetery. During his happy years, Mozart lived in Figarohaus, which has been turned into a memorial. The annual **Vienna Mozart Festival** is an invitation to a musical encounter with the musical genius at the Vienna Konzerthaus.

Musical genius

Fritz Muliar (1919 – 2009)

Actor

»Švejk is dead« was the headline of the news magazine »Focus« over its obituary for the actor Fritz Muliar. Muliar played the role of the »good soldier Švejk« in the 1972 film version of Jaroslav Hašek's world famous novel so well that he was identified with the literary character from then on — and conversely as well: many people only recognized and still recognize Muliar's version of **»Švejk«**. Moreover, the similarity to Josef Lada's illustrations of Hašek's »The Good Soldier Švejk« to the actor is unmistakable.

Fritz Muliar was born in Vienna on December 12, 1919. At the age of 16 he began to study acting at the conservatory of Vienna. His first roles were in comedies in small theatres like »Der liebe Augustin« and »Simpl«. During World War II Muliar was condemned to death for demoralizing the military forces, but he was put on probation and sent to the eastern front. From 1949 on he lived in Vienna again and appeared in the Raimund Theatre, the »Simpl«, from 1974 to 1990 at the Burg Theatre and was part of the ensemble at the Theatre in the Josefsstadt. He celebrated 70 years on the stage in 2006. He also appeared in many films and TV productions. The title role in the TV series »The Adventures of the Good Soldier Švejk« made him famous in the entire German-speaking region.

Muliar was also known for his ability to imitate a Czech accent in German, which was called »Böhmakeln« and was part of the local Viennese culture; he was especially known for his Yiddish humor. As the son of a Jewish jeweller he published several volumes of Yiddish anecdotes and stories. Fritz Muliar appeared on stage in the Theatre in the Josefsstadt just a few hours before his death. 89 years of age, he played the leading role in »Die Wirtin« (lady pubkeeper), a comedy by Goldoni that was adapted by Peter Turrini. He died in the night of May 4, 2009.

Egon Schiele (1890 – 1918)

Expressionist Painter

Egon Schiele demonstrated an unusual talent for painting at an early age. His mentor was Gustav Klimt. He soon moved on from the Secessionist style to his own personal style, and gave up decorative ornamentation in favour of a strong expressivity. In contrast to many of his contemporaries, he remained for the most part true to representational art, creating nude pictures that depicted the models honestly and unembellished, which earned accusations of pornography and even a jail sentence. Besides self-portraits, he painted his family and other artists and landscapes. In 1918, a year which had brought great success through the exhibit in the Vienna Secession, Schiele died of the Spanish flu. Major works from his close to 2,000 drawings and watercolours can be found in the **Austrian Gallery** in the Upper Belvedere, and in the **Museum Moderner Kunst** (Museum of Modern Art).

Otto Wagner (1841 – 1918)

Otto Wagner set a new direction in the city of his birth through buildings that reflected their function and influenced the work of international architecture in modern times. After studying art in Vienna and Berlin, he was professor at the Art Academy in Vienna from 1894 to 1912, and a member of the Vienna Secession from 1899 to 1905. Whereas his earlier works, such as the villa in Hüllsdorferstrasse no.16, the tenement houses in Universitätsstrasse no.12, and Stadiongasse no.10, are still marked by Historicism, his buildings after the turn of the century were in Jugendstil style. Purpose, material and construction were important along with the decorative sculptural aspects. Wagner's combining of decoration and function was a model for numerous architects, including his students Josef Hoffmann, Joseph Maria Olbrich and Adolf Loos. The **36 stations of the Vienna municipal railway** were built according to Wagner's designs from 1894 to 1897. These structures, most of which have survived, are impressive in the way iron is decoratively combined with stone. At about the same time Wagner also designed the **flood gates** on the Danube Canal. The geometric structure characteristic of his later work is also typified in the granite, marble and glass frontage of the **Österreichische Postsparkasse** (1904 – 1906) on Georg Coch Platz.

Between Historicism and Modernity

! Baedeker TIP

Rejuvenation

For decades, Otto Wagner's Stadtbahnbögen along the Gürtel was a wasteland. Recently, the area between Thalia Strasse and Alser Strasse has been transformed into a trendy cultural and restaurant/bar zone. You can enjoy live music in bars like the Rhiz, Chelsea and B72, and turn night into day with style.

Practicalities

WHAT IS AN *EINSPÄNNER*?
HOW DO YOU GET TICKETS FOR A
CONCERT? WHAT DOES THE BERMUDA
TRIANGLE HAVE TO DO WITH VIENNA?
HERE YOU WILL FIND THE ANSWERS
TO THESE QUESTIONS, AND MUCH
MORE.

Accommodation

Hotels As Vienna is popular all year round, it is advisable to book accommodation in advance. The Vienna Tourist Board, which has a detailed hotel directory available (▶Information), and travel agents can be helpful in arranging accommodation. The quickest method is undoubtedly via the internet hotel booking sites.

Seasonal hotels Seasonal hotels offering cheap rooms are generally student hostels or residence halls located near the city centre that operate as hotels from July to September. An address list is available at the Vienna Tourist Board (▶Information) and at the Austrian National Union of Students (ÖH) (Taubstummgasse 7, A-1040 Vienna, tel. 31 08 88 00).

▶ RECOMMENDED ACCOMMODATION

▶ ① etc. ▶**Plan p. 74/75**
No number, outside the map

▶ **Price categories for double room**
Luxury: over 200 €
mid-range: 100 – 200 €
budget: up to 100 €

LUXURY: over 200 €

▶ ⑧ **Astoria**
1, Kärntnerstr. 32 - 34
A-1010 Vienna
Tel. 515 77
Fax 515 77 582
www.austria-trend.at
128 rooms; internationally renowned hotel in turn of the 20th century style, directly behind the Staatsoper and located in a pedestrian zone.

▶ ⑭ **Bristol**
1, Kärntner Ring 1
A-1015 Vienna
Tel. 51 51 60
Fax 51 51 65 50,
www.starwoodhotels.com
140 rooms, directly opposite the opera, still permeated by the spirit of the Belle Époque, offers exclusive accommodation and service. The greats of the international world of music meet here – as Leonard Bernstein once did.

▶ ⑮ **Grand Hotel**
1, Kärntner Ring 9
A-1010 Vienna
Tel. 51 58 00, fax 515 13 10
www.grandhotelwien.com
205 rooms; opened in 1870, not only the rooms and suites evoke an impeccable ambience, but also the grand ballroom and the two top-class restaurants, »Le Ciel« and »Unkai«.

▶ ⑰ **Palais Coburg**
3, Schwarzenbergplatz 9
A-1010 Vienna
Tel. 51 81 80, fax 51 81 81 00
www.palais-coburg.com
The classical-style palais near the City Park offers its guests 35 suites, most of them two-storied, a pleasant wine bistro with a garden pavillion and a large spa.

Le Meridien is highly modern

ⓝ **Le Meridien Vienna**
1, Opernring 13
A -1010 Vienna
Tel. 58 89 00, fax 588 90 90 90
www.vienna.lemeridien.com
294 rooms; Le Meridien is located between the Ringstrasse and the Academy. An historic façade hides a modern design concept with an abundance of light being the central element. The Shambala Restaurant offers international cuisine.

① **Plaza Vienna**
1, Schottenring 11
A-1010 Vienna
Tel. 31 39 00, fax 31 39 02 20 09
www.hilton.com
218 rooms; part of the Hilton chain; the rooms and suites have choice furnishings.

Rathaus Wein & Design
8, Lange Gasse 13
A-1080 Vienna
Tel. 400 11 22, fax 400 11 22 88
www.hotel-rathaus-wien.at
Its 39 rooms are dedicated to top Austrian vintners; the corresponding wines are to be found, appropriately enough, right in the rooms. The recently opened hotel is located a few steps from the Rathaus. The furnishings are modern and tasteful.

⑨ **Sacher**
1, Philharmonikerstr. 4
A-1010 Vienna
Tel. 514 56, fax 51 45 78 10
www.sacher.com
157 rooms and suites
See page 279 on Austria's most famous hotel.

MID-RANGE: 100 – 200 €

Altstadt Vienna
7, Kirchengasse 41
A-1070 Vienna
Tel. 522 66 66, fax: 523 49 01
www.altstadt.at; 42 rooms
Very nice pension in a restored patrician house near the Museum Quarter and the Biedermeier district of Spittelberg. Stylishly and comfortably furnished.

Vienna Hotel, Restaurants and Entertainment

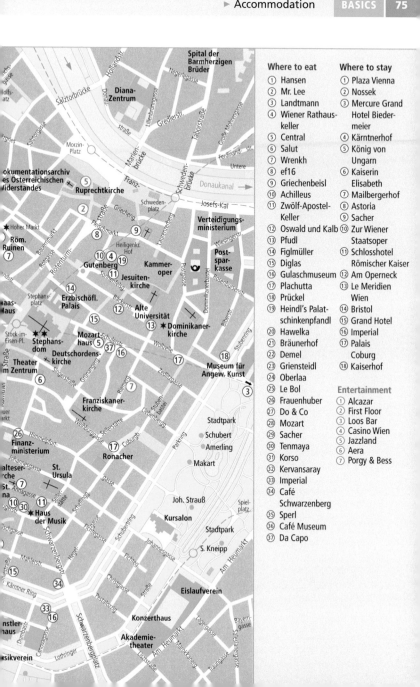

Where to eat

① Hansen
② Mr. Lee
③ Landtmann
④ Wiener Rathaus-keller
⑤ Central
⑥ Salut
⑦ Wrenkh
⑧ ef16
⑨ Griechenbeisl
⑩ Achilleus
⑪ Zwölf-Apostel-Keller
⑫ Oswald und Kalb
⑬ Pfudl
⑭ Figlmüller
⑮ Diglas
⑯ Gulaschmuseum
⑰ Plachutta
⑱ Prückel
⑲ Heindl's Palat-schinkenpfandl
⑳ Hawelka
㉑ Bräunerhof
㉒ Demel
㉓ Griensteidl
㉔ Oberlaa
㉕ Le Bol
㉖ Frauenhuber
㉗ Do & Co
㉘ Mozart
㉙ Sacher
㉚ Tenmaya
㉛ Korso
㉜ Kervansaray
㉝ Imperial
㉞ Café Schwarzenberg
㉟ Sperl
㊱ Café Museum
㊲ Da Capo

Where to stay

① Plaza Vienna
② Nossek
③ Mercure Grand Hotel Bieder-meier
④ Kärntnerhof
⑤ König von Ungarn
⑥ Kaiserin Elisabeth
⑦ Mailbergerhof
⑧ Astoria
⑨ Sacher
⑩ Zur Wiener Staatsoper
⑪ Schlosshotel Römischer Kaiser
⑫ Am Operneck
⑬ Le Meridien Wien
⑭ Bristol
⑮ Grand Hotel
⑯ Imperial
⑰ Palais Coburg
⑱ Kaiserhof

Entertainment

① Alcazar
② First Floor
③ Loos Bar
④ Casino Wien
⑤ Jazzland
⑥ Aera
⑦ Porgy & Bess

Ascent into the Imperial

Tel. 512 19 23, fax 513 22 28 33
www.karntnerhof.com
44 rooms; situated in the historic
centre, this is an old hotel with a
cosy atmosphere.

► ⑥ **Kaiserin Elisabeth**
1, Weihburggasse 3
A-1010 Vienna
Tel. 515 26, fax 51 52 67
www.kaiserinelisabeth.at
63 rooms; stylish first class hotel in
the heart of the city.

► ⑤ **König von Ungarn**
1, Schulerstr. 10
A-1010 Vienna
Tel. 51 58 40, fax 51 58 48
www.kvu.at
33 rooms; hotel with a tasteful
ambience and an impressive inner
courtyard.

► ⑱ **Kaiserhof**
4, Frankenberggasse 10
A-1040 Vienna
Tel. 505 17 01
Fax 505 88 75 88
www.hotel-kaiserhof.at; 74 rooms
The award-winning hotel is centrally located yet quiet, and has
floors for non-smokers.

► ⑯ **Imperial**
1, Kärntner Ring 16
A-1015 Vienna
Tel. 50 11 00, fax 50 11 04 10
128 rooms; these noble premises
were built for the Duke of
Württemberg in 1869, and four
years later the luxury hotel managed to open in time for the World
Exhibition. Austria's visitors of
state have been residing here since
the time of the emperors.

► ④ **Kärntnerhof**
1, Grashofgasse 4
A-1010 Vienna

► ⑦ **Mailbergerhof**
1, Annagasse 7
A-1010 Vienna
Tel. 512 06 41, fax 512 06 41 10
www.mailbergerhof.at
48 rooms; first class establishment
in the Annagasse, where meals are
served in the cosy courtyard garden during summer.

► ⑪ **Mercure Grand Hotel
Biedermeier Wien**
3, Landstraßer Hauptstraße 28
A-1030 Vienna
Tel. 71 67 10 10, fax 71 67 15 03
www.arcorhotels.at
201 rooms; the structure, renovated in its original Biedermeier style
and with a unique shopping arcade, promises comfort at its best.

► ⑪ **Best Western
Römischer Kaiser**
1, Annagasse 16
A-1010 Vienna

Tel. 51 27 75 10, fax 512 77 51 13
www.bestwestern.at
24 rooms; listed Baroque palace
with delightfully furnished rooms.

BUDGET: up to 100 €

▶ Altwienerhof
15, Herklotzgasse 6
A-1150 Vienna
Tel. 892 60 00, fax 89 26 00 08
www.altwienerhof.at
32 rooms and suites
Individually arranged rooms with
a tendency toward the romantic;
restaurant and an exquisite wine
cellar and vinotheque.

▶ Academia
8, Pfeilgasse 3 a
A-1080 Vienna
Tel. 43 14 01 76, fax 43 14 01 76 20
www.academia-hotels.co.at
260 rooms; the hotel is situated in
a quiet neighbourhood with bar
and roof terrace. Open from July 1
until September 30.

▶ Arcotel Bolzmann
9, Boltzmanngasse 8
A-1090 Vienna
Tel. 31 61 20, fax 31 61 28 16
www.arcotel.at
70 rooms; the hotel is quietly
situated a short walk away from
the Liechtenstein Museum. Trendy
»in« spots can be reached in a few
minutes of walking; also the
Ringstrasse is only a ten minute
walk away.

▶ ② Nossek
1, Graben 17
A-1010 Vienna
Tel. 533 70 41, fax 535 36 46
www.pension-nossek.at
30 rooms; cultivated pension in
the pedestrian zone, a few steps
away from St Stephen's Cathedral

Arcotel Bolzmann is located near to the Ringstrasse

▶ ⑩ Zur Wiener Staatsoper
1, Krugerstr. 11
A-1010 Vienna
Tel. 513 12 74, fax 513 12 74 15
www.zurwienerstaatsoper.at
22 rooms; hotel in a historic
building near to the state opera.

▶ ⑫ Am Operneck
1, Kärntner Str. 47
A-1010 Vienna
Tel. 512 93 10, Fax 512 98 10 20
7 rooms; centrally located, nice
pension across from the opera.

▶ Faist
18, Schulgasse 9
A-1180 Vienna
Tel./fax 406 24 05
www.kronline.at
7 rooms; small but nice B&B
in an old Viennese house from
1869.

▶ Kugel
7, Siebensterngasse 43
A-1070 Vienna

Tel. 523 33 55, fax 523 33 555
www.hotelkugel.at
Located near the city centre, old
Viennese atmosphere, rooms with
all the conveniences

YOUTH HOSTELS

▶ **Jugendgästehaus der Stadt
Vienna Hütteldorf-Hacking**
13, Schloßberggasse 8
Tel. 877 15 01, fax 87 70 26 32
www.oejhv.or.at

▶ **Jugendherberge
Myrthengasse**
7, Myrthengasse 7
Tel. 523 63 16, fax 523 58 49
www.oejhv.or.at

▶ **Schloßherberge am
Wilhelminenberg**
16, Savoyenstr. 2
Tel. 481 03 00, fax 481 03 00 13
www.oejhv.or.at

CAMP SITES

▶ **Aktiv Camping
Neue Donau**
22, Am Kleehäufl
Tel. 202 40 10, fax 202 40 20
www.wiencamping.at
Open mid-April – mid-Sept

▶ **Vienna-Süd**
23, Breitenfurterstr. 269
Tel. 867 36 49, fax 867 58 43
www.wiencamping.at
Open Easter and June – Aug

▶ **Vienna-West**
14, Hüttelbergstr. 80
Tel. 914 23 14, fax 911 35 94
www.wiencamping.at
Open March – Jan

▶ **Camping Rodaun**
23, An der Au 2
Tel. 888 41 54
open end of March – Nov

Arrival · Before the Journey

Getting to Vienna

By car
from the UK

The route from London to Vienna is a distance of around 1435km/
899mi, and easy motorway driving almost all the way. Without taking rest stops, you could manage it in 15 hours, not counting the
ferry journey across the Channel, from Dover to Calais. The recommended route is from Calais to Bruges and Antwerp in Belgium,
crossing briefly into Holland before passing into Germany near
Aachen. Heading past Cologne, follow the motorway signs to
Nürnberg, and then turn off for the motorway in the direction of
Passau and Prague. The motorway signage is very clear. On crossing
into Austria shortly after Passau, continue on the A25 motorway in
the direction of Vienna.

Tolls All Austrian autobahns and some expressways charge fees and drivers
need to buy a motorway **vignette**, which costs €7.60 for ten days and
€21.80 for two months. You can buy them at petrol stations and at
the border.

The airport **Vienna-Schwechat** lies 19km / 12mi outside Vienna and can be reached from more than 40 European airports, as well as some trans-Atlantic ones. There are direct flights from London (2hrs 10min) and New York (9hrs). Those who prefer to fly cheaply can try to catch a flight with a »low cost carrier« like Air Berlin (www.airberlin.com) or Germanwings (www.germanwings.com). See also companies such as EasyJet and Ryanair. Overseas visitors should check www.flightcentre.com for flight connections from outside Europe. Austrian Airlines, Air Canada and British Airways all have international routes to Vienna from overseas. Austrian Airlines is worth checking for its twice weekly flights from London's City Airport direct to Vienna.

By air

The most convenient connection from the airport to the city centre/ Wien Mitte is the **City Airport Train**. It runs daily every half an hour from 5.37am – 11.36pm. Non-stop travel time: 16 minutes, tel. 252 50. The **Vienna Airport Lines** express buses travel from the airport to Schwedenplatz/Postgasse in the city, 5am – 0.30am and in the opposite direction from 5.30am – 1am. In addition, there is a shuttle bus from the airport to the west und south train stations from 5.30am – 11.10pm, and the journey takes around 30min. Taxis can be found north of the arrivals hall.

Arriving by train in Vienna gets you to either the Südbahnhof (south railway station) or the Westbahnhof (west railway station) and the most useful information on rail connections and prices from the UK can be found at www.seat61.com. Ideally, you would take the Eurostar (www.eurostar.com) from London to Paris and change there for a direct train to Vienna, a journey that can be made in one day. Another good source of information on European rail connections is www.raileurope.com. Travellers from overseas might find it worthwhile buying a Eurailpass (www.raileurope.com) before arrival, if planning to travel widely by train. Those of any nationality and under the age of 25 can also enjoy unlimited travel in Europe in specified selected zones by purchasing an InterRail pass. Travel offices in Vienna's West and South stations are helpful for arranging accommodation, if you have not booked before arrival.

By rail

There are international coach connections between the UK's major cities and Vienna offered by National Express for Eurolines. For booking and information see www.nationalexpress.co.uk or, in the UK, phone 01582-400694.

By bus

A return ticket from London to Vienna costs in the region of £100. Buses arrive either at Südtirolerplatz 16 or at the Erberg Underground Station. Luggage is limited to one suitcase and one item of hand luggage. A wonderful new service for independent travellers is offered by www.busabout.com, which sells hop-on-hop-off bus passes for Europe. Their service includes route planning and accommodation finding assistance.

▶ ADDRESSES

AIRLINES

▶ Air Canada
Argentinierstr. 2
Tel. 58536 3040; www.aircanada.ca

▶ Austrian Airlines
3, corner of Invalidenstr./
Marxerbrücke
Tel. 05 17 66 10 00; www.aua.com

▶ British Airways
Kärntner Ring 10
Tel. 79567 567, www.ba.com

▶ Lufthansa
6, Mariahilfer Str. 123
Tel. 08 10 10 25 80 80
fax 587 39 32; www.lufthansa.at

▶ Swiss
1, Marc-Aurel-Str. 4
Tel. 08 10 81 08 40
www.swiss.com

▶ Flight Information
Tel. 700 72 22 33

BUS COMPANIES

▶ Eurolines
Erdbergstrasse 202
Tel. 7982900, www.eurolines.at

▶ Blaguss-Reisen
23, Richard-Strauss-Str. 32
Tel. 61 09 00
Hotline: tel. 50 18 01 00
www.blaguss.at

AUSTRIAN FEDERAL RAILWAYS

▶ Train information (24hr)
Tel. 05 17 17
www.oebb.at

SHIP CONNECTIONS

▶ Austria Werbung
Holiday service
4, Margaretenstr. 1
Tel. (UK) 0845 101 18 18
Fax 888 66 20
www.austria.info/uk

By boat From May to September, the ships of the Blue Danube Schifffahrt GmbH (DDSG; ▶ Information) ply the old imperial travel route from Linz, by way of Melk and Krems, to Vienna, a route steeped in tradition. Information about the ship connections can also be obtained from Österreich Werbung, the national tourist organization (www.austria.info), and Austrian Information (▶Information).

By bicycle Athletic tourists can cycle from Passau along the Danube to Vienna. The bike path, about 320km/199mi long and well sign-posted, is mostly downhill and leads through the delightful Danube Valley past the historically rich castles of the Wachau. Information is supplied by the Österreichische Bundesbahn (Austrian Federal Railway at www.oebb.at). The nearest international airport for reaching Passau is Munich and many airlines will transport your bike as part of ordinary luggage if you follow their requirements, available from the relevant airline.

Entry and Exit Regulations

Since Austria joined the **Schengen Agreement** in 1998, there has been no passport control on the German-Austrian border crossing. The authorities, however, continue to recommend having your travel documents with you because spot checks are randomly carried out. All travellers arriving by air, rail or bus need a valid passport, including children.

National driving licenses and vehicle documents must be brought along. It is recommended having an international green insurance card. It is required that vehicles bear an oval national identity sticker if they do not have European vehicle registration plates.

Travel documents

According to EU regulations, as of July 2004, dogs and cats are required to have a veterinarian-attested **pet passport** while travelling within EU countries. It contains, among other things, a government certification of the veterinarian letter or certificate of health (at most 30 days old), a certified rabies vaccination given at least 20 days, but not more than eleven months, prior to entry, as well as a passport photo. In addition, the animal must have a microchip or a tattoo. Muzzles and leashes must be brought along.

Pets

The member states of the European Union (EU), including Austria, form a common economic region in which the movement of goods for private purposes is largely duty-free. Nevertheless the following **maximum amounts** apply: 800 cigarettes, 400 cigarillos, 200 cigars or 1kg/2.2lb smoking tobacco, 10 l/2.6 US gal spirits, 20 l/5.3 US gal intermediate products (e.g. Sherry, Port, Madeira), 90 l/ 23.8 gal wine, of which there is a maximum of 60 l/15.8 US gal sparkling wines, and 110 l/29 US gal beer. Gifts up to 430€ in value (by air) or 300€ in value (by car, bus or train) are also duty-free.

The customs exemption limit for travellers coming from non-EU countries is 550g/1lb 1oz coffee, 100g/3.5oz tea; 200 cigarettes, 100 cigarillos, 50 cigars or 250g smoking tobacco; furthermore 2 l/0.5 US gal wine or other beverages with less than 22 vol % alcohol content as well as 1 l/0.25 US gal spirits with more than 22 vol % alcohol content.

Customs Regulations

Travel Insurance

Before a trip to Austria checking the latest regulations with the relevant health insurance company is recommended, and UK nationals should remember to ask for a European Health Insurance Card (EU EHIC card), available from post offices. It is advisable to purchase a private travel insurance policy which covers the costs of transportation home in the event of an emergency. Even with an EHIC card, a portion of the costs for medical care and medicine must be paid by the patient in most cases. A private health insurance company will assume the costs upon presentation of receipts – though not for all treatments.

Health insurance

Cemeteries

In the **Friedhof der Namenlosen** (Cemetery of the Nameless), 11, Alberner Hafen, between the warehouses and railway tracts on the Danube floodplains, around 100 accident victims and suicides are buried, pulled out of the Danube during the first 40 years of the 20th century. Most of the graves bear no name because many of the victims could no longer be identified, giving the cemetery the name it is known by today, the »Cemetary of the Nameless«.

Today, the **Friedhof St Marx**, 3, Leberstraße 6 – 8 is only a memorial site with 8,000 headstones. It is the only surviving Biedermeier cemetery. Mozart was buried here in 1791, in an unmarked mass grave. Later, the grave could not be found. A cemetery attendant once dressed up the spot where it is thought to have been with obsolete grave decorations – an angel, the stump of a column and a stone tablet - and so it has remained to this day. The cemetery was used from 1784 to 1873, until the opening of the Central Cemetery. The **Hietzinger Friedhof**, 13, Maxingstraße 15, with its well-cared for grounds of over 14,000 graves, stretches out on the fringe of the Schönbrunn Palace park. Besides the mausoleums of the Austrian high nobility, there are a wealth of Empire und Biedermeier tombstones. Among the graves in the cemetery are those of the painter Gustav Klimt, the poet Franz Grillparzer, the architect Otto Wagner, the composer Alban Berg and the dancer Fanny Elssler.

The alleged grave of Wolfgang Amadeus Mozart

The key to the **Israelite Cemetery in the Rossau** can be obtained from the caretaker of the Municipal Home for the Aged at the cemetery entrance (9, Seegasse 11). Vienna's second oldest Jewish cemetery is one of Europe's oldest. It is thought to have been laid out at the beginning of the 16th century – the first one was once located outside the Kärntner city gate and was destroyed in the 15th century. The oldest identifiable gravestone dates back to 1582. When all cemeteries in the outlying villages were closed by order of Emperor Joseph II in 1783, it also affected the cemetery in the Seegasse. When the Danube overflowed in 1784, it destroyed many gravestones. During the Nazi era, the gravestones were removed and in 1943 buried in the Central Cemetery, thus saving them. Some of them were brought back after 1945 and placed on the original site. Up to 1923, **Schubert Park** (18, Gymnasiumstrasse/Semperstrasse) was the Währing district municipal cemetery. During the re-landscaping, one grove with burial sites was left untouched, among them the graves of Ludwig van Beethoven und Franz Schubert.

The **Central Cemetery** in the Simmeringer Hauptstrasse, 11th district, has been Vienna's main cemetery since its opening in 1873 (► p.305).

Children in Vienna

Vienna offers its younger visitors a multitude of attractions and entertainment, from special children's tours or areas in the large museums to the »classic« amusement park, the Prater. Information about events for children and teenagers in Vienna can be found at www.wienxtra.at. For older children, it is worth checking out www.viennahype.at. All the latest about Vienna's nightlife, art and culture and whatever else is on offer can be discovered there.

For little ones

The two big museums in the historic city centre, the **Kunsthistorisches Museum (Art History Museum) and the Naturhistorisches Museum (Natural History Museum)** are also popular amongst children. There are, for example, dinosaur fossils, including the skull of a Tyrannosaurus rex, and an impressive number of mounted animals. The Kunsthistorisches Museum offers tours for children and the Naturhistorisches Museum has a child-

> **!** *Baedeker* TIP
>
> **Baby Breakfast**
>
> Café Stein offers a service every Sunday well into the afternoon to relieve stressed parents. While Mummy and Daddy enjoy an undisturbed breakfast, chat and read the paper, an experienced minder takes care of their offspring in the Kid's Room (9, Währinger Str. 6 – 8, tel. 319 72 41).

⏵ ADDRESSES

CHILDRENS' THEATRES

► **Akzent**
4, Theresianumgasse 16 – 18
Tel. 501 65 33 06

► **Marionettentheater
Schloss Schönbrunn**
Hofratstrakt
13, Schönbrunner Schlossstr.
Tel. 817 32 470
www.marionettentheater.at

► **Niedermair Kindertheater**
8, Lenaugasse 1 a
Tel. 408 44 92
www.niedermair.at

► **Theaterhaus für
junges Publikum**
►theatre and concerts

ren's programme. Children also love this museum's collections; for example, the dinosaurs and the impressive number of stuffed animals. Inside the new **Museum Quarter** there is a museum especially for children, with a touch and feel art exhibition. Children can take an enjoyable journey through the world of technology in the Mini-TMW in the **Technisches Museum** (Museum of Technology). Older children like the musical electronic experiments in the new **Haus der Musik** (House of Music).

For those who like creepy and scary things, Vienna's most notorious crimes can be investigated in the **Kriminal Museum**. Naturally, things are a little less violent in the **Circus and Clown Museum** and in the **Teddy Bear Museum**.

The children's museum in **Schönbrunn Palace** offers an invitation to take a trip into the past. Young visitors can experience close-up what things were like at the imperial court with the Hapsburgs.

Activities   The number one entertainment venue for children is the **Prater** with its many amusement rides. The traditional merry-go-rounds are also suitable for small children. In addition, a miniature railway runs around the fairground. Young visitors also have fun in the **Schönbrunn Tiergarten** (zoo) with an elephant park and seal feeding. The **maze and the labyrinth** also attract children. Once upon a time, only the imperial family strolled through the maze, now it is open to everyone.

Electricity

The Austrian mains carry 220 volt alternating current. As a rule, European norm connector plugs can be used.

Emergency Numbers

Tourists in Vienna who need urgent medical assistance can use the hotline number 513 95 95. In cooperation with the Viennese Chamber of Doctors, the 24-hour free service will put you in touch with the appropriate doctor or specialist.

Medical Hotline

● MOST IMPORTANT EMERGENCY NUMBERS

► **Police**
Tel. 133

► **Fire Department**
Tel. 122

► **Medical Assistance**
►Health

► **Breakdown Service**
►Transport

Entertainment

The **Bermuda Triangle** is what the Viennese call the »nightlife district« between St Stephen's Cathedral and the Danube, around Schönlaterngasse and Bäckerstrasse, all the way to St Ruprechtkirche, because whoever »disappears« here is usually gone for a while; even when they do show up, they often cannot remember anything. The localities around the Vienna Ring in the **Stadtbahnbögen** (arches under the elevated underground) are no less »exciting«. This area has experienced a revival after urban renewal, with many bars and clubs springing up.

Nightlife

● NIGHTLIFE ADDRESSES

BARS

► **Alt Wien**
1, Bäckerstrasse 9
Tel. 5125222
A long-standing favourite among students and a great place to find out what's going on around the city.

► **Alcazar**
1, Bösendorferstr. 2
Tel. 504 35 45

Stylish cocktail bar with a touch of luxury that still retains a cosiness about it.

► **Café Berg**
9, Berggasse 8, tel. 3195720
Close to Schottentor Underground station, Vienna's top gay bar offers a relaxed and very cool atmosphere.

► **First Floor**
1, Seitenstettengasse 5

Vienna offers its guests innumerable bars and cafés, like this one in the Bermuda Triangle

Tel. 533 78 66
One of the city's best cocktail bars; the huge aquarium behind the bar is a real eye-catcher.

► **Loos Bar**
1, Kärntner Str. 10
Tel. 512 32 82
This Jugendstil bar designed by Adolf Loos is wonderful and draws locals as well as the tourists.

► **Planter's Club**
1, Zelinkagasse 4
Tel. 533 33 93 15
Bar in colonial period style with a huge selection of spirits and whiskies. R.E.M., Mick Jagger and others have been guests here.

► **Strandbar Herrmann**
3, Herrmann Park
This trendy bar on the canal is designed like a beach bar, with real sand and deck chairs.

► **Café Willendorf**
6, Linke Wienzeile 102
Tel. 5871789
One of Vienna's longest established gay and lesbian bars with a great courtyard for summer evenings.

► **Stylez**
7, Neubaugasse 10
Tel. 990 75 83
During the day a café, in the evening a club, though most people sit instead of dance. Occasionally fashion shows are presented.

CLUBS · NIGHTLIFE

► **Arena**
3, Baumgasse 80
Tel. 798 85 95
Two entertainment halls in a former slaughterhouse and a brilliant open-air area make this club a significant venue for live music.

► **B 72**
8, Hernalser Gürtel
Stadtbahnbögen 72/73
Tel. 409 21 28
The club continually stages concerts during the week; admission is free at weekends.

► **Chelsea**
8, Lerchenfelder Gürtel
Stadtbahnbögen 29 - 31
Tel. 407 93 09
Club and live music with pop and underground, the Chelsea is considered the place to hang out in the party scene.

► **Flex**
1, Donaukanal, Augartenbrücke
Tel. 5337525
Unpretentious club with a famous sound system that also stages live acts and offers a changing roster of international DJs. No strict dress code and the outdoor area is an added attraction.

► **Meierei**
3, Stadtpark
Am Heumarkt 2 a

Tel. 714 61 59
Idyllic beer garden with seating for close to 300.

► **Rhiz**
8, Lerchenfelder Gürtel
Stadtbahnbögen 37/38
Tel. 409 25 05
An »in« venue that presents concerts, podium discussions and readings.

► **Volksgarten**
1, Burgring 1
Tel. 5324241
One of the capital's most popular clubs and a great place to dance or just hang out at the long bar.

CASINO

► **Casino Wien**
Kärntner Str. 41
Tel. 51 24 83 60
The Vienna Casino is located in the renovated Palais Esterhàzy in the Kärntnerstrasse. Those who want to try their luck can choose between roulette, black jack, poker and more.

Live music in Jazzland

ROCK · POP · JAZZ

▸ **Aera**

1, Gonzagagasse 11
Tel. 533 53 14
Breakfast is served here until 4pm at weekends and various sports events are transmitted live.

▸ **Birdland**

3, Am Stadtpark 1
Entrance: Landstraßer Hauptstr. 2
Tel. 219 63 93
Top acts perform here and the hot tips are mainly from the fields of jazz, pop and World music.

▸ **Jazzland**

1, Franz-Josefs-Kai 29
Tel. 533 25 75
Vienna's oldest jazz cellar is beneath a church, where every kind of jazz is played.

▸ **Riverboat Shuffle**

MS Schlögen
Tel. 715 15 25
In summer you can dance away on the ship to jazz and swing. Reservations required.

▸ **Szene Wien**

11, Hauffgasse 26
Tel. 7493341
A great place for live music ranging from jazz and reggae to rock and pop and always worth checking out. More info at www.szenewien.com.

Etiquette and Customs

Golden Heart

The legendary and much extolled »Golden Heart« that true-blue Viennese like to boast of is sometimes hard to detect by visitors and those who move here – the Viennese can be famously grumpy too. So what are its characteristics?

Viennese Schmäh or Humour ▸

One feature is undoubtedly the idiosyncratic and somewhat calculating humour that flows so easily from the locals' mouths, and which they call »Schmäh«. Another is the curious combination of a collective inferiority complex and a defiant self-satisfaction that historians versed in psychology attribute to the experience of being at the centre of an empire for centuries and then suddenly finding themselves in a little country left lying at the outermost fringe of free Europe for two generations. The Baroque manner the Viennese use to express themselves should always be taken with a pinch of salt and the **show of formal etiquette** should not be taken too literally. The same holds true for the biting wit that the Viennese like to wield. It is not always meant literally or personally and can be defused in an instant with a decent amount of charm. The Viennese like a **lively duel of words** for its own sake, but their notorious **griping** and frequently expressed fatalism and melancholy should rarely be taken at face value. Appearance and reality, seriousness and frivolity, the real world and play-acting are two sides of the same coin for the citizens of this once high Baroque imperial city. Their penchant for – mostly

Viennese Wit ▸

obscure – titles and for the **observance of old-fashioned proprieties** that sometimes appear down-right absurd, confuses non-Viennese because it is so anachronistic (best example is the hand kiss). There is no harm in excess politeness though, and visitors can easily enter into the Baroque spirit by joining the Viennese in dressing up to the nines for cultural and social events like concerts, the theatre, and evenings at the opera or ball.

It is a fact that the Viennese have an especially intimate relationship with death. Unlike some popular clichés, this one is true without exception. Need proof? If your language skills are up to it, listen closely to the words of their mournful songs after a few glasses of *Heurigen*. Wine that »will still be around when you are no more«, the »gown that will be sold to get to heaven«, and »the *Fiaker* that will carry you off when you die« are all frequently mentioned. Or listen to the Viennese when they go into raptures about the »schöne Leich« – the beautiful funeral that every ordinary person hopes will be the climax of their lives, an event when a magnificent funeral cortege and crowds of mourners are accompanied by music, impassioned eulogies and an opulent funeral feast. It was not by chance that Sigmund Freud came up with the **death drive** right here, in his home town. A popular proof of the Viennese death wish was always its place in the suicide statistics but, after being second only to Hungary for decades, the capital has now sunk to »just« a mid-range position. The Viennese appear to be getting happier – albeit reluctantly!

◄ Death

So that the holidays won't be memorable for the wrong reasons, we'll explain some of the most important rules of etiquette

Festivals, Holidays and Events

Festivals

It is worth taking a look at the programme of events published monthly by the Wiener Tourismus (►Information). In addition, it is also reprinted in »Hallo Wien – Guide Book« and in »Wien Magazin«. The Vienna tourist information website (see Information) is best for up-to-date listings. All pertinent information about the events that are taking place in the near future and how to obtain tickets can be found under www.wien-vienna.at and www.wien.info.

▶ FESTIVALS AND EVENTS

HOLIDAYS

January 1: New Year
January 6: Epiphany
Easter Monday
May 1: Labour Day
Ascension Day
Whit Monday
Corpus Christi
August 15: Assumption Day
October 26: National Holiday
November 1: All Saints Day
December 8: Immaculate Conception
December 25-26: Christmas

Debutants at the Opera Ball

JANUARY

► **New Year's Eve Concerts**
Concerts by the Vienna Philharmonic, the Vienna Symphony and the Hofburg Orchestra.

FEBRUARY

► **Opera Ball**
Celebrities from all over the world are guests at this famous event, which always takes place on the last Thursday of Fasching (carnival). Tickets tel. 513 15 13
www.wiener-staatsoper.at

► **International Dance Weeks**
Top dancers present a repertoire spanning classic ballet and waltz performances all the way to postmodern dance. The artists can be admired in February and March as well as in July and August.
Tel. 523 55 58 34

MARCH

► **Sounds of Easter**
At Easter, the Vienna Philharmonic and other orchestras perform pieces appropriate to the occasion. Ticket tel. 5 88 85

APRIL

▶ Vienna Spring Festival

The sound of classic notes fills the air in the Konzerthaus until mid-May. Tel. 24 20 02
www.konzerthaus.at

▶ Mozart Concerts

The Vienna Mozart Orchestra, together with other internationally-known musicians, play pieces by the musical genius until October. www.mozart.co.at

MAY

▶ Vienna Festival Weeks

Each year, the Vienna Festival Weeks (Wiener Festwochen) present the classic, the contemporary and the avant-garde.
Tel. 58 92 20
www.festwochen.at

JUNE

▶ KlangBogen Wien

Compositions from Baroque to the present can be heard between June and September at the »KlangBogen Wien«, including classical concerts in the arcaded courtyard of the Rathaus, as well as chamber music in Schönbrunn

---

! Baedeker TIP

Film Fun Open Air

On summer evenings, movie buffs can indulge their passion for film under an umbrella of stars. Open air cinemas offer a programme that changes daily, including the »Arena Sommerkino« (www.arena.co.at), the »Kino unter Sternen« (www.kinountersternen.at) and the »Tribüne Krieau« (www.tribunekrieau.at).

Palace and much more.
Tickets tel. 5 88 85
www.klangbogen.at

▶ Concordia Ball

Johann Strauss wrote some waltzes for this ball. The dancing takes place in the Rathaus, and also in the open air in the Arkadenhof.
Tel. 533 75 09
www.concordia.at

▶ Danube Island Free Festival

Open air festival –»Europe's biggest youth party« –, offers rock and pop music with no entrance charge.
www.donauinselfest.at

The festival weeks are always well attended

JULY

▸ **Jazz Festival Vienna**
Interpreters of jazz and its frontiers perform in the Staatsoper, in the Volkstheater and at open air concerts.
Tel. 712 42 24;
tickets tel. 319 06 06
www.viennajazz.org

▸ **Musikfilmfestival**
Famous opera films and live recordings of legendary concerts are shown outside on Rathausplatz until September. Entrance is free.
www.wien-event.at

AUGUST

▸ **Folk Festival**
The annual event with stars from the world of international music and entertainment and a huge fireworks show to end it with a bang. Tel. 728 05 16, www.prater.at

OCTOBER

▸ **Festival de Jeunesse**
The festival of Austria's musical youth offers the well-known and the new and presents music in all its manifestations.
Tel. 35 84 20 05, www.jeunesse.at

▸ **Viennale**
The highlights of Austrian and international film-making annually await the public at this film festival.
Tel. 52 65 94 70
www.viennale.at

DECEMBER

▸ **Kaiserball (Emperor's Ball)**
The Hofburg's annual invitation to dance into the New Year to waltzes and operettas in its palatial rooms.
Tel. 587 36 66 23
www.hofburg.com

Food and Drink

Everything but one-sided
The success of Viennese cooking lies in its diversity. The varied recipes betray the Southern German, Bohemian, Hungarian, Croatian, Slovenian and Italian influences of the former multi-national state. The Schnitzel was adopted from Milan, desserts from Bohemia, goulash from Hungary, smoked meats and the Bauernschmaus (farmer's feast) from the Alpine regions. The menu, peppered with dialect expressions, is neither light nor low in calories, but uses many natural products. The aforementioned **meat dishes and dessert pastries** enjoy quite a reputation. The range of freshwater fish and the quality of the **venison dishes** during the Wildbrettwochen (game weeks) from October to November are amazing.

> ! *Baedeker* TIP
>
> **Sociable Campus**
> During the 1990s, a large number of university institutes moved into the immense, extravagantly restored complex of the old General Hospital (Allgemeines Krankenhaus, AKH). In the summer, the budding academic community gathers in the courtyards - mostly in the evenings - in *Beislns* (Austrian dialect for small restaurant), bars and open-air pubs. Visitors can enjoy relaxed, affordable meals here, even if they are not students (entrance: Spitalgasse and Alser Straße).

Undoubtedly Vienna's most famous dish, the Schnitzel

Meanwhile, the lighter **»New Viennese Cuisine«**, along the lines of the French »nouvelle cuisine«, is gaining more and more devotees. Even if you are conversant in German, coming face to face with an authentic Viennese menu will leave you at a loss, more often than not. To help make choosing among the delicacies a less daunting task, a closer look at some culinary specialties follows.

Fischbeuschlsuppe is a **soup** with fish roe and vegetables. Beef soup is readily embellished with the addition of marrow dumplings, semolina dumplings and noodles of various kinds. Further additions to soups include small crisp pea-like drops of choux pastry (Backerbsen), Schöberl, which is cut out of sponge mixture, and strips of savoury pancake called *Fridatten*. A *Semmel* or *Weckerl*, as rolls are called in Vienna, is usually served as well.

The world famous **Wiener Schnitzel** is a breaded veal cutlet usually   Meat served with potato salad and *Häuptelsalat* (head of lettuce salad) or with cucumber salad (Gurkensalat) or tossed salad. The recipe is originally from Milan; linguistically, Schnitzel is derived from the German word »schneiden« (to cut or slice). *Garniertes Rindfleish* or *feines Rindfleish* is understood to be boiled **beef**, usually garnished with vegetables or with various side-dishes. *Tafelspitz* (boiled fillet of beef), number one of the culinary delights, is most often served with *Apfelkren* (apple horseradish).

! **Baedeker** TIP

Delicious Buchteln

Fantastic *Buchteln* can be enjoyed after 10pm in »Hawelka«, a cosy coffee house steeped in tradition (1, Dorotheergasse 6). The »Sperl« (6, Gumpendorfer Str. 11), also a Viennese coffee-house institution, is just as famous for this pastry.

Beinfleisch as well as *Tellerfleisch* and *Kruschpelspitz* (Kruschpeln = gristle) are marbled loin steaks, usually accompanied with chive sauce. *Lungenbraten* is stewed loin roast in a thick sauce; Viennese *Esterházy Rostbraten* is beef ribs prepared, like its Swabian counterpart, with lots of onions. Substantial amounts of pepper and paprika are characteristic of goulash and *Paprika Huhn* (paprika chicken), both imported from Hungary, though the latter is made with cream. *Jungfernbraten* is baked **loin of pork** with cumin; *Krenfleisch* is a suckling pig boiled with the rind and served with horseradish. *Kaiserfleisch* is smoked suckling pig spare ribs, the same as *Kasseler Rippen*; *Stelze* is knuckle of pork; *Geselchtes* means smoked; minced meat is called *faschiertes*; and *Schöpsernes* is mutton. Viennese *Beuschl* is **calves' lungs**, heart and spleen braised in vinegar; whereas *Lüngerl* are strips of calves' lungs and heart cooked in vinegar. Popular **poultry dishes** are stuffed goose breast (*Ganselbrust*), capons in anchovy sauce, pheasant in a mantle of bacon, and roasted snipe. *Backhendl* are breaded chickens, *gespickte Kalbsvogerln* are small larded beef roulades. Hamburger style meat patties are termed *fleischlaberl*. **Wiener** sausages are called »Frankfurters« (as in the USA), though in Frankfurt they are called »Wiener«. Among the **game dishes** worth a mention are above all wild boar in cream sauce with *Serviettenknödel* (dumplings), *Hirschragout mit Speck* (stag ragout with bacon), *Rehrücken* (saddle of venison) in a root marinade and *Hasenrücken* (saddle of hare) in wine sauce.

Fish Dishes Typical fish dishes are, besides the already mentioned *Fischbeuschlsuppe*, carp with garlic butter, *Fogosch Filet* (filet of zander) broiled in bacon or with paprika sauce, *gedünsteter Wels* (steamed catfish) and *Zwiebelfisch* (onion fish).

Vegetables *Heurige Erdäpfel* are **new potatoes**, *geröstete Erdäpfel* are sautéed potatoes. *Fisolen* stands for green beans, *Karfiol* is cauliflower, *Paradeiser* are tomatoes, *Sprossenkohl* are Brussels sprouts, *Kukuruz* is maize or corn, *Kren* is horseradish, *Häuptelsalat* is head of lettuce salad, *Vogerlsalat* is lamb's lettuce, *Risipisi* is rice with green peas and *Schwammerl* are mushrooms.

Pastries and Desserts The tasty **Viennese pastries** are mostly of Bohemian or Czech origin and were created at a time when calories had not yet been invented. **Strudel**, thinly stretched pasta or buttered dough with fruit, *Topfen* (a fresh cheese), poppy seeds, meat or other fillings, is considered Austria's favourite dessert. Among the most popular variations are *Millirahmstrudel* (cream strudel) with vanilla sauce and apple strudel, which can be garnished with *Schlagobers* (whipped cream). *Palatschinken* or *Topfenpalatschinken* are a sweet, filled egg pancake; the much vaunted **Kaiserschmarrn** is strips of sliced raisin pancake fried in sugar and butter. **Topfenknödel** are dumplings with a filling of stewed plums, the *Zwetschkenröstern*; *Germknödel* or *Powidl* are yeast dough dumplings filled with unsweetened plum jam sprinkled with poppy seeds. Also, don't miss trying an apricot dumpling or the *Powidltaschtkerln*, as well as the *Buchteln* or *Wuchteln*, all filled, steamed yeast dumplings. And, of course, the ***Dobostorte***, a sponge cake filled with chocolate cream that simply must be tried; to top it all, treat yourself to a piece of the legendary chocolate cake filled with apricot jam, the ***Sacher-Torte***.

Drinks

The preferred beverage besides **beer** (1 *Seidl* or *Seitel* = 0,35l; *Pfiff* = half a Seitel) is **wine** (a *Vierterl* = 0,25 l / 0.24 qt or an *Achterl* = 0,125 l / 0.12 qt), which comes primarily from Lower Austria and the Burgenland. Wine mixed with soda water is called »g'spritzt«. Among the best known varieties of wine that can be sampled in one of the countless wine taverns in Grinzing are Grüner Veltliner, Rheinriesling, Weißer Burgunder, Traminer, Welschriesling, Neuburger, Müller-Thurgau, Zierfandler, Rotgipfler, Gumpoldskirchner, Blaufränkischer, Blauer Portugieser and Blauer Burgunder.

Restaurants · Coffee Houses

The Agony of Choice

Vienna offers an enormous number of gastronomic facilities, from the inexpensive *beisl* and the corner eateries up to luxurious gourmet temples and the exclusive sites of »New Viennese Cuisine«. A **tip** of about 10% of the bill is customary.

You do not simply order a coffee in a **coffee house**. You select your special preference from among the different variants, though the basis of all specialties is always espresso, and a glass of water is always served with the order.

VIENNESE COFFEE VARIATIONS

Großer/Kleiner Brauner	espresso with little milk
Einspänner	»Schwarzer« in a glass with whipped cream
Eiskaffee	the coffee glass is filled halfway with vanilla ice cream, filled up with strong »Schwarzer« and topped with cream
Fiaker	double espresso with kirsch liquor and whipped cream
Franz Landtmann Kaffee	double espresso with brandy, coffee liquor, whipped cream and cinnamon
Franziskaner	espresso with whipped cream and chocolate sprinkles
Kaffee Sobiesky	double espresso with vodka and honey

Maria Theresia	double espresso in a glass with orange liquor and whipped cream
Melange	half coffee, half foamed milk
Mokka gespritzt	espresso with a shot of brandy or rum
Großer/Kleiner Schwarzer	espresso without milk
Türkischer	Turkish-style mocha in a small copper coffee pot
Überstürzter Neumann	whipped cream is put in a cup and »topped« with a double espresso
Verlängerter	espresso is poured into a coffee cup, which is then filled up with water

The »Einspänner« is not the only coffee served with a glass of water

RECOMMENDED RESTAURANTS AND CAFÉS

► ① etc. ►Plan p.74/75
without no.: outside of the plan

► **Price category per three course meal**
expensive: over 50 €
moderate: 20–50 €
inexpensive: up to 20 €

AUSTRIAN CUISINE

► ⑭ **Figlmüller**
1, Wollzeile 5, tel. 512 61 77
This popular eatery near the Stephansdom serves huge Wiener Schnitzel, among other things, and produces its own wine.
(Moderate)

► ⑧ **ef16**
1, Fleischmarkt 16
Tel. 513 23 18
The excellent service at Fleischmarkt 16 brings Austrian delicacies with an Italian touch to the table. (moderate)

► ⑧ **Griechenbeisl**
1, Fleischmarkt 11
Tel. 533 19 77
Old historic Viennese restaurant in a tower with seven small, individually-styled rooms serves excellent international cuisine. The façade is decorated with the figure of »lieber Augustin« (dear Augustin, a 17th century Viennese minstrel). Artists and writers have immortalized themselves on the walls of the »Mark Twain room«, where the writer reportedly wrote his *The Million Pound Note*.
(Moderate)

► ⑯ **Gulaschmuseum**
1, Schulerstr. 20
Tel. 512 10 17

Goulash is offered in 15 varieties and is very good. The favourites are the beef goulash served with potatoes and a spicy fish goulash with fried egg and sausage.
(Moderate)

► ① **Hansen**
1, Wipplingerstr. 34
Tel. 532 05 42
A restaurant decorated with a lot of plants that offers light international cooking and is located in the basement of the Vienna stock exchange. In summer, the guests are drawn outside by its attractive courtyard garden. (moderate)

► ㉛ **Korso**
1, Mahlerstr. 2
Tel. 51 51 65 46
A choice gourmet restaurant with a very fine atmosphere that has deservedly received three toque blanches (chef's caps) from GaultMillau. (expensive)

► **Meisel**
15, Hütteldorfer Str. 66
Tel. 982 02 29
The world of beer is taken seriously here. In summer, Viennese and vegetarian cooking can be enjoyed in the small sidewalk café.
(Inexpensive)

► ⑫ **Oswald und Kalb**
1, Bäckerstr. 14
Tel. 512 13 71
A mixture of restaurant and modern bar, where celebrities meet; excellent traditional fare.
(Moderate)

► ⑬ **Pfudl**
1, Bäckerstr. 22

THE FIR TWIGS ARE UP!

Just like the fiacre, the »Heurige« is a part of Vienna. The term means, on the one hand, a new wine and, on the other, the tavern where the wine is served.

What would Vienna be without its Heurige? An evening spent with a delicious wine in one of the atmospheric wine restaurants is simply a part of the Austrian capital. »Heuriger« is not to be confused with »Federweißer« or »Suser« wine – served as »Sturm« in Austria – because the young Heurige is the wine of the most recent harvest that is taken from the barrel and sold in spring. After Martini (November 11), it is termed »old wine«. In 1784, Emperor Joseph II allowed the privately-run wine taverns to sell the wine they produced themselves on 300 days of the year and, since 1998, they are allowed to trade all year round. A fir twig or branch hanging above the door (»Buschenschank«), which is a legally protected trademark, means that only local wine from Vienna or neighbouring communities is served, while »Heurigen« is not a trademark and can be used by any restaurant. Wine is produced and bottled on 6,2 sq km/ 2,4 sq mi in Vienna, more than in any other European capital.

Heurige Villages

The most famous »Buschenschanken« (wine taverns) are to be found in the west of the city, in the former villages of Grinzing, Sievring, Nussdorf, Neustift and Heiligenstadt, in the hills of the Vienna Woods; and on the north side of the Danube, in Stammersdorf and Strebersdorf below the Bisamer hill. Information boards in the wine-growing villages announce which taverns are open. As Hugo Wiener once said, whether you go to a Heurige for a good reason or not, you are bound to make friends, end an evening of concert music with a glass of Grüner Veltliner, enjoy the bliss of a first date in a romantic Schanigarten or simply sample the taste of a lively young wine. The ambience of the Burschenschanke is simple, yet extremely friendly; the wine is served in glasses with handles and the food is usually good traditional home-cooking. Even if the legendary zither and tavern music is rarely heard in »authentic« Heurigen, music is occasionally made here too.

Tel. 512 67 05
A *Beisl* rich in tradition with good home cooking. (moderate)

▶ ⑰ **Plachutta**
1, Wollzeile 38
Tel. 512 15 77
Restaurant with traditional *Tafelspitz* broiled beef specialities like *Kruspelspitz* and *Hüferschwanzel* in a sophisticated ambiance. Reservations are recommended. (Moderate)

▶ **Steirereck**
3, Am Heumarkt 2 A
Tel. 713 31 68
Gourmet temple with unusual creation and cultivated wine cellar. Reservations necessary! (Expensive)

▶ ④ **Viennese Rathauskeller**
1, Rathausplatz 1
Tel. 405 12 10
New Viennese cuisine in several salons and rooms in the town hall's vaulted cellar. In the summer an »Austrian Dinner Show« is held several times a week: *Schrammelmusik* and operetta melodies along with a three-course menu. (reservations necessary; moderate)

▶ **Zu den drei Buchteln**
5, Wehrgasse 9, tel. 587 83 65
Restaurant with good Bohemian cooking and Bohemian beer. (Moderate)

▶ **Zu den drei Husaren**
1, Weihburggasse 4
Tel. 512 10 92
Viennese cuisine brought to perfection in a relaxed atmosphere accompanied by piano music. (Expensive)

FISH RESTAURANTS

▶ ㉜ **Kervansaray**
1, Mahlerstr. 9
Tel. 512 88 43
Excellent fish dishes and lobster bar. (moderate)

Friendly service in the »Drei Buchteln«

COFFEE, COMMUNICATION, CULTURE

The Viennese coffee house has been an institution for centuries. Not only is the art of coffee making cultivated there, but the coffee house has been the focus of Viennese intellectual and cultural life since the beginning of the 19th century. Poets, painters and musicians met there.

The Viennese coffee house coffee housesis an institution and much more. Like nowhere else in the world, it has for centuries been the home of the intellect, an indispensable meeting place for the artistic and literary world, and of all those who, as the eloquent editorialist Alfred Polgar once said, »need company to be alone«. Literary schools were born and discarded, political developments and scientific discoveries authoritatively discussed, and new directions in art, music and architecture had their beginnings in the coffee house. Georg Kolschitzky of Poland is often named as the first to be granted an imperial franchise as a »Kaffeesieder« or proprietor of a coffee house in 1683. The resourceful Kolschitzky, courier and Turkish translator, was the one who brought news of the arrival of the reserve army led by the Polish king Sobieski to Andreas von Liebenberg, the mayor of Vienna during the second Turkish Siege. It was undoub-

Herr Hawelka serves his guests personally.

tedly the Turks who introduced coffee into south-eastern Europe, but the first coffee houses were opened by Armenian merchants. The ones who actually established the first coffee houses are considered to be Johannes Deodato, a secret agent of the Court Council of War with a shrewd business sense, who was the first to be granted the right to serve coffee in 1685, and Isaak de Luca (or Sahal Lucasia) from Yerevan, who introduced coffee brewing as a trade in 1697.

Coffee varieties galore

Simply ordering »a coffee« in a Viennese coffee house is bound to confuse the waiter, because that would be about as precise as going into a tobacconist's – called a »Trafik« in Vienna, by the way – and asking for a pack of cigarettes. The sheer endless permutations of coffee preparation, their nuances and refinement, are the basis of Viennese coffee's fame. Terms like Melange, Einspänner, Schwarzer, Kapuziner and the Schale Gold (see p.92) already give an idea of the proportions of coffee, milk and cream that can be mixed together. This knowledge is essential for a half-way expert order, but often exceeds even the imagination of those cultivated visitors for whom an espresso or a cappuccino have long since ceased to be just exotic foreign words. Moreover, having a coffee in a café is not the »purpose but the means to an end«. In other words, you don't go to a coffee house to eat, but rather for »intellectual nourishment« afterwards.

Melange, one of the many Viennese coffee specialities

Adolf Loos designed the Café »Museum«, which was recently restored to its original state.

Literary Café

The literary café, the term popularly identified with the coffee house abroad, was always characterized by the individual establishment and its regular costumers. The coffee house rose to be the centre of Vienna's intellectual life during the Biedermeier period when illustrious artists and poets like Franz Grillparzer and Moritz von Schwind gathered in the »silver coffeehouse« and the waltz kings Strauss and Lanner filled the concert cafés with their melodies. At the latest by the Fin de Siècle era, Vienna's literary history and coffee house culture were inseparably bound together.

Famous Cafés

Around 1890, Café Griensteidl was the meeting place for the writers Arthur Schnitzler and Hugo von Hofmannsthal, the eloquent cultural critic Karl Kraus, the architect Adolf Loos and

the revolutionary Leon Trotsky. By the end of the First World War, however, its leading role was usurped by Café Central, where Karl Kraus, Egon Friedell and Alfred Polgar were regular customers. According to Polgar, the literary café of those times stood for »a world-view whose innermost essence was not to view the world«. During the late 1920s and early 1930s, the noble »Herrenhof« was the most important meeting place of writers and do-gooders. Hermann Broch, Robert Musil, Franz Werfel, Joseph Roth and Sigmund Freud drank their Melanges and played chess in the spacious café, which closed in

A slice of Sacher-Torte along with coffee

1960. Café Museum, which Adolf Loos designed in the style of an American bar in 1907, was frequented by the then yet unknowns, Franz Léhar and Oskar Kokoschka, while in the over-crowded Café de Europe you would come across middle-class people during the day and the demimonde at night – along with the »ladies who worked both sides«. After 1933, the political immigrants from Germany chose this coffeehouse for their nocturnal meetings – among them Bert Brecht – before most of the regulars were forced to go into exile in Paris, London or the USA.

The Spirit of the Past

Though not the creative institution of former days, the coffee house of the early 21st century is still related to these establishments. It is important to differentiate between the in-cafés around the Hofburg, like Central, Griensteidl and Landtmann, and those of the locals that have been saved from days long gone, in which time is still spent calmly leafing through newspapers, playing billiards or chess, or engaging in a good, long »Tratscherl« (chat). The spirit of the classic era still breathes in the old-fashioned Café Bräunerhof, where the malcontent Thomas Bernhard spent his mornings reading the paper. Legendary oases of »Gemütlichkeit« are the Museum café, where the masters of Vienna's Jugendstil once discussed new directions in art; the lovingly restored Sperl, populated since 1880 by artists and theatre people; Hawelka café, famous for its filled pastries, was an artists' café in the 1950s, and remains a meeting place of intellectuals; and then there is the rather quiet Café Grillparzer. With such a large selection, it is really left to personal preferences where best to discover the Viennese phenomenon that is the coffee house.

Vienna also offers international cuisine

VEGETARIAN COOKING

▶ ⑦ **Wrenkh**
1, Bauernmarkt 10
Tel. 533 15 26
A restaurant with excellent whole food and vegetarian dishes. (moderate)

FAR EASTERN FOOD

▶ ㉚ **Tenmaya**
1, Krugerstr. 3
Tel. 512 73 97
Japanese gourmet cooking in an authentic ambiance, many menu variations (moderate)

▶ ② **Mr. Lee**
1, Dr.-Karl-Lueger-Ring 10
Tel. 535 48 02
Sushi, noodles and grilled food near the university, the parliament and the Hofburg. (inexpensive)

FRENCH CUISINE

▶ ㉕ **Le Bol**
1, Neuer Markt 14
Tel. 0699 10 30 18 99
French bistro atmosphere with delicious cooking. (inexpensive)

▶ ⑥ **Salut**
1, Wildpretmarkt 3
Tel. 533 13 22
Culinary delights, above all fish; tasteful setting. (moderate)

GREEK COOKING

▶ ⑩ **Achilleus**
1, Köllnerhofgasse 3
Tel. 512 83 28
Fish specialties, inexpensive Greek and Mediterranean cooking, with good lunch menus. (moderate)

▶ **Taverna Lefteris**
3, Hörnesgasse 17
Tel. 713 74 51
Well chosen range of Greek tavern classics, from tzatziki to moussaka; Greek music live every Tue. (moderate)

HEURIGE (wine taverns) · BUSCHENSCHANKEN (wine restaurants)

▶ **Reinprecht**
19, Coblenzgasse 22
Tel. 320 14 71
The vineyard is located in a

monastery over 300 year old, and offers a spacious garden and *Schrammelmusik*.

► **Schilling**
21, Langenzersdorfer Str. 54
Tel. 292 41 89
Choice wines from their own vineyard and a specialty buffet that can also be enjoyed in a garden planted with fruit trees.

► **Schübel-Auer**
19., Kahlenberger Str. 22
Tel. 370 22 22
Popular posh *Heurigen*; the Philharmonia-Schrammeln perform »Hausmusik« in the tavern in June (music performed at home by family and friends in the 18th-19th centuries).

► ⑪ **Zwölf-Apostel-Keller**
1, Sonnenfelsgasse 3
Tel. 512 67 77
Most popular *Heurigen* in the inner city.

ITALIAN COOKING;

► **Il Mare**
7, Zieglergasse 15
Tel. 523 74 94
Small, classic pub; the pizzas are among the best in the city. (moderate)

► **Da Capo**
1, Schulerstr. 18
Tel. 512 44 91
Comfortable atmosphere and outstanding food; reservations are necessary. (moderate)

COFFEE HOUSES

► ㉑ **Bräunerhof**
1, Stallburggasse 2
Tel. 512 38 93
Coffee house rich in tradition,

---

i **Good for meals**

- Demel: the classic with aristocratic air where you can see the confectionery being made
- Figlmüller: best place for Schnitzel lovers
- Griechenbeisl: 500 year-old tradition beneath an atmospheric vaulted ceiling
- Hawelka: much acclaimed Bohemian meeting place, small and very cosy
- Landtmann: Ringstrasse café par excellence, urban, celebrities, beautiful terrace
- Kevansaray: finest fish dishes
- Korso: Grand Cuisine opposite the Opera House

---

which the writer Thomas Bernhard liked to frequent.

► ㊱ **Café Museum**
1, Operngasse 7
Tel. 586 52 02
Clear forms and high quality materials replace the decorative accessories in this café designed by Adolf Loos.

► ⑤ **Central**
►Freyung

► ㉒ **Demel**
►p.181

► ⑮ **Diglas**
1, Wollzeile 10
Tel. 51 25 76 50
This sidewalk garden café offers delicious home-made cakes, flans and gateaux, and outstanding pastries.

► ㉗ **Do & Co**
1, Albertinaplatz 1
Tel. 532 96 69
Stylish café in the Albertina, offering a great view from its terrace; a small selection of dishes is also offered.

㉖ Frauenhuber
1, Himmelpfortgasse 6
Tel. 512 83 83
Red plush imbues this traditional coffee house with a special charm.

㉓ Griensteidl
►Michaelerplatz

⑳ Hawelka
1, Dorotheergasse 6
Tel. 512 82 30
Student and artist gathering place rich in tradition with typical Viennese charm.

㉝ Imperial
1, Kärntner Ring 16
Tel. 50 11 03 89

Café Museum – popular with students

Piano music is played in the afternoons; delicious home-made flans and gateaux.

③ Landtmann
1, Dr.-Karl-Lueger-Ring 4
Tel. 532 06 21
This traditional Viennese café is popular with theatre people and prominent politicians and has a beautiful terrace.

㉘ Mozart
1, Albertinaplatz 2
Tel. 513 08 81
Coffee house with out-door seating and very good pastries.

㉔ Oberlaa
1, Neuer Markt 16
Tel. 513 29 36
Delicious baked goods and confections.

⑱ Prückel
1, Stubenring 24
Tel. 512 61 15
The café has supplied all the top people in town since 1903. It attracts many guests with its famous pastries, as well as with its concert programme.

㉙ Sacher
►p.289

㉟ Sperl
6, Gumpendorfer Str. 11
Tel. 586 41 58
Under heritage protection, this cosy coffee house is where Vienna's best melanges are served (hot coffee with foamed milk).

㉝ Schwarzenberg
1, Kärntner Ring 17
Tel. 512 89 98
Café with an attractive terrace.

Health

● USEFUL ADDRESSES

PHARMACIES

▶ **Pharmacy Emergency Service**
Tel. 15 50

▶ **Internationale Apotheke (International Pharmacy)**
1, Kärntner Ring 17
Tel. 512 28 25

FIRST AID FOR TRAVELLERS

▶ **Health Consult**
1, Schottenstift, Freyung 6
Tel. 535 64 64
Mon – Thu 8am – 6pm
Fri 8am – 1pm

EMERGENCY SERVICE

▶ **Ambulance**
Tel. 144

▶ **Medical Emergencies**
Tel. 141

▶ **Dental Emergencies**
Tel. 512 20 78

▶ **Poisoning Information Headquarters**
Tel. 406 43 43

▶ **Emergency Numbers**
▶p.85

Information

● USEFUL ADDRESSES

ENGLISH LANGUAGE WEBSITES

▶ **www.austria.info**
Whet your appetite for Austria with this Austrian tourist office site. Lots of practical information as well as brochure request line.

▶ **www.info.wien.at**
Tourist information specifically for Vienna, including hotel booking portal, the latest events programme and much more.

IN VIENNA

▶ **Vienna-Tourismus**
1, Albertinaplatz/
corner of Maysedergasse
A-1025 Vienna
Daily 9am – 7pm
Vienna-Hotels & Info:
Tel. 245 55, Fax 24 55 56 66
www.wien.info

▶ **Austrian Holiday Information**
5, Margaretenstr. 1
A-1040 Vienna
Tel. 08 10 10 18 18

▸ **For travellers by boat**
Blue Danube Schifffahrt GmbH
(DDSG)
1, Handelskai 265
(in the shipping centre)
A-1020 Vienna
Tel. 58 88 00, fax 58 88 04 40
www.ddsg-blue-danube.at
There is another landing on the
Danube Canal between Marien-
brücke and Schwedenbrücke.

▸ **wienXtra-Jugendinfo**
1, Babenberger Str. 1
A-1010 Vienna
Tel. 17 99; www.wienxtra.at
Mon – Sat, noon – 7pm
Information about cheap accom-
modation, events etc.

▸ **wienXtra-Kinderinfo**
7, MuseumsQuartier/Hof 2
Tel. 40 00 84 400
www.wienxtra.at/kinderinfo
Tue – Thu, 2pm – 7pm, Fri–Sun
10am–5pm

EMBASSIES

▸ **In the UK**
Austrian Embassy
18 Belgrave Mews
London SW1X 8HU
Tel. (020) 7235 3731, fax (020)
7344 0292; www.bmeia.gv.at
Mon-Fri 9am-5pm

▸ **In USA**
Austrian Embassy:
Washington, D.C.
3524 International Court N.W.
Washington D.C. 20008
Tel. (202) 895-6700

Austrian Consulate:
Los Angeles
11859 Wilshire Bl, Suite 501
Los Angeles, CA 90025
Tel. (310) 444-9310

Austrian Consulate:
Chicago
400 N. Michigan Av, Suite 707
Chicago, IL 60611
Tel. (312) 222-1515

Austrian Consulate:
New York
31 E. 69th St.
New York, NY 10021
Tel. (212) 737-6400

▸ **In Canada**
Austrian Embassy
445 Wilbrod St
Ottawa ONKIN 6M7
Tel. 613 789
email: Ottawa-ob@bmeia.gv.at

▸ **UK Embassy in Vienna**
Jaurèsgasse 10
1030 Vienna
Mon-Fri 9.15am-12.30pm and
2pm-3.30pm
Tel. 71613 5333
email: viennaconsularenquiries
@fco.gov.uk

▸ **US Embassy in Vienna**
Parkring 12a
1010 Vienna
Mon-Fri 8am-11.30am
Tel. 31339 7535
email: consulatevienna@state.gov

▸ **Canadian Embassy in Vienna**
Laurenzerberg 2, 3rd floor
1010 Vienna
Mon-Fri 8.30-12.30 and 1.30-3.30
Tel. 531 38 3000
email: vienn-visa
@international.qc.ca

▸ **Australian Embassy in Vienna**
Mattiellistrasse 2-4
1040 Vienna
Tel. 1-506 740
email: austemb@aon.at

Language

GERMAN

General

Yes / No	Ja / Nein
Perhaps. / Maybe.	Vielleicht.
Please.	Bitte.
Thank you. / Thank you very much.	Danke. / Vielen Dank!
You're welcome.	Gern geschehen.
Excuse me!	Entschuldigung!
Pardon?	Wie bitte?
I don't understand.	Ich verstehe Sie / Dich nicht.
I only speak a bit of ...	Ich spreche nur wenig ...
Can you help me, please?	Können Sie mir bitte helfen?
I'd like ...	Ich möchte ...
I (don't) like this.	Das gefällt mir (nicht).
Do you have ...?	Haben Sie ...?
How much is this?	Wieviel kostet es?
What time is it?	Wieviel Uhr ist es?
What is this called?	Wie heißt dies hier?

Getting acquainted

Good morning!	Guten Morgen!
Good afternoon!	Guten Tag!
Good evening!	Guten Abend!
Hello! / Hi!	Hallo! Grüß Dich!
My name is ...	Mein Name ist ...
What's your name?	Wie ist Ihr / Dein Name?
How are you?	Wie geht es Ihnen / Dir?
Fine thanks. And you?	Danke. Und Ihnen / Dir?
Goodbye! / Bye-bye!	Auf Wiedersehen!
Good night!	Gute Nacht!
See you! / Bye!	Tschüss!

Travelling

left / right	links / rechts
straight ahead	geradeaus
near / far	nah / weit
Excuse me, where's ..., please?	Bitte, wo ist ...?
... the train station	... der Bahnhof

... the bus stop	... die Bushaltestelle
... the harbour	... der Hafen
... the airport	... der Flughafen
How far is it?	Wie weit ist das?
I'd like to rent a car.	Ich möchte ein Auto mieten.
How long?	Wie lange?

Traffic

My car's broken down.	Ich habe eine Panne.
Is there a service station nearby?	Gibt es hier in der Nähe eine Werkstatt?
Where's the nearest gas station?	Wo ist die nächste Tankstelle?
I want	Ich möchte ...
... liters / gallons of ...	Liter / Gallonen (3,8 l) ...
... regular	.... Normalbenzin.
... premium.	... Super.
... diesel.	... Diesel.
... unleaded	... bleifrei.
Full, please.	Volltanken, bitte.
Help!	Hilfe!
Attention!	Achtung!
Look out!	Vorsicht!
Please call ...	Rufen Sie bitte ...
... an ambulance.	... einen Krankenwagen.
... the police.	... die Polizei.
It was my fault.	Es war meine Schuld.
It was your fault.	Es war Ihre Schuld.
Please give me your name and address.	Geben Sie mir bitte Namen und Anschrift.
Beware of ...	Vorsicht vor ...
Bypass (with road number)	Ortsumgehung (mit Straßennummer)
Bypass (Byp)	Umgehungsstraße
Causeway	Brücke, Pontonbrücke
Construction	Bauarbeiten
Crossing (Xing)	Kreuzung, Überweg
Dead End	Sackgasse
Detour	Umleitung
Divided Highway	Straße mit Mittelstreifen
Do not enter	Einfahrt verboten
Exit	Ausfahrt
Hill	Steigung / Gefälle / unübersichtlich (Überholverbot)
Handicapped Parking	Behindertenparkplatz
Junction (Jct)	Kreuzung, Abzweigung, Einmündung
Keep off ...	Abstand halten ...
Loading Zone	Ladezone
Merge (Merging Traffic)	Einmündender Verkehr

Narrow Bridge	Schmale Brücke
No Parking	Parken verboten
No Passing	Überholen verboten
No Turn on Red	Rechtsabbiegen bei Rot verboten
U Turn	Wenden erlaubt
No U Turn	Wenden verboten
One Way	Einbahnstraße
Passenger Loading Zone	Ein- und Aussteigen erlaubt
Ped Xing	Fußgängerüberweg
Restricted Parking Zone	Zeitlich begrenztes Parken erlaubt
Right of Way	Vorfahrt
Road Construction	Straßenbauarbeiten
Slippery when wet	Schleudergefahr bei Nässe
Slow	Langsam fahren
Soft Shoulders	Straßenbankette nicht befestigt
Speed Limit	Geschwindigkeitsbegrenzung
Toll	Benutzungsgebühr, Maut
Tow away Zone	Absolutes Parkverbot, Abschlepp-zone
Xing (Crossing)	Kreuzung, Überweg
Yield	Vorfahrt beachten

Shopping

Where can I find a ...?	Wo finde ich ... eine / ein ..?
pharmacy	Apotheke
bakery	Bäckerei
department store	Kaufhaus
food store	Lebensmittelgeschäft
supermarket	Supermarkt

Accommodation

Could you recommend ... ?	Können Sie mir ... empfehlen?
... a hotel / motel	... ein Hotel / Motel
... a bed & breakfast	... eine Frühstückspension
Do you have ...?	Haben Sie noch ...?
... a room for one	... ein Einzelzimmer
... a room for two	... ein Doppelzimmer
... with a shower / bath	... mit Dusche / Bad
... for one night	... für eine Nacht
... for a week	... für eine Woche
I've reserved a room.	Ich habe ein Zimmer reserviert.
How much is the room	Was kostet das Zimmer
... with breakfast?	... mit Frühstück?

Doctor

Can you recommend a good doctor?	Können Sie mir einen guten Arzt empfehlen?
I need a dentist.	Ich brauche einen Zahnarzt.
I feel some pain here.	Ich habe hier Schmerzen.
I've got a temperature.	Ich habe Fieber.
Prescription	Rezept
Injection / shot	Spritze

Bank / Post

Where's the nearest bank?	Wo ist hier bitte eine Bank?
ATM (Automated Teller Machine)	Geldautomat
I'd like to change dollars/pounds into euros.	Ich möchte Dollars/Pfund in Euro wechseln.
How much is ...	Was kostet ...
... a letter ...	... ein Brief ...
... a postcard ...	... eine Postkarte ...
to Europe?	nach Europa?

Numbers

1	eins	2	zwei
3	drei	4	vier
5	fünf	6	sechs
7	sieben	8	acht
9	neun	10	zehn
11	elf	12	zwölf
13	dreizehn	14	vierzehn
15	fünfzehn	16	sechzehn
17	siebzehn	18	achtzehn
19	neunzehn	20	zwanzig
21	einundzwanzig	30	dreißig
40	vierzig	50	fünfzig
60	sechzig	70	siebzig
80	achtzig	90	neunzig
100	(ein-)hundert	1000	(ein-)tausend
1/2	ein Halb	1/3	ein Drittel
1/4	ein Viertel		

Restaurant

Is there a good restaurant here?	Gibt es hier ein gutes Restaurant?
Would you reserve us a table for this evening, please?	Reservieren Sie uns bitte für heute Abend einen Tisch!

The menu please!	Die Speisekarte bitte!
Cheers!	Auf Ihr Wohl!
Could I have the check, please?	Bezahlen, bitte.
Where is the restroom, please?	Wo ist bitte die Toilette?

Frühstück / Breakfast

Kaffee (mit Sahne / Milch)	coffee (with cream / milk)
koffeinfreier Kaffee	decaffeinated coffee
heiße Schokolade	hot chocolate
Tee (mit Milch / Zitrone)	tea (with milk / lemon)
Rührei	scrambled eggs
pochierte Eier	poached eggs
Eier mit Speck	bacon and eggs
Spiegeleier	eggs sunny side up
harte / weiche Eier	hard-boiled / soft-boiled eggs
(Käse- / Champignon-)Omelett	(cheese / mushroom) omelette
Pfannkuchen	pancake
Brot / Brötchen / Toast	bread / rolls / toast
Butter	butter
Zucker	sugar
Honig	honey
Marmelade / Orangenmarmelade	jam / marmelade
Joghurt	yoghurt
Obst	fruit

Vorspeisen und Suppen / Starters and Soups

Fleischbrühe	broth / consommé
Hühnercremesuppe	cream of chicken soup
Tomatensuppe	cream of tomato soup
gemischter / grüner Salat	mixed / green salad
frittierte Zwiebelringe	onion rings
Meeresfrüchtesalat	seafood salad
Garnelen- / Krabbencocktail	shrimp / prawn cocktail
Räucherlachs	smoked salmon
Gemüsesuppe	vegetable soup

Fisch und Meeresfrüchte / Fish and Seafood

Kabeljau	cod
Krebs	crab
Aal	eel
Schellfisch	haddock
Hering	herring

Hummer	lobster
Muscheln	mussels
Austern	oysters
Barsch	perch
Scholle	plaice
Lachs	salmon
Jakobsmuscheln	scallops
Seezunge	sole
Tintenfisch	squid
Forelle	trout
Tunfisch	tuna

Fleisch und Geflügel / Meat and Poultry

gegrillte Schweinerippchen	barbecued spare ribs
Rindfleisch	beef
Hähnchen	chicken
Geflügel	poultry
Kotelett	chop / cutlet
Filetsteak	fillet
(junge) Ente	duck(ling)
Schinkensteak	gammon
Fleischsoße	gravy
Hackfleisch vom Rind	ground beef
gekochter Schinken	ham
Nieren	kidneys
Lamm	lamb
Leber	liver
Schweinefleisch	pork
Würstchen	sausages
Lendenstück vom Rind, Steak	sirloin steak
Truthahn	turkey
Kalbfleisch	veal
Reh oder Hirsch	venison

Nachspeise und Käse / Dessert and Cheese

gedeckter Apfelkuchen	apple pie
Schokoladenplätzchen	brownies
Hüttenkäse	cottage cheese
Sahne	cream
Vanillesoße	custard
Obstsalat	fruit salad
Ziegenkäse	goat's cheese
Eiscreme	icecream
Gebäck	pastries

Gemüse und Salat / Vegetables and Salad

gebackene Kartoffeln in der Schale	baked potatoes
Pommes frites	french fries
Bratkartoffeln	hash browns
Kartoffelpüree	mashed potatoes
gebackene Bohnen in Tomatensoße	baked beans
Kohl	cabbage
Karotten	carrots
Blumenkohl	cauliflower
Tomaten	tomatoes
Gurke	cucumber
Knoblauch	garlic
Lauch	leek
Kopfsalat	lettuce
Pilze	mushrooms
Zwiebeln	onions
Erbsen	peas
Paprika	peppers
Kürbis	pumpkin
Spinat	spinach
Mais	sweet corn
Maiskolben	corn-on-the-cob

Obst / Fruit

Äpfel	apples	Birnen	pears
Aprikosen	apricots	Orange	orange
Brombeeren	blackberries	Pfirsiche	peaches
Kirschen	cherries	Ananas	pineapple
Weintrauben	grapes	Pflaumen	plums
Grapefruit	grapefruit	Himbeeren	raspberries
Zitrone	lemon	Erdbeeren	strawberries
Preiselbeeren	cranberries		

Getränke / Beverages

Bier (vom Fass)	beer (on tap)
Apfelwein	cider
Rotwein / Weißwein	red wine / white wine
trocken / lieblich	dry / sweet
Sekt, Schaumwein	sparkling wine
alkoholfreie Getränke	soft drinks
Fruchtsaft	fruit juice
gesüßter Zitronensaft	lemonade
Milch	milk
Mineralwasser	mineral water / spring water

Literature

Fiction **Graham Greene**, *The Third Man*, Penguin, USA, 1999.
Austrian literature is often obscure and heavy-going, weighed down by the nation's complicated and tragic history and an excess of experimental writing. An excellent introduction to Vienna's complex cultural heritage, however, is Graham Greene's *The Third Man*, originally written as a filmscript and set in Vienna.

Traveller's tales **Frances Trollope** *Vienna and the Austrians* describes a winter spent in the great city in 1838.

Carl Domeltsch *Our Famous Guest: Mark Twain in Vienna* (1992) is an American academic study of Twain's sojourn in fin-de-siecle Vienna, linking the author's despair during his later years with the cultural nihilism he encountered in Vienna at the turn of the 19th century.

i **Vienna in Film**

- *Sissi*, an emotionally romantic film adaptation of the life of the world famous Austrian empress with Romy Schneider in the title role.
- *The Third Man*, a cult film about the writer Holly Martins, who pursues the murderer of his friend through Vienna.
- *Amadeus*, Mozart's final 10 years seen through the eyes of his rival Antonio Salieri.

Christian Brandstätter, *Vienna 1900: Art, Life and Culture* (2006) is a beautifully illustrated coffee table book with interesting analysis.

Gordon Brook-Shepherd, *The Austrians: A Thousand Year Odyssey* (1997) provides a helpful overview of the country's history

Hella Pick, *Guilty Victim: Austria from the Holocaust to Haider*, investigates the country's role during one of its darkest eras.

Money

Euro The Euro (€) has been the official currency in Austria since 2002.

Cash dispensers (ATMs) Money can be withdrawn from Austrian cash machines (Bancomat) around the clock with credit or bank cards – and the correct pin number – without any problems. Most international **credit cards** are accepted by banks, hotels, restaurants, car hire companies and individual businesses.

When a card is **lost**, the loss should immediately be reported to the police and the card blocked with your bank to prevent misuse. The same is true of mobile telephones.

To **report lost or stolen credit cards** call the relevant number: American Express 0800 900 940; Diners Club 501 35 14; MasterCard 0800 218 235; Visa 0800 200 288. It is recommended to keep your card details and emergency phone numbers separate from your wallet so you have the information to hand if needed.

Museums and Memorials

Entrance to Vienna's municipal museums is free every Friday until noon, unless a special exhibition happens to be taking place.

▶ MUSEUM ADDRESSES

HISTORY ·
CULTURAL HISTORY

▶ **Alte Backstube (Old Bakery)**
8, Lange Gasse 34
Opening times of the coffee house: Tue – Sat 11am – midnight, Sat from noon, Sun noon – 11pm
The bakery, located in a beautiful Baroque building, was in operation from 1701 until 1963. The bakery has been part of the Josefstadt district museum since 1965 and displays the traditional »tools« of the baker.

▶ **Alte Schmiede (Old Blacksmiths' Shop)**
▶Schönlaterngasse

▶ **Armenisches Klostermuseum (Armenian Monastery Museum)**
▶Mechitarist monastery

▶ **Bestattungsmuseum (Funeral Museum)**
4, Goldeggasse 19
Mon – Fri noon – 3pm by appointment only, tel. 50 19 50
Expensive funeral paraphernalia for a luxuriously staged »schöne Leich« (beautiful funeral), palls and the ornate livery of the »Pompfüneberer« (as morticians are called in Vienna), can be seen here, as well as an alarm for the apparently dead and a reusable »Retoursarg« coffin, introduced by Emperor Joseph II. As soon as the wooden coffin was over the open grave, a bolt mechanism was released and the corpse fell into the grave. Under pressure from public opinion, however, the imperial order was recalled in 1784.

Historical transportation to the final resting place

▶ **Dokumentationsarchiv des Österreichischen Widerstandes (Documentation Centre of Austrian Resistance)**
▶Böhmische Hofkanzlei (Bohemian Court Chancellery)

▶ **Foltermuseum (Torture Museum)**
6, Flakturm, Esterházypark
Daily 10am–6pm
On display inside the anti-aircraft tower's air-raid shelter are 60 historical instruments of torture, punishment and execution. In addition, there is an information section by Amnesty International attached.

▶ **Freud Museum**
▶there

▶ **Glasmuseum (Glass Museum)**
1, Kärntner Str. 26
Mon–Fri 9am–6pm,
Sat 9am–5pm
The museum is located in the Lobmeyr glass store.

▶ **Globenmuseum (Globe Museum – as in world maps)**
▶Freyung, Palais Mollard-Clary

▶ **Haus der Musik (House of Music)**
1, Seilerstätte 30
Daily 10am–10pm. The visitor is invited to hear, see and feel music in the palace of Archduke Karl. Aural experiences await inside a huge instrument and the possibility of virtually directing or composing your own music. Thanks to numerous interactive installations, anyone can effortlessly make music. In addition, historical information is offered. Some of Vienna's most important musicians–Mozart, Schubert, Beethoven, Johann Strauß, Haydn, Mahler and Schönberg–are presented in their social environment in music-filled rooms.

▶ **Heeresgeschichtliches Museum (Museum of Military History)**
▶there

Archduke Franz Ferdinand was shot in this vehicle, today on display in the Military Museum

▶ **Hermesvilla**
▶Lainzer Tiergarten (zoo)

▶ **Jüdisches (Jewish) Museum**
▶there

▶ **Hofmobiliendepot – Möbel Museum Wien (Imperial Furniture Collection)**
7, Andreasgasse 7
Tue – Sun 10am – 6pm
The collection developed out of the former Court furniture depository, which was responsible for the management and repair of the imperial furniture and furnishings. Furniture, carpets, paintings and lamps, all from the former imperial palaces, provide a complete impression of the different eras. In addition, special exhibits of furniture design and photography are presented.

▶ **Kriminalmuseum (Crime Museum)**
▶Leopoldstadt

▶ **Lipizzaner Museum (Spanish Riding School)**
▶Hofburg

▶ **Museum of the Institute for the History of Medicine**
▶Josephinum

▶ **Museum für Angewandte Kunst (Museum of Applied Arts)**
▶there

▶ **Museum für Verhütung und Schwangerschaftsabbruch (Museum of Contraception and Pregnancy Termination)**
15, Mariahilfer Gürtel 37
Tel 0699 178 178 04
www.verhuetungsmuseum.at

Wed – Sun 2pm – 6pm
Extensive exhibit in a museum that is one of a kind worldwide

▶ **Museum für Völkerkunde (Museum of Ethnology)**
▶Hofburg

▶ **Museum für Volkskunde (Museum of Folk Life)**
8, Laudongasse 15 - 19
Tue – Sun 10am – 5pm
The museum is housed in the former Schönborn garden palace. On display are models of traditional settlements, houses and farms, pictures and cartograms, traditional living rooms with country household items, costumes, jewellery and musical instruments from the 16th to the 19th centuries.

▶ **Pathologisch-Anatomisches Bundesmuseum (Pathological-Anatomical Museum)**
▶Josephinum

▶ **Prater Museum**
▶Prater

▶ **Sammlung Alter Musikinstrumente (Collection of Musical Instruments)**
▶Hofburg

▶ **Sammlung Religiöse Volkskunst (Collection of Religious Folk Art)**
1, Johannesgasse 8

! *Baedeker* TIP

www.kunstnet.at
This internet address provides comprehensive information about current exhibits, galleries, auctions and art dealers.

The entrance to the Kunstforum

Wed. 10am – 5pm
The former Ursuline monastery displays, among other things, an original monastery pharmacy.

► **Sammlung der Medizinischen Universiät Wien (Collection of the Medical University of Vienna)**
P. 215 (Josephinum)

► **Schatzkammer des Deutschen Ordens (Treasury of the Teutonic Knights Order)**
  ►Deutschordenshaus

► **Alt-Wiener Schnapsmuseum (Old Vienna Schnapps Museum)**
12, Wilhelmstr. 19
min. 10 persons, only by appointment, tel. 815 73 00
High proof drinks ranging from »Schönbrunner Gold« enriched with real gold leaf to chili-flavoured »Viennese Blood«.

► **Silberkammer (Imperial Silver Collection)**
  ►Hofburg

► **Bank Austria Kunstforum (Bank of Austria Art Forum)**
1, Freyung 8
Daily 10am – 6pm, Wed until 9pm

► **Ernst Fuchs Museum**
14, Hüttelbergstr. 26
Mon – Fri 10am – 4pm,
Tel. 914 85 75
In a villa built by Otto Wagner between 1886 and 1888 the works of the main exponent of »fantastic realism« Ernst Fuchs are exhibited.

▶ **Fälschermuseum
(Museum of Forgery)**
3, Löwengasse 28, tel. 715 22 96
www.faelschermuseum.at
Tue – Sun 10am – 5pm
Opposite the Hundertwasserhaus
the »Werkstätte für Kunst & Architektur« shows famous masters
of art hsitory – as forgeries.

▶ **Kunsthalle Wien
(Art Hall Vienna)**
▶Museum Quarter

▶ **Kunst Haus Wien
(Art House Vienna)**
▶there

▶ **Kunsthistorisches Museum
(Art History Museum)**
▶there

▶ **Liechtenstein Museum**
▶there

▶ **Museum Mittelalterlicher
Kunst
(Museum of Medieval Art)**
▶Belvedere

▶ **Museum Moderner Kunst
Stiftung Ludwig Wien
(Modern Art at the
Ludwig Wien Foundation)**
▶Museum Quarter

▶ **Schottenstift
(Benedictine Monastery)**
▶Freyung

▶ **Secession**
▶there

▶ **Otto Wagner Wohnung
(Apartment)**
7, Döblergasse 4
Mon – Fri 9am – noon,
July – Sept by appointment only

Tel. 5 23 22 33
A considerable amount of Otto
Wagner (1841 – 1918) memora-
bilia is on display. He was one of
Austria's most famous architects.

LITERATURE · FILM

▶ **Heimito von Doderer
Gedenkstätte / Memorial Site**
Alsergrund District Museum
9, Währinger Str. 43
Wed 9am – 11am (except July,
Aug) Sun 10am – noon
The museum presents the life and
works of the writer Heimito von
Doderer (1896 – 1966).

▶ **Esperanto Museum**
▶Freyung, Mollard-Clary Palace

▶ **Filmmuseum**
▶1, Augustinerstr. 1
(in the building of the Albertina)
Guided tours: by appointment
only, tel. 533 70 54 10
Films shown regularly

▶ **Stifter Museum**
Manuscripts and first editions of
the writer Adalbert Stifter can be
seen in the ▶Schubert Museum
affiliated Stifter Museum; in addition, there are some remarkable
landscapes painted by the writer.

▶ **Third Man Museum – 3mpc**
4, Pressgasse 25
Sat 2pm – 6pm
Tel. 586 48 72, www.3mpc.net
The museum is dedicated to the
classic film »The Third Man«,
which was made in Vienna in
1949.

MUSIC

▶ **Beethoven Memorial Sites**
▶Baedeker Tip p.59 and Heiligenstadt

other memorial sites:
Eroica-Haus
19, Döblinger Hauptstr. 92
Fri 3pm – 6pm and by appointment, tel. 50 58 74 70
Beethoven worked here in 1803 and 1804, primarily on his Third Symphony; among the items displayed is the first print of this score.
6, Laimgrubengasse 22
tours by appointment only
Tel. 371 40 85
He lived here in 1822 and 1823.

► Brahms Gedenkraum (Brahms Memorial Room)

A room on the first floor of the ►Haydnhaus is dedicated to Brahms, and is furnished with pieces of furniture and everyday items from his last flat. A small pictorial documentation on the life and works of the composer complete the exhibit.

► Figarohaus

►there

► Haydnhaus

6, Haydngasse 19
Tue – Sun 9am – 6pm
Joseph Haydn acquired the house in the little Steingasse in 1793, and lived there until his death in 1809. The oratorios »The Creation« and »The Four Seasons« were written here. Concerts are also given here.

► Lehár-Schikaneder-Schlössl

19, Hackhofergasse 18
by appointment only, tel. 318 54 16
Emanuel Schikaneder, the author of »The Magic Flute«, lived here from 1802 until 1812. In 1932, the operetta composer Franz Lehár purchased the house and composed »Giuditta« here. A small museum is set up in one room.

► Arnold Schönberg Center

3, Schwarzenbergplatz 6
Palais Fanto
Opening times: Mon – Fri
10am – 5pm
Tel. 712 18 88, www.schoenberg.at
The foundation presides over the famous composer and painter's estate and organizes eshibits and concerts.

► Schubert's death chamber

4, Kettenbrückengasse 6
Tue – Sun 9am – 12.15
1pm – 4.30pm
The History Museum has arranged the rooms in which Franz Schubert spent his last days into a memorial site for him and his brother Ferdinand.

► Johann Strauss Apartment

Praterstr. 54,
Tue – Thu 2pm – 6pm
Fri – Sun 10am – 1pm.
These are the rooms in which Johann Strauss (son) wrote his lilting »The Blue Danube« waltz in 1867, which explains the name »Donauwalzerhaus« (Danube Waltz House). On view are documents from the life of »the Waltz King« as well as personal items.

NATURE · TECHNOLOGY

► Feuerwehrmuseum (Vienna Fire Department Museum)

►Am Hof

► Haus des Meeres – Aqua Terra Zoo Wien (House of the Sea Aquarium – Aqua Terra Zoo Vienna)

6, Esterházypark
Daily 9am – 6pm, Thu until 9pm
Close to 6,000 live animals can be observed here. The tropical and Mediterranean aquariums and the

tropical greenhouse are impressive.

► **Naturhistorisches Museum (Natural History Museum)**
►there

► **Planetarium**
►Prater

► **Strassenbahnmuseum (Tram Museum)**
3, Ludwig-Koeßler-Platz
May – Sept, Fri-Sun 9am – 4pm

► **Technisches Museum (Museum of Technology)**
►there

► **Uhrenmuseum (Clock Museum)**
►there

► **Urania Observatory**
1, Urania-Str. 1
Wed, Fri, Sat 8pm, April – Sept
9pm, Sun 11am; closed in August
Info tel. 729 54 94 10
The observatory offers tours when the sky is clear, as well a look through the telescope and computer graphics.

► **Waffensammlung (Weapons Collection)**
►Hofburg

Post and Communications

Post office business hours are Mon-Fri 8am-noon and 2pm-6pm.   Post Offices
The main post office (1, Fleischmarkt 19) is open until 10pm and
the railway post offices are open until late evening.

Stamps can be purchased in post offices and tobacco shops – called   ◄ Postal Rates
»Trafik« in Vienna. Standard letters (up to 20g/0.7oz) and postcards
to within the EU cost 0.55 €, but rates regularly increase.

The public telephone boxes all now only operate with **phone cards**.   Telephone
Coin-operated phones can still be found in cafés and post offices.
Telephone cards with 50 and 120 tariff units are available at post offices and tobacco shops (Trafik).

COUNTRY CODES

► **From outside Austria**
to Vienna: 00 43/1

► **From Austria**
to UK: 00 44
to USA: 00 1

to CANADA: 00 1
to AUSTRALIA: 00 61

INFORMATION

Austria: tel. 11 82 00
Other European countries:
tel. 11 82 02

Prices and Discounts

Vienna Card
The Vienna card (currently €18.50) gives you reduced rates in many museums for 72 hours. In addition, it includes unlimited use of Vienna's Underground, buses and trams, discounts in cafés, restaurants and many shops. The card is available from the Vienna Tourist Board (► Information), at the ticket counters of the Wiener-Linien and in hotels (www.wienkarte.at).

Combination tickets
In order to see the Hapsburger art treasures make use of one of the combination tickets offered by the Kunsthistorisches Museum: The ticket for **»Schätze der Hapsburger«** to visit the Kunsthistorisches Museum and the treasure chamber currently costs €18; the **»Imperialen Sammlungen«** (€21) also includes the Wagenburg in Schönbrunn.

Sisi Ticket
The Sisi Ticket (22.50 €) is valid for entrance to the Sisi Museum, the Imperial Apartments and the Imperial Silver Collection in the Hofburg. Also included in the price is the »Grand Tour« through all 40 rooms open to the public in Schönbrunn Palace, and entrance to the Imperial Furniture Collection.

 WHAT DOES IT COST?

3-course meal
from €15

Simple meal
from €7

Cup of coffee
€2,50

One-way ticket
€1.80

Soft drink
€2.20

Double room
from €50

Print Media

Newspapers
Naturally, all of the major Austrian newspapers are available in Vienna. The major international English-language newspapers can be found in many Trafiks (tobacco shops). The **most-read newspaper** in Austria is the conservative »Kronenzeitung«. Other important newspapers are the »Kurier«, »Die Presse« and »Der Standard«.

»Austria Today« is an English-language daily newspaper available on-line at www.austriatoday.at. The Viennese listings magazine »Der Fal-ter« is easy enough to understand, even if you don't really read German.

Shopping

Among the traditional things to take home from Vienna are the timeless **traditional costumes and sports articles**. Austrian ski and winter fashions are always in demand. **Antiques and crafts**, such as **items of worked gold and lead crystal**, fine **Augarten and Herend porcelain** or rustic **Gmundener pottery** and delicate **petit-point embroidery** are popular. There is also a wide range of haute couture and youthful fashion. In the opinion of many, Viennese patisseries and confectioneries sell the best **sweets** and the most enchanting boxed chocolates. Golden brown *Kaiserschmarrn* and fluffy *Gugelhupf*, rosy *Punschkrapferln* (pastry soaked in rum with a pink icing) and fluffy *Topfengolatschen* (pastry filled with fresh cheese) make for ideal sweet souvenirs, if you can resist eating them before the flight home. Finally, it is well worth acquiring one of the eminently drinkable Austrian **white wines** from a wine shop.

Souvenirs

Elegant, exclusive shops can be found in the inner city around St Stephen's Cathedral in the Kärntner Strasse, on the Graben, as well as along Kohlmarkt, Tuchlauben, Wollzeile, Spiegelgasse and Neuer Markt. A second, less expensive shopping zone is in the Mariahilfer Strasse, where the department stores Generali Center, Stafa and Gerngroß have their stores.

Shopping Boulevards and Department Stores

You can also purchase antiques

Antiques A large number of **antique dealers** can be found in the narrow side streets west of the Graben, in the Bräunerstrasse, Stallburggasse, Dorotheergasse, Plankengasse, Spiegelgasse and Seilergasse.

A smaller area of antique shops has also established itself south of the cathedral in the Singerstrasse, on Franzplatz, Himmelpfortgasse, Annagasse, Akademiestraße, Walfischgasse and Mahlerstrasse. The antiques range from individual items of medieval art to pieces of Jugendstil art and the Wiener Werkstätte.

Street Markets The »Standler« as vendors are called here, as well as farmers from the surrounding countryside offer a colourful picture with their mountains of fresh fruit and vegetables at Vienna's **farmers' markets**. Besides traditional pastries, cheese specialties and meat and sausages, you will also find crockery, clothes and the occasional flea market item.

A special attraction is also offered by the **seasonal markets**, such as the *Fastenmarkt* before Easter in the Kalvarienberggasse, the Easter market on the Freyung and the magical *Adventszauber* and *Christkindl* markets on Rathausplatz, on Spittelberg, and on the Freyung, during the weeks leading up to Christmas.

⏵ ADDRESSES

ANTIQUES

▶ **Dorotheum**
1, Dorotheergasse 17
▶there

▶ **Entzmann & Sohn**
1, Seilerstätte 21
Old prints and engravings

▶ **Reinhold Hofstätter**
4, Bräunerstr. 12
A large assortment of costly furniture, paintings and sculptures, as well as arts and crafts

ART AND ANTIQUE MARKETS

▶ **Market on the Danube Canal**
1, On the old town side of the Danube Canal promenade between Augarten bridge and Aspern bridge
May – Sept Sat 2pm – 8pm
Sun from 10am
Art, crafts and antiques

▶ **Old Viennese Art and Antique Market**
Am Hof
Mar – mid-Nov Fri, Sat
10am – noon
Antique dealers and second-hand bookseller set up their stands around the Mariensäule.

ANTIQUARIAN SHOPS

▶ **Inlibris**
1, Rathausstr. 19
The »market leader among Austrian second-hand booksellers« sells primarily old Austrian books and prints.

▶ **Nebehay**
1, Annagasse 18
Books and prints from the 16th to the 19th centuries, manuscripts, drawings and watercolor paintings

ENGLISH BOOKSHOPS

► British Bookshop
1, Weiburggasse 24-26
email: weiburggasse@
britishbookshop.at

► British Bookshop
1, Mariahilferstrasse 4
email: mariahilf@
britishbookshop.at

► Shakespeare & Company
1, Sterngasse 2
email: booksellers@
britishbookshop.at

CONFECTIONERS·PATISSERIES

► Altmann & Kühne
1, Am Graben 30
The specialty of this traditional shop is hand-rolled miniature sweets, including chocolate-dipped nut brittle, raspberry-filled chocolates and pistachio marzipan, packed in little hatboxes and miniature chests of drawers.

► Demel
►there

► Manner Shop
►Baedeker Tip, p.291

► Sacher Confiserie
1, Philharmonikerstr. 4
The most famous sweet delight is without a doubt the *Sachertorte*; packaged in different sizes in wood for transport. The dream in chocolate, produced according to a secret recipe, is sold from 9am until 11pm.

DELICATESSEN

► Da Conte Alimentari
1, Kurrentgasse 2
Italian specialties await the gourmet in this shop

► Meinl am Graben
1, Am Graben 19
The large selection is the attraction in this well-known delicatessen supermarket. The restaurant on the first floor with its fried goose liver, venison and all kinds of other culinary delicacies is a real invitation to eat.

GLASS

► Lobmeyr
1, Kärntner Str. 26
The shop offers hand-blown crystal of the highest quality. There is also a glass museum on the premises

CERAMICS · PORCELAIN

► Augarten-Porzellan
1, Stock-im-Eisen-Platz 3 - 4
Finest porcelain, glass and table-linen

► Pawlata
1, Kärntner Str. 14
Gmundner pottery

JUGENDSTIL

► Kunsthandel Kaesser
1, Krugerstr. 17

► Backhausen
1, Schwarzenbergstr. 10
There is a small Wiener Werkstätten museum attached to the shop.

MARKETS

► Augustiner-/ Rochusmarkt
3, between Landstraßer Hauptstr. and Maria-Eis-Gasse
Named after the Augustinian monastery that was torn down in 1812, but today it is better known under the name »Rochusmarkt«.

Vienna is a great place to go window shopping

MEN'S FASHION

▶ **Claudio Pascalini**
1, Freisingergasse 1
Exclusive apparel from designers like Fendi, Versace and Armani

▶ **Don Gil**
1, Kärntner Str. 14
You'll find good and pricey designer clothing in each of the 6 shops

▶ **House of Gentlemen**
1, Kohlmarkt 1
Elegant fashions for the gentleman; the original interior was done by Adolf Loos

JEWELLERY

▶ **Bachner**
1. Kärntner Ring 9 - 13
Precision watches from the world's best watchmakers

▶ **Caesar's Juwelen**
1, Graben 26
Finely-crafted designer pieces are what you'll find here. The façade was designed by the Viennese architect Hans Hollein

▶ **Galerie Slavik**
1, Himmelpfortgasse 17
Modern jewelry by international designers for people with money

▶ **Schullin & Söhne**
1, Kohlmarkt 7
The façade of this exclusive shop was designed by Hans Hollein.

SHOES

▶ **Ludwig Reiter**
1, Mölkersteig 1
Tremendously long-lasting hand-crafted shoes have been created here since 1885.

▶ **Naschmarkt**
▶there

▶ **Flohmarkt (Flea Market)**
▶Naschmarkt

WOMEN'S FASHION

▶ **Disaster Clothing**
7, Neubaugasse 7 and
7, Kirchengasse 19
Affordable Austrian designer fashions

▶ **Flo**
4, Schleifmühlgasse 15 a
Treasure trove of designer clothing and accessories

▶ **Rieger**
1, Judengasse 9
(and other shops)
Designer fashion, some of it kooky, at reasonable prices

► **Zak**
1, Kärntner Str. 36
One of the nicest shoe salons in
Vienna

TOYS

► **Das Spielzeug**
16, Thaliastraße 78
Imaginative toys for big and small

► **Spielkistl**
3, Landstr. 2
Captivating things for children of
all ages

TRADITIONAL COSTUMES

► **Resi Hammerer**
1, Kärntner Str. 29 - 31
Traditional costumes and urban
fashions

► **Tostmann**
1, Schottengasse 3 a
The shop specializes in dirndls
made of the finest textiles. Even
Caroline of Monaco has shopped
here.

WINE

► **Vinissimo**
6, Windmühlgasse 20 a
Outstanding wines; bistro

► **Wein & Co.**
1, Jasomirgottstr. 3
Wine shop & with a comprehensive collection of top wines

Sport and Outdoors

There are two football clubs in
Vienna that play in the Austrian
national league (Bundesliga): **SK
Rapid Wien** and **FK Austria Wien**.
They are the most successful clubs
in Austria, though not very successful internationally.

There are lots of activities for
hikers in and around Vienna. The
Vienna Tourist Board (► Information) has put together numerous
routes in a leaflet about **hiking in
and around Vienna** , which not only details the individual circular
hiking paths marked on a small outline map, but also the starting
points (specifying public transport), duration and length, as well as
places that serve food and drink.

> ! *Baedeker* TIP
>
> **»Through the night, through the city«**
> With this motto, a huge roller blading/inline
> skating spectacular gets underway every Friday
> evening in the warm summer months. The 12km/
> 7.5mi car-free route runs from Heldenplatz in
> Pulk, first via the Ringstrasse, and then for 1.5
> hours through the inner districts. No registration
> necessary, simply show up! Participation is free.
> Start is at 9pm. More information at
> www.wien.gruene.at/skater.

The Vienna City Marathon takes place annually in the spring. The   **Vienna City**
42km/26mi route passes Schönbrunn Palace and the Prater and fin-   **Marathon**
ishes, appropriately enough, at Heldenplatz (Heroes' Square).

◉ ADDRESSES

FOOTBALL

▶ **Gerhard Hanappi Stadium**
14, Keißlergasse 6
SK Rapid Wien football club's
home stadium

▶ **Franz Horr Stadium**
10, Fischhofgasse 12
Tel. 688 81 50
Home stadium of FK Austria Wien
football club

HORSE-RACING

▶ **Trabrennbahn Krieau**
2, Nordportalstr. 247
Tel. 72 80 04 60
www.krieau.at
Season runs Sept – June

ICE-SKATING

▶ **Wiener Eislaufverein**
3, Lothringerstr. 22
Tel. 71 36 35 30

Ice Skating Every year between the end of January and the beginning of March, Rathausplatz is transformed into a skating rink. You will see traditional »ice skating« as well as the latest fashionable sport of **curling**. The skating rink is also used for a variety of other events, such as concerts, music clubs on ice and much more.

Bungee Jumping The daring can plunge a record height of 152m /499ft from the Donau Turm (tower). In operation on Saturdays and Sundays from April to October.

Theatre and Concerts

Programme preview, tickets The Vienna Tourist Board distributes a monthly events calendar (▶ Information); furthermore, the monthly programme is printed in city guide and listing magazines published monthly (▶Festivals, holidays and events). Tickets can be purchased at advance booking offices or directly at the theatres.

◉ INFORMATION AND ADDRESSES

ADVANCE TICKET SALES

▶ **Bundestheater Advance Booking Office**
Tickets for the Staatsoper, Burgtheater, Volksoper and Akademietheater
1, Operngasse 2, Tel. 514 44 78 80
www.bundestheater.at

▶ **Vienna Ticket Service**
1, Börsegasse 1
Tel. 534 170, fax 534 17 26

▶ **Wien-Ticket**
Advance booking office for Theater an der Wien, Ronacher Theater and Raimund Theater

Culture: visitors in front of the Theatre in Josefstadt

Wien-Ticket pavilion at the opera
1, Herbert-von-Karajan-Platz
Credit card bookings
Tel. 588 85
www.wien-ticket.at

▶ **Vienna Classic**
Kundenzentrum
1, Karlsplatz 1
Tel. 890 53 97, fax 890 53 97 97
www.viennaclassic.com

▶ **Wiener Sängerknaben
(Vienna Boys' Choir)**
Hofmusikkapelle
1, Hofburg, Schweizerhof
Tel. 533 99 27 75
Tickets for the Sunday concerts in
the Burgkapelle (start 9.15am);
ticket pick-up Fri 11am – 1pm,
3pm – 5pm or Sun
8.15am – 8.45am in the Burgkapelle; ticket sales at the Burgkapelle box office on Fridays
11am – 1pm, 3pm – 5pm for the
following Sunday.

THEATRE

▶ **Akademietheater**
3, Lisztstr. 1

Tel. 514 44 47 40
www.burgtheater.at

▶ **Ateliertheater**
1, Burggasse 71
Tel. 524 22 45
http://kpc.server101.com/atelier-
theater

▶ **Burgtheater**
▶there

▶ **Ensemble Theater
am Petersplatz**
1, Petersplatz 1
Tel. 535 32 00
www.ensembletheater.at

▶ **Theater in der
Josefstadt**
8, Josefstädter Str. 26
Tel. 42 70 03 00
www.josefstadt.org

▶ **Theaterhaus für junges
Publikum – Dschungel Wien**
8, Museumsplatz 1
Tel. 522 07 20,
www.dschungelwien.at

▶ **Volkstheater**
7, Neustiftgasse 1
Tel. 52 11 14 00
www.volkstheater.at

COMEDY

▶ **Kammerspiele**
1, Rotenturmstr. 20
Tel. 42 70 03 00
www.josefstadt.org

▶ **stadtTheater Walfischgasse**
1, Walfischgasse 4
Tel. 512 42 00
www.stadttheater.org

▶ **Komödie am Kai**
1, Franz-Josefs-Kai 29
Tel. 533 24 34
www.komoedieamkai.at

CABARET

▶ **Theater Drachengasse**
1, Fleischmarkt 22
Tel. 513 14 44
www.drachengasse.at

▶ **Kabarett Niedermair**
8, Lenaugasse 1 A
Tel. 408 44 92
www.niedermair.at

▶ **Theater Kabarett Simpl**
1, Wollzeile 36
Tel. 512 47 42
www.simpl.at

OPERA · BALLET

▶ **Staatsoper**
▶there

▶ **Volksoper**
9. Währinger Str. 78
Tel. 513 15 13
www.volksoper.at

▶ **Wiener Kammeroper**
1, Fleischmarkt 24
Tel. 512 01 00 77
www.wienerkammeroper.at

MUSICAL · OPERETTA · REVUE

▶ **Theater an der Wien**
▶Naschmarkt

▶ **Raimundtheater**
6, Wallgasse 18
Tel. 588 85
www.musicalvienna.at

▶ **Ronacher-Theater**
1, Seilerstätte 9
Tel. 51 41 10
www.musicalvienna.at

CONCERT VENUES

▶ **Konzerthaus**
3, Lothringer Str. 20
Tel. 24 20 02 11
www.konzerthaus.at

▶ **Musikverein**
Karlsplatz 6
Tel. 505 81 90
www.musikverein.at

Time

Austria is in the Central European Time (CET) zone; European daylight savings time (CET + 1 hour) is March through October.

Tours and Guides

This bus runs daily past the most important sights such as St Stephen's Cathedral and the Prater. It serves its 15 bus stops hourly from 9am to 4.30pm. The complete tour lasts about three hours. Sightseeing information is given at each stop in English and German. The 2-day ticket is available in hotels and on the busses.

Hop on Hop off

Viennese guides offer walks led by experts focusing on close to 50 different subjects. The tours cover historic **medieval Vienna** above and below ground, the Habsburg highlights, **Jugendstil architecture** and Hundertwasser's architectural milestones, as well as touring ancient alleyways and quiet, typically Viennese courtyards, legendary coffee houses, princely palaces and the homes of the great composers. You can also retrace »Sisi's« footsteps and those of other famous and not-so-famous women, locate sights from »The Third Man« and discover **Viennese legends** and criminal chronicles. Other tours provide insight into the life of Sigmund Freud and **Jewish Vienna** at the turn of the 20th century. Last but not least, there are also »culinary« walks on the programme.

Guided City Walking Tours

Historic form of transport in front of a historical backdrop: Fiaker at the Burg

● CITY TOURS

BUS TOURS

▶ **Vienna Sightseeing Tours**
4, Weyringergasse 28 A
Tel. 712 46 830
www.viennasightseeingtours.com

▶ **Cityrama Sightseeing**
1, Börsegasse 1/
Tiefer Graben 25
Tel. 534 130
www.cityrama.at

▶ **Stattwerkstatt**
9, Kolingasse 6
Tel. 317 33 84

Tours offering an alternative, offbeat view of the city

BICYCLE EXCURSIONS

▶ **Pedal Power**
Ausstellungsstr. 3
Tel. 729 72 34
www.pedalpower.at

▶ **Bike & Guide**
Tel. 212 11 35
www.bikeandguide.com

Where and when the 1-2hr walks take place can be discovered in the Vienna Tourist Board brochure (▶ Information), the daily newspapers and the monthly Vienna programme, or by calling 894 53 63.

Fiaker   The famous horse-drawn carriages known as *Fiaker*, also called *Zeugl* by the Viennese, have been plying the streets of Vienna since the end of the 17th century. In recent years, the number of **Fiakers** has risen to 140. The **Fiaker stands** are on Stephansplatz, to the north side of the cathedral, in Augustinerstrasse in front of the Albertina, and on Heldenplatz in front of the statue of Archduke Karl.

Guided Bicycle   Sporty types can take to the saddle daily between May and September around 10am for an approx. 3-hour tour of the city with various tour organizations.

Boat Excursions   The Blue Danube Schifffahrt GmbH (DDSG, ▶ Information) offers roundtrip boat excursions on the Danube. Points of departure are Schwedenplatz and the Reichsbrücke (bridge). The ship that Hundertwasser designed in 1995, the »Vindobona«, sails daily from the KunstHausWien by way of Schwedenplatz to the Nussdorf weir and locks and back (c1.5 hrs). »Große Donaurundfahrten« (extended Danube cruises) and »Abendliche Tanzfahrten« (evening dance cruises) depart from Schwedenplatz, past UN City to the Freudenau power plant and back (c4 hrs). Oldies night and *Heurigen* wine-tasting cruises, evening cruises by candlelight with formal buffet und live music are also offered during the summer.

Transport

By Car

The **speed limit** on Austrian Autobahns for private vehicles and mo- torcycles is 80mph/130kmh, for vehicles with trailers 62mph/ 100kmh. Noise pollution legislation limits speed during the hours of 10pm to 5am, and is set at 68mph / 110kmh; exceptions are the A 1 from Salzburg to Vienna and the A 2 from Vienna to Villach. The speed limit for vehicles and motorcycles on country roads is 62mph /100kmh, for vehicles with trailers with a weight up to 750kg / 1654lb it is 62mph / 100kmh; with a weight above that, it is 50mph / 80kmh. Within the city limits, where honking is banned, the speed limit for all vehicles is 31mph / 50kmh.

Traffic Regulations

The legal **blood alcohol limit** is 0.5 per thousand. **Safety belts must be used** on all seats. Children under 12 must sit in the rear; child- ren's safety seats are required. A hazard warning triangle and a warn- ing vest in case of a breakdown are compulsory.

Motorcycle and moped riders must wear **protective helmets**, carry a first aid kit and drive with dimmed headlights during the day.

◄ Motorcycle riders

Vienna's entire inner city is a fee-paying **short parking zone**, where a maximum of 1.5hrs is allowed. Pay and display tickets for 30, 60 and 90 minutes can be obtained at the sales points of the Vienna munici- pal transport, in train stations, in tobacco Trafiks and banks. Dis- abled visitors may park in short- term parking zones for an un- limited amount of time by display- ing the appropriate certificate be- hind the windscreen. A list of car parks is available from the Vienna Tourist Board (►Information) and on the internet (www.wkw.at/gara- gen). From December 15 to March 30 there is a general **ban on park- ing** in all streets between 8pm and 5am that have tramway tracks, to facilitate the removal of snow in case of heavy snowfall.

◄ Parking

> **!** *Baedeker* TIP
>
> ### Oldtimer Tour
>
> A ride with a vintage tram (1929 model) is a must for all aficionados of historic track vehicles. From May through October there are nostalgic 2.5hr tours through Vienna. Departures are Sat 1.30pm, Sun and Fri 11.30am and 1.30pm from the Otto Wagner Pavilion on Karlsplatz. Infor- mation and tickets are available at the Karlsplatz Underground station (tel. 790 94 40 26).

There is a **higher basic tariff** for trips at night (11pm – 4am), and on Sundays and holidays. In addition, a surcharge is levied for radio taxis and trips to the airport.

Taxi

Local Public Transport

There are 24-, a 48–hour and 72-hour **season tickets** that are valid everywhere in Vienna for the specified period of time after valida-

Tickets

Vienna Public Transport Map

U1 Underground Lines
S 1 Municipal Railway
CAT City Airport Train
S Local Railway Vienna-Baden
Wiener Linien Customer Centre U3 station Erdberg)
i Wiener Linien Information Offices
V Ticket Offices
P+R Airport Park & Ride
■■■■ U2 extension (2008)

WIENER LINIEN
Die Stadt gehört Dir.

Oberdöbling
Krottenbachstr.
Gersthof   Nußd
Währing
Vol
Michelbeuer
Allg. Krankenha
Hernals
Kendler-straße **P+R**
Ottakring
U3 V   Hütteldorfer-Straße
V   Johnstraße
Breitensee   Schwegler-straße
Penzing   **S 50**
Purkersdorf Sanatorium Weidlingau
S 45
S 15   Gumpendorfer Straße
S 50   Unter St. Veit Braun-schweigg.
Hadersdorf **U4**   **V**   **V**
Hütteldorf
Ober St. Veit   Hietzing (Tiergarten) Schönbrunn Meidling Hauptstraße Langenfeldg.
V i
Speising   Philadelphiabr.
Meidling
Hetzendorf   Tscherttegasse
Am Schöpfwerk
Atzgersdorf   Alterlaa **V**
Erlaaer Straße
Liesing   Perfektastraße
S 9 P+R   Siebenhirten **U6 P+R**

www.wienerlinien.at

© Wiener Linien, Mai 2007

◉ ADDRESSES

TELEPHONE
TAXIS

▶ **Calling Radio Taxis**
Tel. 313 00, 401 00, 601 60
C & K Airport Service:
Tel. 444 44

AUTOMOBILE
CLUBS

▶ **ÖAMTC**
(Austrian Automobile Club)
Tel. 71 19 90, www.oeamtc.at
Breakdown service: tel. 120

▶ **ARBÖ**
(Austrian Car Driver and
Cyclist association)
Tel. 853 53 50
www.arboe.or.at
Breakdown service:
Tel. 123

ÖPNV

Wiener Linien
Tel. 790 91 00
www.wienerlinien.at

CAR HIRE

The best prices can always be had
by booking hired cars in advance.
See Holiday Autos
(www.holidayautos.com) or
easyCar (www.easycar.com).
Also, Avis (www.avis.at);
Europcar (www.europcar.at) and
Hertz (www.hertz.at).

▶ **Avis**
Reservations in Vienna:
Tel. 08 00 08 00 87 57
www.avis.com

▶ **Europcar**
Reservations in Vienna:
Tel. 866 16 33

▶ **Hertz**
Reservations in Austria:
Tel. 79 54 20
www.hertz.com

BICYCLE HIRE

▶ **Hochschaubahn**
2, Prater 113
Tel./fax 729 58 88

▶ **Pedal Power**
2, Ausstellungsstr. 31
Tel. 729 72 34

BICYCLE
PATH MAP

▶ **ARGUS (Coalition for**
Environmentally Friendly
Urban Transport)
4, Frankenberggasse 11
Tel. 505 09 07
Fax 505 09 07 19
www.argus.or.at
Opening times: Mon – Fri
2pm – 7pm, Sat 9am – 1pm
The complete ARGUS map for
cyclists is also available in book-
stores.

tion. There is also a shopping ticket, a season ticket valid from Monday through Saturday from 8am to 8pm. In addition, there is an 8-
day ticket that can be used on any 8 days as an all-day ticket; it can
also be used for several persons travelling together – just validate one
strip per person per day. All tickets entitle the bearer to unlimited

travel with or without transfers. Single tickets for single journeys are sold as **strip tickets** for 4 journeys. The tickets can be purchased at the ticket sales offices of the Vienna Transport Authority, in Trafiks, in the vehicles themselves (tram, bus), from vending machines (in the Underground) and in hotels.

It is well worth buying a Vienna Card (►Prices and Discounts). Children under six ride for free on public transport and children under 15 pay half price and they also ride for free on Sundays and holidays, as well as during school holidays. There are special discounted tariffs for school children, apprentices, students and seniors.

Vienna Card

21 night bus routes run the whole week from 12.30am to 5am, every 15 or 30 minutes.

Nightline buses

By Rail

Trains run from Westbahnhof to West Austria, Germany and Switzerland. The terminal of the Südbahn and Ostbahn covers the area of southern Austria and countries like Hungary, Slovenia and the Slovak Republic.
The regions of north-western Austria and the Czech Republic can be reached from the Franz Josef railway station.

The »City Express Trains« offer good connections (»Austro-Takt«). For example, they run hourly during the day from Vienna to Salzburg and Graz and every two hours to Villach and Innsbruck.

City Express Trains

By bicycle

Vienna now has a fully developed network of bicycle paths of over 900km /560mi. In Austria cyclists must yield **right of way** to cars at road junctions without traffic lights.
Bicycles can be transported on the Underground at the following times (ticket necessary): Saturdays after 2pm, all day Sundays and holidays; July to August Mon-Fri 9am – 3pm and after 6.30pm, Saturdays after 9am, all day Sundays and holidays.

Travellers with Disabilities

Vienna-Tourism's webpage (www.wien.info) has tips for travellers with disabilities in the section »Specials« under the heading »Vienna for Visitors with Disabilities«. The hotels listed cite their special facilities, like extra-wide swinging doors. There is also information on hiring wheelchairs.

Internet

When to Go

Vienna is always in season – that is why the legendary *Heurige* wine taverns are almost all licensed for the whole year. The coffee houses offer their own special charm to budding writers, daydreamers and interested observers of the local scene at any time of year. The capital on the Danube is magical in spring, when the parks blossom and temperatures are pleasant enough for a good long stroll through the city and the outdoor cafés have already opened. The **Vienna Festival Weeks** present the first cultural highlight of the year. In the months July through September, the musical events of the Vienna **Summer Music** take over from the popular Festival Weeks. During these months, Vienna also offers real bathing pleasures within the city, on the Donauinsel (Danube Island) and along the old Danube, as well as countless possibilities for delightful excursions into the surrounding countryside. When autumn comes to Vienna so do the new productions of the renowned **stages of theatre and music**. Finally, the winter, alongside everything else, is first and foremost **ball season**.

In Season All Year Round

Vienna lies in a transitional zone moving from oceanic to continental climates. The temperature seldom falls below –5 °C / 23°F in winter; the average temperature in January is 2 °C/36 °F. It is seldom above 30 °C / 86°F in summer; the average temperature has levelled off at 20 °C / 68°F. There are often showers, especially in summer, but hardly ever continuous rain. A slight wind blows almost steadily, which is known as the »Viennese Breeze«.

Climate

← *Fall is the season for visiting a »Heurigen«*

Tours

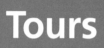

HOFBURG OR ST STEPHEN'S CATHEDRAL –
THE CITY'S SIGHTS LIE SO CLOSE TOGETHER THAT
VIENNA CAN COMFORTABLY BE EXPLORED
ON FOOT.

Vienna Plan

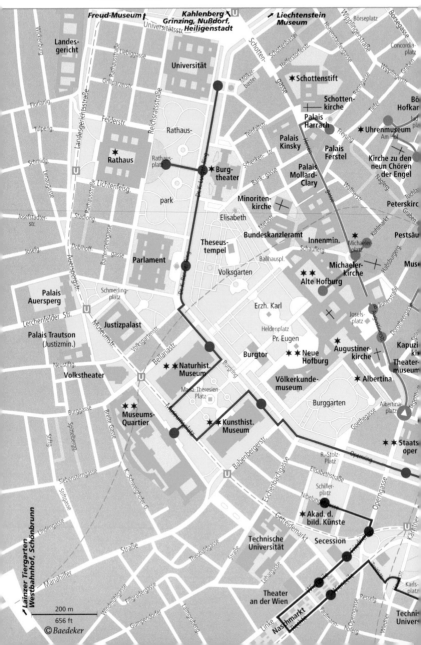

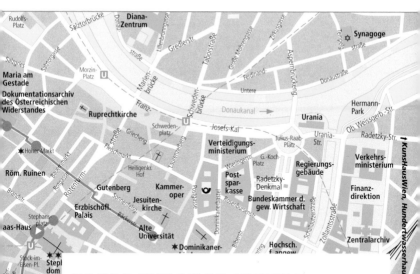

TOURS THROUGH VIENNA

Tours through ViennaFour walks and countless sights, which you can just glance at or visit in depth. We will add a few tips for a coffee break along the way.

TOUR 1   **In the Heart of Vienna**
A varied walk from St Stephen's Cathedral to squares, churches and interesting neighbourhoods. ► page 147

TOUR 2   **Power and Politics: In and around the Hofburg**
The Hofburg is the focal point of this tour – with its extensive museums and priceless collections, a must for every visitor to Vienna. ► page 149

TOUR 3   **The Splendour of Historicism**
The Ringstrasse was built in the late 19th century and is an incomparable showpiece. The recent Museum Quarter has more than art to show. ► page 150

TOUR 4   **Karlsplatz and Surroundings**
Karlskirche is the focal point of the Karlsplatz; it is the most important Baroque sacred structure in Vienna. ► page 152

Getting Around in Vienna

Coach and horses A trip to Vienna demands sturdy shoes because practically all of Vienna's sights can be explored on foot. Most of the attractions are along or within the Ring, meaning in the city centre or district 1. The **historic city centre** encompasses about 2 sq km / 1 sq mi, and is the starting point of every tour. Furthermore, a large part of the city centre has been pedestrianized. Alternatively – though not exactly cheap – you can explore by taking a **Fiaker** or horse-drawn carriage. This option offers a nostalgic tour of the city and there are several places where coaches can be hired, including at St Stephen's Cathedral, on Heldenplatz, and in front of the Albertina. The tram lines 1 or 2 also offer a comfortable tour of the historic **Ringstrasse** with its magnificent buildings, whose construction began in the middle of the 19th century to replace the demolished city wall. The lines run along the boulevard passing parliament, the Rathaus, university, Burgtheater and the great museums. The ride is also a trip through art history, because the architectural style of the Ringstrasse covers everything from Classical to Gothic, and Renaissance to Baroque.

> ! **Baedeker** TIP
>
> **Otto Wagner Tour**
> The »suburban line« between the districts of Hütteldorf and Döbling that was reopened for public transport in 1987, is a real attraction. Its bridges and tunnels, and above all its stations, were designed as one in Art Nouveau style by Otto Wagner.

The **Prater's** leisure park spreads out on the other side of the Danube Canal and offers footpaths leading off in all directions and fun in the so-called Wurstelprater, with its taverns and amusement attractions. Beyond the **Gürtel**, a ring road that encircles the former villages that grew up outside the old city wall, there are new hot spots of Viennese nightlife which can be found in pubs along the Stadtbahnbögen, along the Lechenfelder and the Hernalser Gürtel.

Finally, there is the »**second city**« on the opposite side of the Danube. Along with New York and Geneva, Vienna is now the third UN headquarters, and its modern administrative complex known as **UN City** has been developing since the 1970s. The towering high-rise buildings can hardly be called architectural highlights, but buildings such as the Millennium Tower, Andromeda Tower and the technology centre Tech Gate do present an interesting contrast to historic Vienna.

How long to stay? ► An extended weekend is perfectly suited for a trip to the city. Most of the hotels are located within the Ring or only a few minutes from the Ringstrasse, and the selection is huge. Moreover, in the summer months, when business travellers are not so prevalent, some hotels offer bargain prices. Getting to Vienna is also quick and easy in these days of cheap flights.

Tour 1 In the Heart of Vienna

Start and destination: St Stephen's Cathedral　**Duration:** 1/2 day

This tour begins at Vienna's most famous landmark, which is St Stephen's Cathedral, and offers plenty of variety. It alternates between lively shopping boulevards and quiet spots, passing churches and memorials, going into the former Jewish district, and then on to the old university quarter.

The tour through the innermost part of the historic city touches Vienna's oldest sites. The Medieval Virgilkapelle was excavated at the Gothic ❶ ✷✷ **St Stephen's Cathedral**, towering in the heart of the old city. In the ❷ ✷ **cathedral and Diocesan Museum** next door, the cathedral's most precious items are on display. Continue by walking down the busy ❸ **Kärntner Strasse**, one of the city's important shopping boulevards. Turn west to Neuer Markt. The unclothed figures

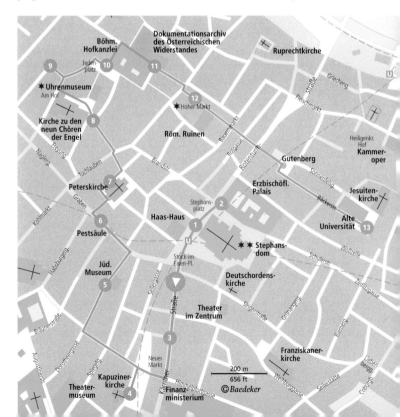

of the river deities on the Donner fountain, named for its creator, Georg Raphael Donner, were once a source of displeasure for Maria Theresa. The Kapuzinerkirche stands on the square with its ❹ ✳ **Imperial Crypt**, in which most of Austria's rulers are buried. Take Plankengasse, which leads to the Dorotheergasse, where the ❺ ✳ **Jewish Museum** is to be found. Almost directly opposite is Hawelka, a typical Viennese coffee house and an excellent place for a break. Across the ❻ **Graben** is Petersplatz with the Baroque ❼ ✳ **Peterskirche**. Further north is ❽ **Am Hof**, a city square dominated by the Baroque church »Zu den neun Chören der Engel« (Nine Choirs of Angels). Right next to it is the ❾ ✳ **Uhrenmuseum (Watch Museum)**, which is worth touring. The Holocaust Memorial by Rachel Whiteread close by on ❿ **Judenplatz** is a reminder of the murder of 65,000 Viennese Jews during the Nazi period. The Wipplingerstrasse can be reached by walking further to the north-east, where the ⓫ **Böhmische Hofkanzlei (Bohemian Court Chancellery)** stands. The Documentation Centre of Austrian Resistance (Dokumentationsarchiv des Österreichischen Wiederstandes) is housed in the old Rathaus opposite. The Wipplingerstrasse leads south-east to ⓬ ✳ **Hohe Markt**, Vienna's oldest square. The Bäckerstrasse leads into the ⓭ **old university quarter**, with the Baroque Jesuitenkirche, the former university church. And finally, coming in from the east, we find ourselves once again at St Stephen's Cathedral.

They come in droves, but the Hofburg is so spread out that visitors soon lose themselves between the individual wings of the building

Tour 2 Power and Politics: Hofburg and Surroundings

Start and Destination: from the Albertina to the Freyung

Duration: min. 4 hours

The middle point of this walk is the Hofburg, one of the most important sights in Vienna with its considerable museums and valuable collections, and a must-see on the schedule of every trip to Vienna.

The walk begins on Albertinaplatz, where the recently restored ❶ ✶ **Albertina** stands. Walk along Augustinerstrasse to Lobkowitzplatz, where a visit can be paid to the ❷ ✶ **Theatre Museum**. The walk passes the Gothic ❸ ✶ **Augustinerkirche,** with its Classical, pyramid-shaped marble memorial for the Archduchess Maria Christina von Sachsen-Teschen by Antonio Canova, and finally reaches ❹ ✶ **Josefsplatz** with a memorial to the monarchs.

A passageway leads from here into the ❺ ✶✶ **Hofburg**, the former residence of the Austrian rulers with the old and new Hofburg, innumerable museums, the Spanish Riding School and the Austrian National Library.

Further north of Josefsplatz is ❻ ✶ **Michaelerplatz**, where a rest can be made to sample some of Vienna's many coffee specialties in the famous Café Griensteindl, or in the celebrated ❼ ✶ **Demel** coffeehouse around the corner. Adolf Loos caused a scandal in 1911 by doing away with all ornamentation on its façade.

Walking down the Herrengasse will eventually lead to the ❽ **Freyung**, where the originally Gothic Schottenkirche and the Schottenstift with its collection of 15th to 18th century paintings is located. Also on the square is the Ferstel Palace with Café Central, which is a Viennese institution.

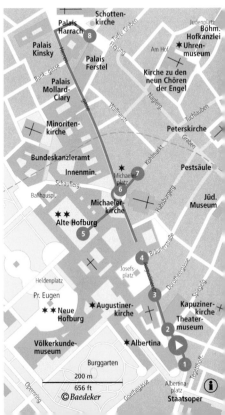

Tour 3 The Splendour of Historicism

Start and Destination: From the Museum für Angewandte Kunst (Museum of Applied Arts) to the University

Duration: min. 4 hours

After Emperor Franz Joseph had given orders to demolish Vienna's old ramparts, the Ringstrasse, a magnificent boulevard unequalled in Europe, was created. A unique ensemble was also achieved in recent years when numerous museums, including the museums of natural history and art history, moved into 60,000 sq m / 196,850 sq ft of the Baroque Imperial Stables. A stopover for refreshments can be made in one of the large number of restaurants and cafés in the Museum Quarter.

The walk begins at the ❶✶ **Museum für Angewandte Kunst** on the eastern side of the Ring. Head in a southerly direction through the ❷**city park** with its many monuments.

The ❸✶✶ **Staatsoper (state opera)**, one of the world's largest music theatres, stands where Kärntner Ring becomes Opernring. Opernring continues and turns into Burgring, and on the left side further down, Burgring becomes Maria Theresien Platz. Here stands the ❹✶✶ **Kunsthistorische Museum (Art History Museum)**, with its displays of world-class exponents; opposite is the ❺✶✶ **Naturhisto-**

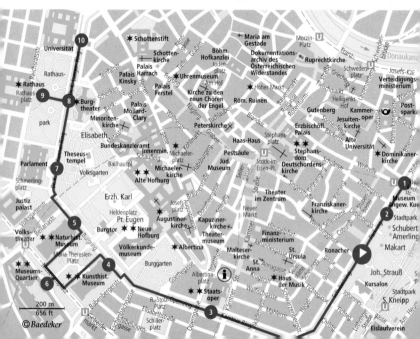

Need a break? Vienna's cafés are waiting for you!

risches Museum (Natural History Museum), whose scientific collections are among Europe's most important. The triad of museums is completed by the totally innovative ❻✳✳ **Museums Quartier (Museum Quarter)**, a centre of contemporary art and cultural activities that also owns outstanding collections of modern art. The MUMOK (Museum für moderne Kunst Stiftung Ludwig Wien), a museum of modern art, is now housed in a purpose-built structure together with the Museum des 20. Jahrhunderts (Museum of the 20th Century), and the Sammlung Leopold (Leopold Collection) which was acquired by the city in 1994. Walk along the Burgring in a northerly direction, which leads into the Dr.-Karl-Renner-Ring. Here the Volksgarten (▶ Hofburg) public park opens up, the second largest green space in the inner city. The Classical ❼✳ **parliament** building, built in Greek style, can be seen across from the Volksgarten. Further along the Ring is the famous ❽✳ **Burgtheater**, one of the most important German language stages. The Café Landtmann located in

the immediate vicinity is a fine place to take a break. Across the way stands the prestigious neo-Gothic ❾✳ **Rathaus**, which can be viewed on a guided tour. The ❿**university** (▶ old University quarter), built in Italian Renaissance style by Ferstel, is at the end of this part of the Ring.

Tour 4 Karlsplatz and Surroundings

Start and Destination: From the Stadtbahn (light railway) pavilions to the Akademie der bildenden Künste (Academy of Fine Arts)

Duration of tour: min. 4 hours

It goes without saying that the walks described here can only cover a portion of the sites in a great city like Vienna, but Karlsplatz should be included in every sight-seeing programme, not because of the square itself, which is of little interest, but for the buildings here and in the neighbourhood.

First, take a look at the ❶✳ **Jugendstil pavilions by Otto Wagner** at the Karlsplatz underground station. The famous ✳ **Musikverein building** has fantastic acoustics. The ❷✳ **Vienna Museum Karlsplatz** is recommended to those who are interested in the city's history. Right next to it is the ❸✳ **Karlskirche**, Vienna's most significant Baroque church. The building of the ❹**Secession** west of Karlsplatz can be recognized by the gilded laurel tree on the dome; inside, the Jugendstil painter Gustav Klimt's Beethoven frieze can be admired. From there, it is only a few steps to the colourful and lively ❺ **Naschmarkt** with its food stalls and flea market. Otto Wagner erected two tenement houses (nos. 38 & 40) in the parallel running Linke Wienzeile in 1898/1899. The eye-catcher here is no longer the Piano Nobile, but rather the whole basement, which has been architecturally emphasized as an independent commercial area. Wagner had the face of the apartment building known as the ❻**Majolikahaus** covered with tiles. The ❼**Café Museum** is on the way to the last sight on the walk. Adolf Loos decorated the interior of the artists' café, which met with bitter opposition from traditionalists because of its plain and simple furnishings. The end of the tour is the ❽✳ **Akademie der bildenden Künste** on nearby Schillerplatz, with its significant collection of paintings.

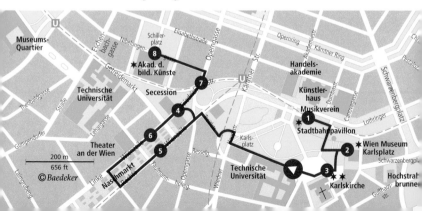

Excursions

There are sites well worth taking a short trip to visit within a radius of 35km/22mi, such as beautiful wine-growing villages and the vast countryside of the Vienna Woods.

A little further out

26km/16mi south of Vienna lies Baden, a spa town steeped in tradition, where Schubert, Liszt and Stifter stayed. People still come for the thermal baths and sprawling spa gardens or to visit the casino and the harness horse racing track.

◄ Baden bei Wien

The popular wine village of Gumpoldskirchen, 18km/11mi to the south, is visited first and foremost to enjoy a glass of *Heurigen* in one of its cosy taverns or wine restaurants.

◄ Gumpoldskirchen

The major attraction of Heiligenkreuz, 34km / 21mi south-west of Vienna, is the **monastery** of the same name founded in 1133, Austria's second oldest Cistercian abbey. Many members of the House of Babenberg found their last resting place in the order's Romanesque-Gothic church.

◄ Heiligenkreuz

Klosterneuburg, 12km/7.5mi north of Vienna, is visited for its Augustinian Abbey, whose founding dates back to the 12th century. Certainly not to be missed is the famous **Verdun Altar** (1181), one of the finest examples of high medieval enamel and gold work in existence, which is in St Leopold's Chapel inside the monastery. Austrian art after 1945 can be admired in the **Sammlung Essl (Essl Collection)**.

◄ Klosterneuburg

Austria's largest wine-growing district is bounded to the north by the Czech Republic, in the east by the Slovak Republic and in the south by Marchfeld. The Waldviertel (Wooded Quarter) adjoins to the west, which is separated from the wine district by the extended ridge of Manharts Mountain. Mainly wine is cultivated on the fertile loess slopes of the wide valleys; in addition, there are widespread fields of sugar beet and wheat. Grüner Veltliner, Blauer Portugieser, Neuburger, Rheinriesling, Müller-Thurgau and Blaufränkisch are the main grape varieties of the region, which can be pleasantly sampled in the pretty little villages where wine taverns and small restaurants tempt travellers to pull over.

◄ Wine-growing district

The Vienna Woods lie to the west of the Austrian capital. Its close to 80 sq km/50 sq mi actually reaches far into the city's urban areas and constitutes Vienna's most popular recreational area. The softly undulating hills of this hilly region form the north-eastern foothills of the Eastern Alps that descend in several terraces down towards the Danube. To the north, the Vienna Woods are a thickly wooded recreational area, a charming picture book landscape with wide hillocks und beech wood forests. Austrian pine dominates in the east and, in the less cultivated south-east, romantically wild gorges can be found.

◄ Wienerwald

The Lainzer Tiergarten forms the eastern end of the Vienna Woods. The **Hermesvilla**, former hunting lodge of Empress Elizabeth built by Karl von Hasenauer, is today used by the Vienna Museum Karlsplatz for changing exhibitions.

◄ Lainzer Tiergarten

Sights from A to Z

VIENNA STANDS FOR CULTURE AND ARCHITECTURE AND ALWAYS INVITES THE VISITOR TO FOLLOW IN THE FOOTSTEPS OF ITS HISTORY. THE BURGTHEATER WAS BUILT IN RENAISSANCE STYLE BY SEMPER AND HASENAUER IN THE 19TH CENTURY.

✱ Akademie der bildenden Künste (Academy of Fine Arts)

G 7

Location: 1, Schillerplatz 3
Bus: 59 A
Internet:: www.akademiegalerie.at

Underground: Karlsplatz (U1, U2, U4)
Tram: 1, 2, 3, 62

The Akademie der bildenden Künste is a highly respected and cele-brated centre of learning for painters, sculptors, graphic artists, stage designers, curators and architects. Its graphic collection and its picture gallery are noteworthy.

Its founder, Peter von Strudel, set up the first art school in his »Strudelhof« following the examples of Italian schools in 1692. The school moved into the building on Schillerplatz in 1876 that **Theophil Hansen** had built in the style of the Italian Renaissance. The academy produced painters like Friedrich von Amerling, Ferdinand Georg Waldmüller, Leopold Kupelwieser, Moritz von Schwind and Egon Schiele.

The professors teaching architecture there set new distinctive architectural directions that influenced the way the city looked. Almost all of the »architects of the Ringstrasse« were academy professors, as was Theophil Hansen who, besides building the academy, built the Musikverein and Parlament. Adolf Hitler tried to gain admission to the academy in 1907, but failed the entrance examination. Even in recent times, professors like Friedensreich Hundertwasser with his Hundertwasserhaus and the KunstHausWien (▶ p.231), and Fritz Wotruba (1907 – 1975) with his Wotruba Church, have caused a stir. The picture gallery was renovated and remodelled from 2008–2010. It reopened September 2010.

Renovation of the picture gallery ▶

The Graphics Collection

🕐 *Opening hours:*
Viewing by appointment,
tel. 588 16 24 00

Before proceeding up to the Graphics Collection in the mezzanine, it is worth taking a look in the auditorium on the ground floor. It is a Classic banquet hall with an ambulatory. The *Fall of the Titans* on the ceiling was painted by **Anselm Feuerbach**. The Graphics Collection attached to the library contains about 40,000 drawings and watercolours and more than 100,000 prints, including unique architectural plans from the builder of the Stephansdom, over 300 nature studies by Friedrich Gauermann and 415 watercolours of flowers by the miniaturist Michael Daffinger.

Another highlight are the prints by the German Romantics, including drawings by Friedrich Overbeck, Heinrich Reinhold and the Olivier Brothers.

Picture Gallery

The Picture Gallery on the first floor of the west wing was originally intended as a collection of teaching aids for art instruction in order to train the students in observation and help them gain a sense of artistic style. The academy was not only a school but also the government authority for the arts and so the stock of pictures was enlarged in the course of the 18th century by »election pieces«. These were the works that every artist had to submit who wanted to become a member of the academy. The first step to becoming a museum gallery of international rank was finally taken when the head of the academy Anton Graf Lamberg-Sprinzenstein died in 1822, and bequeathed his picture collection to the academy. Even today, while the collection continues to grow through purchases and gifts, the character of the academy is at the same time documented by the fact that work is on display by almost all of the artists at present associated with the academy. The exhibition begins in room 4; rooms 1 to 3 are reserved for administrative purposes.

Examples of 15th century works are provided by the *Holy Trinity and Saints*, created by **Simone da Bologna** to crown the middle panel of a late 14th century retable, and the panel *A Miracle by St Nicholas* (c1455) by **Giovanni di Paolo**, probably also part of an altar. Early Dutch painting is represented by *The Coronation of the Virgin* (mid-15th century) by Dieric Bouts. Among the most important works of

Opening hours:
Tue – Sun
10am – 6pm
Tours:
Sun 10.30am,
tel. 58 81 62 25

**Room 4
15th – 16th
century Dutch
and German art**

Academic building in Renaissance style: the Kunstgalerie once housed a collection of teaching aids

Cranach incorporated his self-portrait into the »Holy Family«

the collection is The *Last Judgment Triptych* (after 1504) by **Hieronymus Bosch** with paradise and hell framing the Last Judgement. On display is an important early work *The Holy Family (Rest during Flight)* (c1512) by **Hans Baldung, called Grien** and major works by **Lucas Cranach the Elder** are *The Holy Family* (c1512) and *Lucretia*; (1532), a masterpiece of court salon art for which Cranach was famous.

In room 5 the classical ideal of Italian Renaissance painting is captured in *The Madonna and Child with Angels* (c1480) from Sandro Botticelli's workshop; **examples of Venetian artists** of this era are the fragment of a *Reclining Venus* from Giorgione's workshop and one of Titian's last works, *Tarquin and Lucretia* (c1575). The works documenting the **Baroque style that started in Rome** in the closing years of the 16th century include *The Deliverance of Peter* (c1650) by Mattia Preti and *Still Life* (1675) by Giuseppe Antonio Recco. The Spanish variation is represented by works including **Murillo's** *Boys Playing Dice*.

Room 6 **17th century** **Flemish artists**	Among the collection of works by **Peter Paul Rubens** are the sketches for his ceiling fresco – subsequently destroyed by fire – for the Jesuit Church in Antwerp. **Anthonis van Dyck**, who worked as an independent artist in Rubens' studio, is represented by a self-portrait and a sketch of an *Assumption of the Virgin*; *Paul and Barnabas in Lystra* (1645) by **Jacob Jordaens**, also associated with Rubens, is on display.
Room 7–9 **17th century** **Dutch artists**	Examples of entertaining **genre painting**, typical of Dutch art, are the works of David Vinckboons, Pieter Codde and Dirck Hal, Adriaen van Ostade, Cornelis Bega and Cornelis Saftleben, and architectural paintings by Hendrick C. van Vliet and Jan van der Heyden. **Portrait painting** is represented by Pieter de Hooch's *Dutch Family* (c1660) and **Rembrandt van Rijn's** *Young Woman in an Armchair* (1632); **landscape painting** encompasses works by Jan van Goyen, Jacob van Ruisdael and Cornelia Vroom; **still life painting** is documented by works including those by Jan Davidsz de Heem and Jan Weenix.

Works by Giovanni Battista Tiepolo, Alessandro Magnasco and Gianpaolo Pannini are displayed here. A highlight of the academy's collection are the pictures by **Francesco Guardi**, eight detailed views of Venice and two altar pieces. Moreover, a major work by Pierre Gubleyra is shown, *The Artist's Studio* (c1747). **Austrian painting** of the 18th century includes a portrait of *Empress Maria Theresa* (1759) by Martin van Meytens – one of the directors of the academy – and works by Daniel Gran, Franz Anton Maulbertsch and Johann Martin Schmidt (Kremser Schmidt), the last of the great Baroque painters.

Room 10
18th Century

Austrian Classicism is shown in the works of Friedrich Heinrich Füger, Johann Peter Krafft and Josef Abel. Biedermeier painting is represented by Ferdinand Georg Waldmüller , Friedrich von Amerling and Josef Danhauser, whose painting *The Pupil's Room* shows a classroom in the academy at St Anna, where it was located before its move to the building on the Ring.

Room 11
19th and 20th
century Austrian
Artists

Schiller Memorial

The former Kalkmarkt in front of the Akademie der bildenden Künste was renamed Schillerplatz (Schiller Square) in 1876, with the unveiling of the Schiller Memorial, a work by Johann Schiller from Dresden. The allegorical bronze figures represent the Four Ages of Man, and the reliefs portray Genius, Poetry, Truth and Learning. On the monument, Friedrich Schiller is shown standing with Goethe seated nearby. It is said that turn of the century admirers of Schiller were outraged, but Franz Josef I is supposed to have spoken up in favour of Goethe sitting, saying, "Let the old boy be comfortable ..."

✶ ✶ Albertina

H 6

Location: 1, Albertinaplatz 1
Underground: Karlsplatz (U1, U2, U4),
Stephansplatz (U1, U3)

Tram: 1, 2, 62
Internet: www.albertina.at

With its close to 45,000 drawings and watercolours, around 1.5 million sheets of prints covering five centuries and more than 35,000 books, the Albertina is one of the most important and comprehensive graphics collections in the world. Maria Theresa's son-in-law, Duke Albert of Saxe-Teschen, founded the collection named after him in 1786.

It has been housed in the former Taroucca Palace since 1795. The building was remodelled by Louis von Montoyer between 1801 and 1804. Archduke Carl (1771 – 1845) had state rooms designed by Joseph Kornhäusel that are some of the most luxurious examples of

Classical architecture in Austria. Duke Albert's collection was combined with the print collection of the Imperial Library after the First World War. The Albertina had a glittering reopening in 2003 after almost ten years of reconstruction. Behind the façade that was reconstructed according to the original plans lie the historic **state rooms** and several large exhibition halls covering a total area of 20,000 sq m / 215,278 sq ft, most of which is again open to the public. The state rooms were restored with their magnificent Classical furnishings from 1822. The centre of the 100m/328ft long suite of rooms in the older wing is the **Ball Room** or Museum Room, with Joseph Klieber'smasterpiece of Classical sculpture, the cycle of *Apollo and the Nine Muses*. Following are the grand living quarters of the Habsburgs, including the Gold Room with a Sèvres porcelain table, a gift of French King Louis XVI, the Wedgwood Room with the oldest English porcelain reliefs, and the Purple Audience Room or the Rococo Room. Two to three major themed exhibitions are regularly held in the adjoining museum rooms and newly created display areas. Up to now, they have been dedicated to the world giants of fine arts, such as Rembrandt, Rubens, Dürer and Munch, and were stocked with extremely high quality pieces from its own as well as other collections.

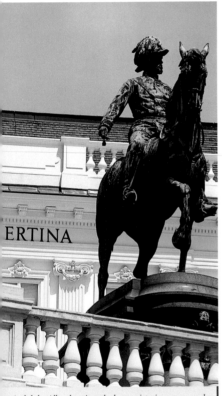
Archduke Albrecht triumphed as a victorious commander

Drawings All major European schools are represented in the drawings. The German School, beginning in the 15th century, includes 145 drawings by Dürer (the Albertina has the largest collection of his works) and works by Holbein the Elder, Baldung Grien, Cranach the Elder, Altdorfer, Kölderer, Menzel, Spitzweg, Feuerbach, Liebermann, Nolde and Käthe Kollwitz. The Austrian School, from the 18th century onwards, includes von Rottmayr, Troger, Kremser-Schmidt, Schwand, Daffinger, Amerling, Alt, Gauermann, Makart, Klimt, Schiele and Kubin. The Italian School, beginning with the early Renaissance, includes Pisanello, Fra Angelico, Lippi, Mantegna, Leonardo, Titian, Raphael, Michelangelo, Tintoretto, Veronese, Guardi, Canaletto and Tiepolo. The Flemish School, from the 15th century onwards, includes drawings by Van Leyden, Breughel the Elder, de Mompaer, Van Dyck and a collection of sketches by Rubens. The Dutch School, with the city schools from the 17th century onwards, includes drawings by Both, Asselijn, Van Goyen, Ruysdael, de Hooch and 70 drawings from all of Rembrandt's creative periods. The French School, from the 16th century onwards, includes examples of work by Clouet, Bellange and Callot, selected drawings by landscape artists Poussin and Lorrain, works by Watteau, Liotard and Fragonard, and pieces by Picasso, Matisse and Chagall. The English School, from the latter half of the 17th century onwards, is represented by Hogarth, Reynolds, Gainsborough and Romney drawings.

> ! **Baedeker TIP**
>
> **Hot and Tasty**
>
> There are »Würstelstände« (sausage stands) all over Vienna for those in need of a quick snack. The »Albertina stand« on the corner of Hanuschgasse and Augustinerstrasse serves its customers until 5am in the morning during ball season, though it doesn't matter if you show up in jeans or a tuxedo.

Print Collection

Among the Print Collection's valuable pieces are a unique collection of 15th century popular prints or xylographs, Dürer's woodcuts and copper engravings, Rembrandt's etchings, original work by Menzel, woodcuts by Munch, first impressions by Goya and works by Picasso and Chagall. The majority of the collection consists of original graphics. Special collections include historical papers, and collections of playing cards, caricatures, illustrated books and portfolios, views, posters and original wood printing plates from the time of Dürer.

Photographic Collection

The foundation of the photographic collection begun in 1999 is based on the collection of the Höhere Grafische Bundeslehr- und Versuchsanstalt (Federal Education and Research Institute for Graphics) sponsored by Josef Maria Eder. It primarily contains scientific photography, but also includes studio photography, early colour photography and pictorial works. Another important part of this archive is the collection of the Langewiesche publishing house, famous for its picture books, emphasising object photography from the 1920's and 30's. The other sections of the collection encompass the origins of the medium up to the present, with a special focus on American photography of the 1960's and 70's.

The Architectural Collection

The Architectural Collection contains about 25,000 plans, sketches and models, among them large mixed lots, bequests and the estates of Francesco Borromini, Johann Bernhard Fischer von Erlach, Adolf Loos, Lois Welzenbacher and others. Pride of place in the collection is taken by the architectural models created by Otto Wagner, Le Corbusier, Mies van der Rohe and Alvar Aaalto.

ALBERTINA

** With almost one million visitors annually since reopening in spring 2003 after an extensive ten-year restoration, the Albertina is Austria's most popular museum. The museum was founded in 1776 while the palace, which was built on one of the last remaining bastions of the city wall, was the residence of Duke Albert von Sachsen-Teschen. Along with exhibits of famous works by artists from Dürer and Rubens to Kokoschka and Picasso, the palace state rooms and the golden chamber can also be toured.

⏲ Opening Hours:
Daily. 10am – 6pm,
Wed until 9pm

① Albrechtsrampe
A flight of steps leads from the Albertina up to the Albrechtsrampe, which is what remains of the once mighty Augustinian Abbey that served as part of the city fortifications. The bastion was pulled down in 1858. The ramp was heavily damaged in 1945 and converted to a flight of stairs in 1952.

② Equestrian Statue
The level section of the ramp is dominated by an equestrian statue of Field Marshall Archduke Albert (1817 to 1895), the victor of the Battle of Custozza (1866) created by Kaspar von Zumbusch in 1899.

③ Titanium Wing
As part of the overall restoration of the Albertina, the prominent architect Hans Hollein redesigned the new stairway with an escalator and a lift. He set a huge flying roof over it, creating a new symbol for the building. The roof, made of eloxized aluminium, and not of titanium as planned, and named the »Soravia Wing« after its sponsors, called the critics of contemporary architecture into action at its dedication.

④ Danubius Fountain
When the fountain erected by Moritz von Loehr was unveiled in 1889, there were ten other figures of white Carrara marble in niches grouped around the main allegorical figures of Danubius and Vindobona. They were the personifications of the tributary rivers Theiss, Raab, Enns, Traun, Inn, Save, March, Salzach, Mur and Drau. Most of these sculptures fashioned by Johann Meixner have been returned to their alcoves.

Striking Feature: The almost 50m/164ft long and 15m/50ft wide roof floats 8m/26ft above the entrance of the new museum.

⑤ State Rooms
Archduke Karl had Joseph Kornhäusel make modifications in sections of the palace in 1822, reworking them in the Classical style.

⑥ Hall of Muses
The main hall of the museum is flanked on both sides by stately apartments. Joseph Klieber created the cycle of *Apollo and the Nine Muses*. The hall served the Habsburg family as a dining hall and ballroom until everything was turned over to the state in 1918.

⑦ Golden Chamber
The Golden Chamber on the gentlemen's side is impressive because of the gilding of its walls and the way its numerous mirrors seem to open up the confining space of the room. The Sèvres table was a gift for Marie Christine, who was married to Duke Albert of Sachsen-Teschen, from her sister Marie Antoinette and King Louis XVI.

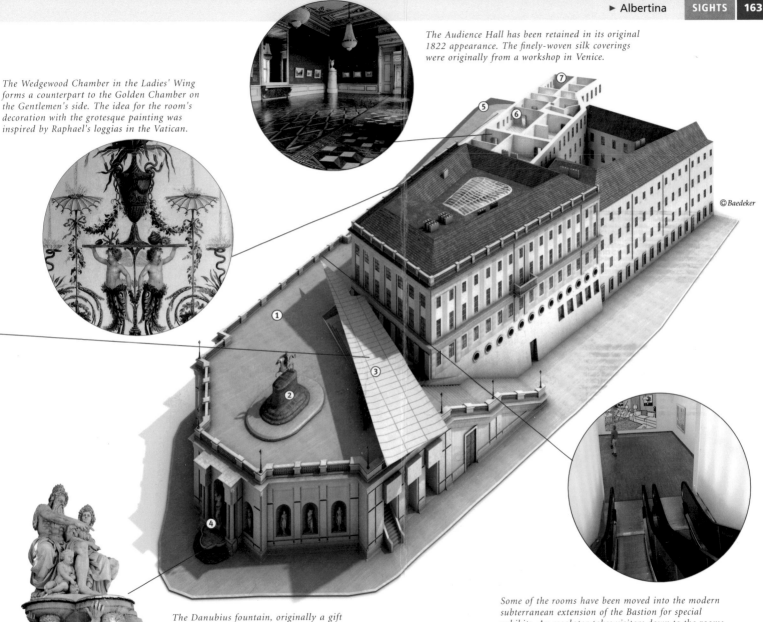

The Wedgewood Chamber in the Ladies' Wing forms a counterpart to the Golden Chamber on the Gentlemen's side. The idea for the room's decoration with the grotesque painting was inspired by Raphael's loggias in the Vatican.

The Audience Hall has been retained in its original 1822 appearance. The finely-woven silk coverings were originally from a workshop in Venice.

©Baedeker

The Danubius fountain, originally a gift from Franz Joseph I to Vienna and reconstructed after 1945, is incorporated into the front side of the Albrechtsrampe.

Some of the rooms have been moved into the modern subterranean extension of the Bastion for special exhibits. An escalator takes visitors down to the rooms.

Monument against War and Fascism

Albertinaplatz is dominated by a monument against war and fascism by the Austrian sculptor **Alfred Hrdlicka** (1988–1991), commemorating the victims of the Nazi regime and those killed by bombs during the Second World War lying in the filled-in air-raid shelters below Albertinaplatz. The stone *Gateway of Violence* symbolizes the terror of the Nazi dictatorship; the base of the gate is from the Mauthausen Concentration Camp quarry. The bronze sculpture of a Jew scrubbing the pavement is a reminder of 12 March 1938 when, following the annexation of Austria by the Nazis, Jewish citizens were forced to scrub off the pro-Austrian slogans painted on the streets with toothbrushes. The barbed wire is meant to recall the hopelessness of the Jews' situation. The large granite stone with Austria's declaration of independence reminds of the persecution and murder of Jews, Slavs, Sinti, Roma and resistance fighters, whereas the statue »Orpheus Entering Hades« is dedicated to the memory of Vienna's bombing victims of the Second World War. There were fierce debates about the setting up of the monument. The Allies felt the square was inappropriate and that is why there is another memorial on ►Judenplatz by the British artist Rachel Whiteread.

Altes Universitätsviertel

(Old University Quarter)

H 6

location: 1, Dr.-Ignaz-Seipel-Platz   **Underground:** Stephansplatz (U1, U3)

The old university, the Aula – the university's new lecture hall – and the university's former church, the Baroque Jesuitenkirche, are all grouped around today's Dr. Ignatz Seipel Platz, one of Vienna's most beautiful squares.

Old University

The old university, founded in 1365 by Duke Rudolf IV, is one of the oldest universities in the German-speaking world. It was moved here in 1425. As a result of the Counter Reformation, Ferdinand II turned over the philosophical and theological faculties to the Jesuits in 1623, and had an academic college built. The building was remodelled and extended in 1725, gaining its present appearance. Franz Schubert attended the college from 1808–1813. Joseph Kornhäusel added the library wing in 1927.

The former **Jesuit theatre** (1650) is on the upper floor. The university is today the main seat of the Jesuit Order.

Jesuitenkirche (Jesuit Church)

The Baroque Jesuitenkirche, the former university church immediately adjacent to the old university, was funded by Emperor Ferdinand II and built by an unknown master builder between 1624 and 1631. Between 1703 and 1705, it was given a two-storey façade in typical early Baroque fashion with figure niches and a central gable, as well as two High Baroque towers crowned with massive domes. The stirring impression the interior makes is due to the illusionary perspective paintings on the barrel vault by **Andrea Pozzo**.

The trompe l'oeil dome stands out, conferring the elongated room with the impression of being a central-plan building. The »optimal position« for the observer is marked by a bright plate in the central aisle.

Maria Theresa had the university's **New Aula** built in 1753, to the west of the Jesuitenkirche according to plans by Jean-Nicolas Jadot de Ville-Issey. Vienna's most outstanding example of secular Rococo has been the **seat of the Österreichische Akademie der Wissenschaften** (Austrian Academy of Sciences) since 1857. The main façade is bounded by corner risalits with fountains, in the middle is an elongated loggia sectioned by columns. Two allegorical figures above the side risalits represent to the left Medicine and to the right Jurisprudence. The interior, magnificently furnished in parts, is not open to the public.

The **University** building (1, Dr.-Karl-Lueger-Ring 1) was built during the »Ringstrasse period«. **Heinrich Ferstel** designed it in the style of the Italian Renaissance, the era that introduced Western science. The »Alma Mater Rudolfina« building was opened in 1884, and renovated in 1953 and 1965. The memorials for famous university lecturers in the arcades of the main

Being gloriously idle: students in front of the university

courtyard include Anton Bruckner, Gerhard van Swieten, Theodor von Billroth, Marie von Ebner-Eschenbach, Ludwig Boltzmann, Anton von Eselsberg, Philipp Semmelweis, Sigmund Freud and the Nobel Prize winners Karl Landsteiner and Julius Wagner-Jauregg.

Am Hof

G/H 6

Location: 1st District
Tram: 1, 2, 3

Underground: Stephansplatz (U1, U3),
Herrengasse (U3)

»Am Hof« is the largest square in Vienna's city centre and is steeped in history. The Romans set up their camp here. The Babenbergs had their first royal palace built »am Hof« between 1135 and 1150, and the tournament square and market place became the stage for glittering festivals that the Minnesinger Walther von der Vogelweide sang of in his verses, »That is the wondrous court at Vienna«.

Emperor Barbarossa stopped off at »Am Hof« on his way to the third crusade in 1189; the Habsburg-Jargellon double wedding was celebrated here and the Jesuits performed edifying plays in front of their church. The princely mint was later built on this site. In 1667, at the end of the Thirty Years War, the Corinthian **column with the bronze figure of Maria Immaculata** was erected in the middle of the square. Her four putti symbolize the victorious defence against war (lion), plague (basilisk), hunger (dragon) and heresy (snake).

Zu den neun Chören der Engel (Nine Choirs of Angels Church The former Jesuit church dedicated to the Nine Choirs of Angels with its striking early Baroque west façade dominates the square. The group of figures on the gable with Mary as queen of the heavenly hosts illustrates the melodious name. In 1782, Pius IV pronounced his blessing *Urbi et Orbi* upon the Viennese from the bal-

Large square with a great power of attraction: the Romans, the Babenbergs, Barbarossa – all put in an appearance »am Hof«

cony above the entrance – the same balcony that was used by Emperor Franz II to proclaim his abdication as Holy Roman emperor and the dissolution of the Holy Roman Empire of the German nation in 1806. The Gothic hall church was built in the 14th century, refurnished in the Baroque style around 1607 and provided, presumably by Carlo Carlone, with its impressive west façade in 1662. It is worth taking a look inside the church at the organ loft, the Maulbertsch frescoes in the second side chapel on the left, the women's altar and the Ignatius Chapel with ceiling frescos by Andrea Pozzo.

The **Märkleinsche town house** (no. 7) was named after its original owner, who had it built between 1727 and 1730 based on a design by Johann Lukas von Hildebrandt. Today the Baroque building houses the headquarters of the Vienna Fire Brigade and the **Feuerwehrmuseum** (Fire Brigade Museum; currently closed for renovations, infotel. 53 19 95 14 44).

Märkleinsches Haus

The **Bürgerliches Zeughaus** (no. 10), the former civilian armoury, is a wonderful example of Baroque architecture that was built around 1530 and extensively remodelled and enlarged in 1731, by Anton Ospel. Mattielli's allegorical figures of Strength and Stamina balancing an enormous globe provide the crowning glory of its magnificent façade.

Zeughaus (armoury)

The **Palais (palace) Collalto** (no. 13) was built around 1680; the façade facing the schoolyard was given a classical form in 1804. A plaque on the building commemorates the fact that Mozart made his first public appearance in Vienna here, in October 1762.

Palais Collalto

Augarten

Location: 2, Obere Augartenstraße 1   **Bus:** 5 A
Tram: 31

Vienna's oldest park, the Augarten, was laid out as an imperial pleasure garden covering 52,000sq m/560,000sq ft in the 17th century. In 1775, at the wish of Emperor Joseph II, it was opened to the Viennese public for their enjoyment as a place of entertainment.

Leopold I's garden palace, the »Alte Favorita« was destroyed during the second siege of the Turks in 1683. Joseph I had a garden pavilion erected on part of the ruins, and it was here that the famous musical matinees took place from 1782, under the direction of Mozart. Later they were also directed by Beethoven (incl. the first performance of the Kreutzer sonata) and Strauss the Elder, and celebrated evenings were held with Richard Wagner and Franz Liszt.

HIGH C IN THE BURGKAPELLE

Some 500 years ago, Emperor Maximilian I wanted to have a boys' choir for his court and so he established a singing school, which brought forth the Vienna Choir Boys, Austria's greatest export hit.

The Vienna Boys' Choir is **world famous**. There are four choirs, each with two dozen voices. A boy must pass a difficult entrance exam before he is accepted into the exclusive organization, whose most famous member was Franz Schubert. The »Golden Throats« not only have to shine vocally, but they must also play an **instrument**. The choir boys have been residing since 1948 in the Baroque Augarten Palais, but they are often away from home, travelling as Austria's ambassadors.

Born to sing

In 1498, Emperor Maximilian I had a **school for a dozen choir boys** set up under the direction of Heinrich Isaac, the Dutch director of music at the court. From that time on, they were under the special protection of the emperor up until the end of the monarchy in 1918. The choir boys wore cadet uniforms with bicorn hats and swords during the time of Emperor Franz Joseph. The sailor's uniforms didn't come into fashion until the choir's re-organization in 1926 by the priest Josef Schmitt, a music enthusiast.

Walt Disney's Film, *Born to Sing*, made the Boys' Choir famous also in America. Naturally, a boy's singing career is very short because when his voice breaks, his career is over. There was gossip in the 1990s about the authoritarian style of up-bringing in the choir and that too much was constantly demanded of the boys. Even the Vienna Opera Director Ioan Holender had his doubts about the boys' singing skill. The former choir boy, Dominik Orieschnig, accused the elite institution of being a »child marketing machinery«.

Until the Voice Changes

The **consequence** since then has been multiple changes of those in management positions and the appointment of a psychological caretaker. At the moment, there are 100 active singers and a few former members in the singing organization, which places particular importance in promoting new talent in order to assure the choir's continued success. For, as one of the choir boys' witty sayings says, »Whoever's voice doesn't break, will be singing until Judgement Day«.

Today, the Augarten porcelain factory display and sales rooms are housed in the former Garden Pavilion. The porcelain factory was founded in 1718 by Claudius du Paquier, the second factory on European soil – Meissen had begun production 10 years earlier. It was turned over to the city in 1744. After its re-founding in 1923, it became municipal property in 1924. Its much acclaimed traditional dinner services with the blue Augarten shield bearing the names Pacquier, Liechtenstein, Prince Eugene and Maria Theresa are known the world over. The most popular export articles are porcelain Lipizzaner horses in all the Spanish Riding School poses, in styles ranging from Rococo to Art Déco and modern. Classic »Viennese characters« based on original models dating back to the era of Maria Theresa are also popular.

✴
Porcelain factory
🕑
Opening hours:
Tours: Mon – Fri
10am and by
appointment, tel.
21 12 42 00
www.augarten.at

The Baroque Augarten Palace has been the boarding school of the famous Viennese Boys' Choir (▶Baedeker Special p. 168) since 1948. A privy councillor had this fine mansion built towards the end of the 17th century using ideas from Johann Bernhard Fischer von Erlach. Emperor Joseph II bought it in 1780, but personally preferred the modest Josephsstöckl as residence, which he had Isidor Canevale build for him in 1781. This building is today the so-called transitional home for Viennese Choir boys. Choir members who have to retire because their voices have broken live here.

Augarten palace

?   **DID YOU KNOW …?**

■ …that girls now also sing in the world famous boys' choir? Since 1997 the Vienna Philharmonic is also no longer the exclusive domain of men.

The Gustinus Ambrosi Museum (Scherzergasse 1 a), also located in Augarten, is part of the Austrian gallery Belvedere and shows works by the sculptor Gustinus Ambrosi (1893 – 1975). The artist created naturalistic portrait busts and colossal sculptures in imitation of Michelangelo. A changing exhibit of contemporary art is in the adjacent **Atelier im Augarten**.

Gustinus Ambrosi Museum

✴ Augustinerkirche (Augustinian Church)

G/H 6

Location: 1, Augustinerstraße 3
Tram: 1, 2, 3

Underground: Stephansplatz (U1, U3),
Herrengasse (U3)

The Augustinerkirche (Augustinian Church) has repeatedly been the scene of great weddings. Archduchess Marie Louise was married here in 1810 to Napoleon I. In 1854, Emperor Franz Joseph stepped up to the altar with Elizabeth (Sissi) of Bavaria, and in 1881, Crown Prince Rudolf wedded Stephanie of Belgium. The church was commissioned by the Augustinian Hermit Friars.

⊕
Opening hours:
daily 8am – 6pm

Dietrich Ladtner of Pirn constructed a Gothic hall church between 1330 and 1339. The choir was added about 1400, and the tower in 1652. The chapel of St George was consecrated in 1351, and the small Loretto Chapel not until 1724. A later refurbishing in Baroque style was removed again in the 18th century, when J. F. Hetendorf von Hohenberg carried out a restoration commissioned by Joseph II in 1785, restoring the original Gothic style.

⊕
Opening hours:
Tours: Sun 12.15pm

The **Loretto Chapel** was once richly decorated with silver, but it was melted down during the Napoleonic Wars. The wrought iron lattice-work dates back to the 18th century. The hearts of the Habsburg monarchs since the time of King Matthias († 1612) have been kept in small silver urns in the **Herzgruft** (Heart Vault), including those of nine emperors, eight consorts and empresses, one king, one queen, 14 archdukes, 14 archduchesses and two dukes. The bones are interred in the Imperial Vault of the Kapuzinerkirche, the internal organs in the catacombs of the Stephansdom. The **Georgskapelle** (Chapel of St George) was built in the 14th century by Duke Otto the Merry, as a meeting place for the Order of St George. Later it was converted into a mortuary chapel and Imperial Field Marshall Daun, the victor of Kolin, lies buried here, as does Maria Theresa's personal physician, Gerard van Swieten. The marble tomb of Leopold II, designed by Franz Anton Zauner in 1799, is empty. The Emperor lies in the Imperial Vault in the Kapuzinerkirche. The **Christinendenkmal** (Christine Memorial) is a highpoint of Classical funerary art. **Antonio Canova's** monumental marble tomb for Archduchess Maria Christina of Saxe-Teschen, the daughter of Maria Theresa, dates from 1798 to 1805. Beneath the apex of the flat pyramid is the spirit of blissful happiness bearing the archduchess' medallion, who also found her final resting place in the Imperial Vault in the Kapuzinerkirche.

★ ★ Belvedere

H 7/8

Location: 4 (Lower Belvedere);3 (Upper Belvedere)
Tram: 71 (Lower Belvedere) 18 (Upper Belvedere)

Underground: Karlsplatz (U1, U2, U4), Taubstummengasse (U1)
Internet: www.belvedere.at

Prince Eugene, who defeated the Turks, had the Palace of Versailles in mind when he had a summer residence built on the abandoned slope of the glacis by the Rennweg in 1700. Lukas von Hildebrandt worked on this, his major work, for 10 years.

The Lower Belvedere, where Prince Eugene actually lived, was completed in 1716. The Upper Belvedere, the palace for official represen-

Glorious majesty: Hildebrandt created his masterpiece in the upper Belvedere

tation on the upper level, was not officially completed until 1724. Both palaces are linked by a magnificent garden that the Parisian landscape artist **Dominique Girard** designed as a terraced park laid out along an axis with cascades and symmetrical flights of stairs bordered on the sides by hedges and avenues, following Hildebrandt's concept. The sculptures adorning the pools lead symbolically from the bottom to the top. The Underworld with Pluto and Prosperina can be seen in the boscage; then, where the cascades are falling, come Neptune and Thetis, the deities of water, together with Apollo and Hercules. From the terrace in front of the Upper Belvedere there is a wonderful view out over the sloping garden to the towers of Vienna beyond, reaching all the way towards the heights of the Wiener Wald (Vienna Woods). After the death of the bachelor prince, his heiress »frightful Victoria«, as the Viennese called her, sold off the entire property without a second thought. The Imperial Court purchased the buildings and the garden in 1752. A plaque in the curator's wing of the Upper Belvedere commemorates the death there of Anton Bruckner, in 1896. The emperor had placed the residential rooms at the disposal of the retired court organist and composer to honour him for his services. Franz Ferdinand, the heir to the throne, lived in the Belvedere between 1894 and 1914. It was in the Marble Chamber of the Upper Belvedere on 15 May 1955, that the foreign ministers of France, Great Britain, the Soviet Union, the United States and Aus-

⊕
Opening hours:
daily 10am – 6pm

tria signed the Austrian State Treaty restoring Austria's independence. Housed in both of Prince Eugene's Baroque palaces, the Lower Belvedere and the Upper Belvedere, is the Austrian Gallery Belvedere with the Museum of Medieval Art, the Baroque Museum and the Gallery of the 19th and 20th centuries.

Lower Belvedere

Barockmuseum

The Austrian Baroque Museum containing a collection of paintings and sculptures from the great age of Austrian Baroque, approximately the period between 1683 and 1780, has been housed in Prince Eugene's residential palace, the Lower Belvedere, since 1923. The museum was reopened after the Second World War, in 1953. The two paintings by Martin Johann Schmidt (called Kremser-Schmidt) in Room 5, *Venus in Vulcan's Forge* and *The Judgment of Midas*, were the two works he turned in for admission to the Viennese Academy. The two-storey high Marble Room (Room 8) with its extremely rich stucco decoration and its painted ceiling by Martin Altomonte depicting the *Triumph of Prince Eugene*, the conqueror of the Turks, is the finest room in the Lower Belvedere. In the centre are the original figures made by **Georg Raphael Donners** for the Providentia Fountain in the Neuer Markt. In what used to be Prince Eugene's state bedroom (Room 10), a ceiling painting by M. Altomonte can be seen, Donner's reliefs for the piscina at St Stephen's, statuettes of Mercury and Venus, a monumental statue of Karl VI and of a nymph. Standing in front of the grotesque paintings in the room of the same name (Room 15) are the character heads by **Franz Xaver Messerschmidt**. The former audience chamber (Marble Gallery, Room 16) displays, like the Marble Hall, the Apotheosis of Prince Eugene. The life-size figures of Greek deities in the alcoves are the work of the Genoese artist Domenico Parodi. The magnificent Gold Chamber (Room 17) is adorned with massive mirrors, which seem to make the room go on for ever. Here stands Balthasar Permoser's *Apotheosis of Prince Eugene*, a marble work carved in Dresden in 1721, commissioned by Prince Eugene himself.

 DON'T MISS

In the Upper Belvedere ...
- Gustav Klimt: *The Kiss* – a fervent embrace, trimmed in gold
- Marble Hall: the most breathtaking panorama of Vienna
- Hans Makart: the series *The Five Senses*
... and in the Lower Belvedere
- Gold Room: state room with the apotheosis of Prince Eugene
- Franz Xaver Messerschmidt: the wittiest »character heads«

Museum Mittelalterlicher Kunst (Museum of Medieval Art)

The collection housed in the Orangery of the Lower Belvedere shows masterpieces of sculpture and panel painting from the 12th to the early 16th century, with an emphasis on 15th century works. The oldest exhibit is the Romanesque **Stammerberg Crucifix**, which dates back to around the mid-12th century and is one of the oldest surviving example of Tyrolean wood carving. The collections of the museum are divided into three sections. Included in the first section are **High Gothic sculptures**. The following works are on display: the Sonntagberger Madonna (c1370), the four stone figures by the Master of Grosslobming (c1375-1385) and major international Gothic works such as the *Wiltener Crucifixion* and the *Master of the Holy Cross*. Furthermore, there are panel paintings by the Albrechtsmeister, the masters of Lichtenstein Palace and by Conrad Laib (crucifixion reredos of 1449).

The only major work in the second section is the intensely colourfully executed »**Znaimer Altar**« dating from 1427. Also there are five panels by the Tyrolean painter and carver Michael Pacher – altar panels from St Lorenzen in Pustertal (c1427) and from the Franciscans' Church in Salzburg (prior to 1498) – and seven pictures by Rueland Frueauf the Elder (1490/1491). Outstanding exhibits in the

A river god stretching his legs: the personification of the Enns River shoulders an oar as a sign of its navigability, on display in the Baroque Museum

third section include the two paintings, *Pietá* and *The Adoration of the Magi*, by the **Schottenmeister** that were once part of the four-sectioned high altar dating from 1469 in the Schottenkirche in Vienna. Also worth noting in this section are the Uttenheimer panel by the teacher of **Michael Pracher**, the Roggendorfer winged altar (c1479/1480), Marx Reichlich's panels from the life of the Virgin, the panel paintings by Urban Görtschacher, including an *Ecce Homo* (1508) and the master of the Krainburg Altar (early 16th century), as well as sculptures by Andreas Lachner (c1518).

Upper Belvedere
(Gallery of the 19th and 20th centuries)

Collections The Gallery of the 19th and 20th centuries in the Upper Belvedere provides an excellent overview of Austrian artistic creativity from the Biedermeier period to Jugendstil (Art Nouveau) and contemporary art.

Ground Floor The ground floor is dedicated to art after 1918, presented in changing exhibitions sourced from the museum's extensive collection. The focus is on Expressionism, New Objectivity (Neue Sachlichkeit) and art after 1945.

First Floor The first floor is reserved for Historicism, Realism, Impressionism, Symbolism and the Viennese Secession. Represented, alongside Austrian artists like Hans Makart and Anton Romako, are international artists like Wilhelm Leibl, Adolf Menzel, Camille Corot, Edouard Manet, Auguste Renoir, Claude Monet, Ferdinand Hodler and Edvard Munch. Moreover, **Austrian art around 1900** is presented within the context of the development of international art, including **Gustav Klimt** and **Egon Schiele**, the main exponents of the Wiener Secession, with a room dedicated to each. There are also works by Oskar Kokoschka, Richard Gerstl, Anton Hanak, Vincent van Gogh, Fernand Khnopff and Max Klinger.

Second Floor Classicism, Romantic and Biedermeier art are presented on the second floor. Included among those works representing Classicism and Romantic art are paintings by Caspar David Friedrich, Ludwig Ferdinand Schnorr von Carolsfeld and Moritz von Schwind, as well as work by **Angelika Kauffmann**, who is primarily known as a portrait painter. The Biedermeier section presents portraits, still life, landscapes and genre paintings. One of the finest landscape artists is **Ferdinand Georg Waldmüller**, the most significant master of Viennese Biedermeier, who became famous through his mastery of painting light (*Large Prater Landscape*). Worthy of mention among the portraitists are above all **Friedrich Amerling**, the favourite Biedermeier artist of the aristocracy and up and coming middle class (*Rudolf von Arthaber and his Children*, 1857), and Waldmüller (*The Eltz Family*).

Smile, ladies, but not as mysteriously as the sphinx in the garden of the Belvedere

Representing genre painting is **Waldmüller** (*Peasant Wedding*), Josef Danhauser (*Wine, Women and Song*), Peter Fendi, Friedrich Amerling (*The Fisher Boy*) and Carl Spitzweg. Still lifes by Waldmüller, Petter, Lauer and Knapp are also noteworthy.

The entrance to the Alpine Garden (Alpengarten), in which a wealth of alpine vegetation can be seen, is in the Upper Belvedere. Opening hours: April – July daily 10am – 6pm.

Alpine Garden

Botanischer Garten (Botanical Garden)

The garden was begun in 1754, when Maria Theresa had medicinal herbs planted on the recommendation of her private physician, Gerard van Swieten. According to one tale, when one of the herbs failed to relieve her complaints, the empress commissioned the physician and botanist Nikolaus von Jacquin to lay out a botanical garden in place of the herbal garden, which the monarch then presented to the university in 1757. During the summer season, visitors can admire thousands of rare plants in the tranquillity of the garden. Particularly worth seeing are the succulent plants, the cultivated strains of orchids and the Australian plant collection in the Sonnenuhrhaus (sundial house).

🕐
Opening hours:
Opening times: Jan/ Feb 9am until nightfall; Mar – Dec from 9.30am

The Hochstrahl fountain on Schwarzenbergplatz

Palais Schwarzenberg

Palais Schwarzenberg, with its superb interior furnishings (Schwarzenbergerplatz 9), was one of the first summer residences built outside Vienna's city walls. Prince Schwarzenberg settled the rivalry between the two great Baroque architects, **Johann Bernhard Fischer von Erlach** and **Johann Lukas von Hildebrandt** in his own way: the first sketches for the shell construction were done by Hildebrandt, finished between 1697 and 1704, and the alterations were undertaken by Fischer von Erlach from 1720 to 1723, whose son Joseph Emanuel was responsible for finishing the palais and laying out the magnificent Baroque gardens. The palace was badly damaged in 1945 and was meticulously restored after the war. However, the frescoes painted by Daniel Gran between 1723 and 1726 could only partially be saved. Today, it is one of Vienna's most beautiful hotels. (currently expected to be closed for renovation until 2011).

Böhmische Hofkanzlei (Bohemian Court Chancellery)

H 6

Location: 1, Wipplingerstraße 7	**Underground:** Stephansplatz,
Tram: 1, 2	Schwedenplatz (U1, U3, U4)

The buildings of the former Bohemian Court Chancellery (Böhmische Hofkanzlei) now serve as the seat of the Constitutional and Administrative Court. The Chancellery was built in Baroque style between 1708 and 1714. Johann Bernhard Fischer von Erlach designed it and Lorenzo Mattielli produced most of the sculpture.

In the year 1752, Maria Theresa commissioned the architect Matthias Gerl with enlarging the building and in 1809 the outer façade was altered. The building was so badly damaged in the war that major reconstruction lasting until 1951 was necessary. A pedestrian passage was added in 1948.

The Documentation Centre of Austrian Resistance

The Documentation Centre of Austrian Resistance (Dokumentationsarchiv des Österreichischen Widerstandes) is located in the **Old Town Hall** (Altes Rathaus, Wipplingerstr. 8). Displayed in its museum rooms are displays on the active opposition to Austro-fascism during the years 1934 – 1938 and exhibits covering the resistance and its persecution under the Nazis in Austria between 1938 and 1945.

⊙
Opening hours:
Mon – Fri
9am – 5pm, Thu
until 7pm

Certainly the decision to set up the documentation centre in the Old Town Hall had little to do with the history of the building. Nevertheless, there are historical parallels. The Old Town Hall was originally the house of a freedom-loving citizen named Otto Haymo. After Emperor Albrecht I was murdered in 1309, a number of influential Viennese citizens, including Haymo, resolved to resist the Habsburg rulers. However, the conspiracy was discovered, the conspirators punished and their property confiscated. Duke Frederick the Fair gave Haymo's house to the town in 1316, and it served as the town hall until 1885. During this time it was remodelled, enlarged and partially rebuilt on several occasions. It was given a Baroque façade about 1700. The doors with the sculptures *Fides publica* and *Pietas* are by **Johann Martin Fischer** and also date from the 18th century. The Andromeda Fountain dating from 1741 with a lead relief of Perseus and Andromeda standing in the west end of the courtyard is one of Raphael Donner's last works.

Salvatorkapelle

Gift of a conspirator – Otto Haymo had sponsored the building of the Salvator Chapel about 1301 (Salvatorgasse 5, entrance through the Old Town Hall). As it formed part of the house which the authorities took over after the failure of the rebellion against Frederick the Fair and converted into the **town hall** (Rathaus), he gave up the chapel as well. In 1871, the church passed into the possession of the Old Catholics. After being severely damaged in the Second World War, it was fully restored in 1972/73. The magnificent Renaissance door is especially noteworthy; dating from around 1520, it is one of the few Renaissance works in Vienna. The statues of knights are copies; the originals are in the Historisches Museum der Stadt Wien (Historical Museum).

✱ Maria am Gestade (Mary on the Strand)

The sacred building known locally as »Maria Stiegen Kirche« (Mary on the Steps) was once situated, as the name implies, directly on the steep banks of the old arm of the Danube (Salvatorgasse 12). It is the Czech national church, and its captivating open work **Gothic cupola** is one of the landmarks of the north part of the old town. The church was originally a wooden place of worship for the Danube raftsmen dating from the 9th century, and its first documented mentioned was in 1158. The present building, with its Gothic stained glass, was essentially constructed between 1394 and 1414. The tower was badly damaged during the Turkish sieges and was restored in the 16th century and extensive restoration work was again carried out in the 19th and 20th centuries. The west front of the church, towering up out of the winding lanes of the old town like the prow of a ship, is not quite 10m/33ft wide but is 33m/108ft high. Inside, two Gothic sandstone figures near the second pillar on the east side of the nave date from the 14th century, while two Gothic panel paintings in the chapel dedicated to Clemens Maria Hofbauer, **patron saint of the city**, are from the 15th century. The organ loft and a stone Renaissance altar in the Johann Perger Chapel are 16th century; the other church furnishings are 19th century work.

Bundeskanzleramt (Office of the Federal Chancellor)

G 6

Location: 1, Ballhausplatz	**Underground:** Herrengasse (U3)
Tram: 1, 3	**Internet::** www.bka.gv.at

»The windows of the beautiful old palais on the Ballhausplatz often cast light onto the bare trees in the garden opposite until late into the evening, and a shudder would grip educated strollers on their way past.

For just as St Joseph permeated the plain carpenter Joseph, the name Ballhausplatz permeated the palace standing there with the secret of being one of the half dozen kitchens where the fate of mankind was being cooked behind drawn curtains«
That is how Robert Musil described the centre of power in *The Man Without Qualities*. For over 250 years, Austrian policy was made at Ballhausplatz and, even today, the Austrian government and the Foreign Ministry have their seats here.

The Bundeskanzleramt, formerly the Privy Court Chancellery, was erected between 1717 and 1719 to plans by **Johann Lukas von Hildebrandt**. It was enlarged by Nikolaus Pacassi in 1766, a side wing to the left was added in 1882, and enlarged even more when the State Archive Building was added in 1902. Damage from the Second World War was not completely repaired until 1950. Powerful chancellors, such as Kaunitz under Maria Theresa, and Prince Metternich under Franz I and Ferdinand I, determined the fate of the country in the Privy Court Chancellery. After Napoleon's downfall, the building was the scene of the **Congress of Vienna** in 1814 and 1815, when Europe was given its new order through diplomacy, debates, disputes and intrigues during glittering ball nights. In 1914, the ultimatum to

Ballhausplatz is where national policy is made: the Federal Chancellery by Hildebrandt

Serbia which led to the outbreak of the First World War was formulated here. It was here, too, that the conservative-authoritarian Federal Chancellor Dolfuss was murdered in the Marmorecksalon during a Nazi coup attempt in 1934. In the same room in 1938, his successor Schuschnigg sealed Austria's fate of being incorporated into Hitler's Germany and resigned at the same time with the closing words »May God protect Austria«. In 1940, Vienna's Nazi district governor, Baldur von Schirach, moved into Ballhausplatz. The Federal Government and Ministry of Foreign Affairs have been located here again since 1945.

Minoritenkirche
(Greyfriars Church or Minorite Church)

Not far from the Bundeskanzleramt stands the former Minorite church on Minoritenplatz. Since 1786, it has officially been called the **»Italian National Church of Mary of the Snows«**, and it has been a Franciscan church since 1957. The first meeting place of the »fratres minores« in Vienna was built here in 1230, a Holy Rood chapel that burned down twice. Duke Albrecht the Wise had today's Gothic hall church built in its place in the 14th century. After a Baroque remodelling, it was given its Gothic appearance again by Ferdinand von Hohenberg between 1784 and 1789. Of particular architectural interest is the **Gothic main door** that was designed by Duke Albrecht's confessor Jacobus, from 1340 to 1345. Giacomo Raffaelli's mosaic copy of Leonardo da Vinci's famous ***Last Supper*** can be seen inside the Minoritenkirche. Napoleon I had ordered the copy at one time –

Gothic Hall Church

he wanted to appropriate the Milan original, take it to Paris and replace it with the Viennese copy. After Napoleon's fall, the Austrian court courteously purchased the work and eventually it was installed in the Minoritenkirche in 1845. The high altar painting by Christoph Unterberger is also a copy; the original »Mary of the Snows« is an object of veneration in Rome.

✴ Burgtheater

G 6

Location: 1, Dr.-Karl-Lueger-Ring
Tram: 1, 3

Underground: Herrengasse (U3),
Rathaus (U2)
Internet:: www.burgtheater.at

Names like Klaus Maria Brandauer, Fritz Muliar, Kirsten Dene, Gert Voss, Thomas Bernhard and Elfriede Jelinek were and are associated with this illustrious theatre. Claus Peymann provided unusual as well as highly controversial productions until 1999.

🕐
Opening hours:
Tours: July, Aug
Mon – Thu 3pm,
Fri – Sun 3pm, 4pm,
Sept – June daily
3pm

Even now an engagement to play at the »Burg«, as the Viennese call this museum-like temple of the theatre arts, is still a high point if not the peak in the artistic career of a German-speaking actor. The theatre was founded by Emperor Joseph II in 1776 as a »Court Theatre«, with instructions to be a German National Theatre. It was later called the »Court and National Theatre«. In 1888, a new theatre on the Ring designed by **Carl von Hasenauer** and **Gottfried Semper** was inaugurated in the presence of Franz Joseph I. Gottfried Semper responded to criticism of the new theatre from the Viennese that »either every theatre has to be rebuilt after 60 years or it has burned down by then«. It happened to the Burgtheater after 57 years, when it caught fire in 1945 and the auditorium was completely destroyed.

! *Baedeker* TIP

Free Literature

Every year in the middle of September it is possible to enjoy the finest of literature in a tent set up next to the Burgtheater. As part of the »Rund um die Burg« festival, famous Austrian authors and newcomers read from their works at half-hourly intervals for 24 hours. Entrance is free. For information on dates and the programme call tel. 205 50 10 or check the daily newspapers.

It was not until 15 October 1955 that the theatre was able to be reopened with Grillparzer's *König Ottokars Glück und Ende* (King Ottokar's Prosperity and Demise). The building is 136m/446ft long and the middle section is 95m/311ft across. The façade rises up to 27m/88ft. The auditorium has seating for 1,285 and standing room for 105 in its stalls, box seats and four steep galleries. The regular season runs from September to June. The exterior of the »Burg« is eye-catching with its many decora-

Formal setting for the frescoes by Klimt and Matsch

tive figures, colossal groups, scenes and busts by the sculptors Tilgner, Weyr and Kundman. The costly interior is fashioned in French Baroque style. The staircase has frescoes by Gustav and Ernst Klimt, as well as by Franz Matsch.

✴ Demel

G 6

Location: 1, Kohlmarkt 14

Internet:: www.demel.at

Underground: Stephansplatz (U1, U2) Herrengasse (U3)

The shop's unmistakable trademark are its waitresses that Helmut Qualtinger celebrated in a couplet as »Demelinerinnen«, and who always wear modest black dresses with white lace collars and address the customers very formally with »Werden schon bedient?« (Has Sir/Madam already been served?).

Emperor Franz Joseph sent for fine cakes and pralines from Demel for his tête-à-têtes with his mistress; whereas his wife, Sissi, was addicted to the shop's fabulous candied violets. Despite all the scandals in recent times, the world famous court confectioner is still considered to be Vienna's finest and most expensive, where irresistible delicacies are produced according to time-honoured recipes. The over 200-year-long history of this illustrious establishment began with the

Opening hours:
daily 10am – 7pm

Württemberg confectioner Ludwig Dehne, who founded the legendary institution in 1785. In 1857, his heirs turned the business over to the apprentice Christoph Demel, whose family made the city palace the most prestigious on the square. In 1917, it was taken over by Anna Demel, who ran it successfully for four decades. Her successor, Klara Demel, married a Baron Berzeviczy, who showed little interest in the tradition-rich shop and put it up for sale after the death of his wife. Austrian entrepreneur Udo Proksch wielded the sceptre from 1972, until he was put behind bars for an insurance fraud which claimed the lives of six seamen and one minister. Eventually, the coffeehouse was sold to the German Günter Wichmann, who declared the business bankrupt in 1993. Despite continual rumours of closure and take-overs, however, visitors can still enjoy their melanges and the »authentic« Demel Sacher torte here.

Opening hours:
daily 11am – 6pm

Attached to the coffeehouse is the **Demel Museum** that tells the history of the former court confectionary and displays sweet works of art made of marzipan.

The agony of choice: deciding on a cake is difficult here

Kohlmarkt

The Kohlmarkt, now a pedestrian zone, links Michaelerplatz and the Graben. Where once wood and coal were sold, there are now elegant boutiques and luxury shops. Two of these, nos. 7 and 8/10, have unconventional façades designed by **Hans Hollein** in post-Modernist style, boldly executed in metal and marble. The fine Art Nouveau façade of the Artaria Publishing House (no. 9), where Chopin lived during his stay in Vienna, is also worth a look.

> ! **Baedeker** TIP

Torte Test

After years of dispute between Hotel Sacher and Demel over the Sacher torte both produce, Sacher now calls their's the »original«, while Demel call their's »authentic«. Test for yourself which of the two variations tastes the best, the one from Demel or the one from Hotel Sacher.

Großes Michaelerhaus

Across from Demel's stands the Großes Michaelerhaus, whose construction around 1720 was commissioned by the Barnabites. The poet **Pietro Metastasio** (1698–1782) lived and died here, and **Joseph Haydn** lived in the attic room for several years from 1750 onwards.

★ Dominikanerkirche (Dominican Church)

H 6

Location: 1., Postgasse 4   **Underground:** Stubentor (U3)
Bus: 74 A   **Tram:** 1, 2, Fresken

The Dominicans were summoned to Vienna in 1226, and had consecrated their first church by 1237. After a series of fires, work began on the construction of a Gothic church between 1283 and 1302, which suffered severe damage in the first Turkish siege of 1529. The present church, the third, was built between 1631 and 1632 and is one of the most beautiful Early Baroque churches in the Austrian capital, whose façade presents an interesting variation on Rome's »Il Gesù« church. Since being raised to the status of a »minor basilica« in 1927, it bears the name »Rosary Basilica ad. S. Mariam Rotundam«. The stunning **frescoes** in the nave are by **Matthias Rauchmiller** (17th century); those in the crossing are by **Franz Geyling** (1836), and those in the choir are by **Carpoforo Tencala** (1676). All of the wall and ceiling paintings in the side chapels were done in the 17th century. The painting above the High Altar, *The Virgin as Queen of the Rosary* by Leopold Kupelwieser (1839), alludes to the establishment of the Feast of the Rosary by Pope Gregory XIII. The chapels are works from the 17th and 18th centuries, the oldest being the Thomas Aquinas Chapel with a painting on the altar-piece from 1638. The most important is the Vincent Chapel with an altar-piece painted by Françoise Roettiers (*St Vincent raising a Man from the Dead*, 1726).

✴ Dom- und Diözesanmuseum

(Cathedral and Diocesan Museum)

H 6

Location: Stephansplatz 6   **Underground:** Stephansplatz (U1, U3)

The museum in Zwettlerhof, adjacent to the Archbishop's Palace, was founded in 1932, remodelled in 1973 and extended in 1985. On display from its collection is religious art from the early Middle Ages to the present day.

🕐 Opening hours:
Tue – Sat
10am – 5pm

The Treasury contains the most valuable items from the Stephansdom, including two Syrian glass vessels dating from the 13th and early 14th centuries, the St Andrew's Cross reliquary and an important 14th century reliquary which was remounted in 1514. Mementos of **Duke Rudolf IV**, »the founder«, who had the church rebuilt in Gothic style, include the chapter seal stamp, a cameo set in the Middle Ages, and his portrait (▶illus. p. 36) and Rudolf's funeral shroud. Other valuable exhibits include a monstrance (1784) by Ignaz Würth, enamelled 12th century tablets with Old Testament scenes, a 9th century Carolingian evangelistary with full-page depictions of the Evangelists. Most prominent among the Gothic painted panels are the works of the master of Maria am Gestade, the upper St Veit Altar based on a sketch by Dürer, and the *Man of Sorrows* by **Lucas Cranach the Elder**. Worth noting among the Gothic sculptures are a relief of the *Deposition from the Cross* and the Erlach and Therberg Madonnas (14th centuries). The museum has a rich collection of early 15th and 16th century sculptures, the most valuable of which are the *Madonna of the Shrine* (early 15th century) and the group sculpture of Anna Selbdritt (c1505) by **Veit Stoß**. The most important Baroque works are by Paul Troger (*St Cassian*), Franz Anton Maulbertsch (*Calvary*), Jan van Hemessen (*Christ Carrying the Cross*) and Kremser-Schmidt (*The Holy Group*).

Donauinsel (Danube Island)

H 1 – N 7

Location: Between Klosterneuburg and the oil port of Vienna-Lobau
Underground: Neue Donau (U6), Donauinsel (U1)

S-Bahn (suburban train): Strandbäder (S1, S2, S3) Lobau, Brücke (S 80)
Tram: 31

The Danube Island, nicknamed »Copa Cagrana« (named after the nearby part of Vienna called Kagran), is the favourite recreational area of the Viennese. It was created in the 1970s during the course of the second regulation of the Danube.

The island was created between the Danube and the New Danube, which was designed as a flood relief channel. It is a local recreational area covering 700ha/1,730acres, including stretches of water, woodland, grass and 42km/26mi of bathing beaches.

Northern Part

The northern part of the Danube Island is a paradise for sailing enthusiasts and surfers, as the wind coming from the Vienna Woods blows the strongest here. There are surfing schools, board rental, surfboard workshops and yacht harbours. Rowing, paddle and electric boats can be hired, though motor boats are not permitted on the New Danube, and there are also bicycles for rent. Bathing beaches invite for a swim and sunbathing, and innumerable restaurants and cafeterias provide sustenance all over the island.

Middle Part

The banks of Danube Island, as befits their function as a flood barrier, are reinforced against flooding with stone and turf pavers of concrete. There are especially prepared bathing beaches with a layer of fine gravel covering the stones and areas with shallow water suitable for children. Worth mentioning in the middle part are the sports fields and regulation-size football pitches, an 800m/2,625ft long water ski lift and a waterslide, and a school for diving, sailing and canoeing.

View of »Copa Cagrana« from the Sunken City

Southern Part Nudists are well provided for in the southern part of Danube Island, and there are specially designed banks providing access to the water for disabled visitors. A 1,500m/4,920ft long cyclodrome offers a place for bicycle and wheelchair races. Next to it are grills for summer barbecues. Anglers can find peaceful places away from the busy beaches, and some of the best fishing spots in Vienna are along the banks of Danube Island. The nature reserve area »Toter Grund« (dead ground) with its reed banks, is also in this part of the island. The southern part of Danube Island can be reached by ferry from the right bank of the Danube at Lindmayer's restaurant (Dammhafen 50), providing at the same time the opportunity to take a look at the **Peace Pagoda**. Elisabeth Lindmayer, the proprietor's daughter, is a Buddhist and it was her wish that the first peace pagoda on European soil be erected here. Monks of the Michidatsu Fujii Order had already erected peace pagodas in Japan, Sri Lanka, India and the USA and this bell-shaped one was created in 1983 – not so much a temple as a monument, which contains an almost 3m/10ft high statue of a seated Buddha.

> ! **Baedeker TIP**
>
> **Celebrations on the Island**
>
> The Danube Island festival is a special event in June. Hundreds of rock and pop musicians perform at »Europe's biggest teen party« – and entrance is free! The food on offer ranges from roast chicken to South American specialities (Infos: www.donauinselfest.at).

✴ Dorotheum

H 6

Location: 1, Dorotheergasse 17
Internet:: www.dorotheum.at

Underground: Stephansplatz (U1, U3)

The Viennese call one of the largest auction houses in the world »Tante Dorothee« (Aunt Dorothy) for short, or simply »Pfandl« (pawn). The origins of the Dorotheum date back to 1707, when Emperor Joseph I founded an office for pawn broking.

The pawn brokerage was moved into the Dorothean Monastery in 1787, which had been consecrated in 1360 and secularized in 1782. It underwent large-scale remodelling and extension in neo-Baroque style between 1898 and 1901. There are around 2,400 auctions a year, handling over 700,000 items, which can first be viewed in the spacious exhibit rooms. The Dorotheum has over a dozen branches in Vienna alone. There are several impressive sections in the main building for furniture, carpets, paintings, craftwork, furs, art, stamps, books and valuables. Experts from all over the world arrive for the four major art auctions in March, June, September and November. There are also things for sale not bound to an auction date. Not only

Desk, oil paintings and the display cabinet are all for sale

interesting, the Dorotheum – which has 14 branch shops in Vienna – is worth a visit simply for the grandeur of its atmosphere (open sales: Mon–Fri 10am–6pm; viewing: Mon–Fri 10am–6pm, Sat 9am–5pm).

Antique lovers will find many **shops** to browse through for treasures in the streets of the neighbouring quarter.

★ Franziskanerplatz

Location: 1 District　　　　**Underground:** Stephansplatz (U1, U3)

The Franziskanerplatz, with its complete 17th/18th century architectural picture including the Franciscan monastery and church, is considered one of the prettiest squares of old Vienna. In Emperor Joseph's day, the horse-drawn diligences used for country tours of up to a hundred miles and more were unharnessed in front of the former inn known as »Zum Grünen Löwen« (The Green Lion).

Nowadays people meet in the »little Café« here for a leisurely chat, or to take a break from shopping with a cream-topped coffee (Melange). The Moses Fountain, with its base like the jaws of a lion, placed here in 1798, used to stand in the courtyard of The Green Lion (no. 6). Johann Martin Fischer designed the lead statue of Moses striking water from the rock.

The Church of St Jerome standing on this idyllic old town square is the only church in Vienna with a Renaissance façade. The church was constructed between 1603 and 1611 on the site of an old 14th century convent of discalced nuns. Father Bonaventura Daum was responsible for the designs of the new building and the tower was added in 1614. Worth noting in the interior is the high altar by **Andrea Pozzo**, consecrated in 1707, with an image of the Madonna and Child from about 1550, which probably came from Grünberg in Bo-

St Hieronymus Franciscan Church (St Jerome)

hemia. Behind the altar is the monks' choir, which is reached by passing through the sacristy. The Capristan Altar (second altar on the left) displays the painting *Martyrdom of St Capristan* by Franz Wagenschön. The Francis Altar (fourth altar on the left) displays a portrait of the church's patron saint by Johann George Schmidt, and on the Cross Altar (third altar on right) is *Crucifixion* by Carlo Carlone, from the first half of the 18th century. The carved Baroque organ from 1643 is Vienna's oldest organ. It has folding doors, which are partly painted, partly carved with artistic figures of saints. According to legend, the Madonna on the reredos, popularly called the »Madonna with the Axe«, was about to be destroyed by iconoclasts, but the axe remained securely stuck. Soldiers then took the »Indestructible Madonna« with them on their campaign against the Turks and attributed their victory at Pest (Hungary) to it.

★ Freud Museum

G 5

Location: 9, Berggasse 19
Tram: 3

Underground: Schottentor (U2), Herrengasse (U3)
Internet:: www.freud-museum.at

The entrance room has been almost exactly recreated, down to the hat and cane in the cloakroom and even the waiting room with the plush upholstery from the turn of the 20th century. For almost half a century, from 1891 – 1938, Sigmund Freud lived in the house at 19 Berggasse.

Opening hours:
Opening times: daily
9am – 5pm, July –
Sept until 6pm

It was here that the Father of Psychoanalysis wrote his ground-breaking works including *The Interpretation of Dreams* (1900), and developed the theory of »Ego and Id« in 1923. The museum managed by the Sigmund Freud Society is not only a historical museum, but also a venue for a continuing response to Freud's life and works. In 1971, the Sigmund Freud Society reconstructed and decorated, in part with original furnishings, the entrance room, waiting room, consulting room and study of the great psychologist's classy 15-room apartment.

Documents and photographs provide information about Freud's career until his emigration to London, where his famous couch now stands. Further exhibits include pieces from Freud's antique collection, most of which was formerly kept in his study, donated to the society by Anna Freud.

Library ►

The library, whose basis was formed by books donated by numerous emigrated analysts, collects psychoanalytical literature in several languages and has now become one of the largest specialist libraries for psychoanalysis in Europe. Documents, films and recordings about the history of psychoanalysis in Austria are preserved in the archives.

Freyung

Location: 9, Berggasse 19
Tram: 1, 3

Underground: Schottentor (U2),
Herrengasse (U3)

In days gone by, the Freyung was the setting for something similar to an amusement fair, where jugglers and other travelling entertainers, market-criers and sweet cake bakers had their stalls. Today the square is primarily known for its Easter Market and pre-Christmas Advent magic.

The Freyung (»free place«) is a triangular public square near the **Schottenstift**, whose name refers to the fact that, like the monastery and the Stephansdom, it had the right to offer asylum to the persecuted. The city palaces around the Schottenstift that define the square's character today were not erected until the 17th and 18th centuries: **Palais Ferstel** (no. 2; see below); **Palais Harrach** (no. 3), exhibition centre for the Kunsthistorisches Museum; and Baroque **Palais Kinsky** (no. 4; see below). Bank Austria's Art Forum (no. 1) presents changing exhibitions worth seeing.

In the middle of Freyung square is the Austria Fountain, a work by **Ludwig Schwanthaler** unveiled in 1846. Its allegorical bronze figures by Ferdinand Miller cast in his Munich foundry represent Austria

Austria Fountain

In 1759, Canaletto painted the Freyung with the Schottenkirche as an open square without the Baroque palaces that frame the square today

! *Baedeker* TIP

The café as a way of life
On entering the Café Central in the Ferstel Palais via Herrengasse, the visitor is greeted by the writer Peter Altenberg sitting at a table directly to the right – not, of course, in person, but as a life-size model. Altenberg was a regular patron and often gave his address as »Wien 1, Café Central«. Franz Werfel, Stefan Zweig, and Karl Kraus made the café famous and turned it into a Viennese institution. Mon – Sat 8am – 10pm.

and the former major rivers of the monarchy: the Po, Elbe, Vistula and Danube. It is noted in the Viennese chronicles that Alma von Goethe, the poet's granddaughter, modelled for the figure of Austria at the age of 17, shortly before she died. After the bronze figure was completed, Schwanthaler supposedly had it filled with cigarettes in Munich for smuggling to Vienna, but was unable to remove them before the statue was put in place. They are thought to be there to this day.

Schottenkirche (Scots' Church)

The 12th century Irish monks invited to Vienna from Regensburg were called Scots because at the time Ireland was known as *Scotia Minore*, and thus the parish church built for the Irish Benedictine monks came by its name of »Our Lady to the Scots« or Schottenkirche. The church has been in the possession of the German Benedictines since 1418. The monastery was founded in 1155 by the Babenberg Duke Henry II Jasomirgott, who chose Vienna as his residence, and construction of the church began in 1177. The church was remodelled in the Gothic style in the 14th and 15th centuries, but it was given a Baroque remodelling in the mid-17th century by **Andrea Allio** and **Silvestro Carlone** and restored at the end of the 19th century. There is a memorial to the founder of the church on its façade. Among altar pieces inside created by Tobias Pock (1651 – 1655), Joachim Sandrant (1652 – 1654) and August Eisenmanger (1887 – 1888), the most beautiful is *Farewell of the Apostles* near the Imperial Oratory. The Baroque memorial for Count von Starhemberg who defended Vienna against the Turks is on the right, behind the Confessors' Chapel, and was created by Joseph Emanuel Fischer von Erlach. The High Altar (1883) was **Heinrich Ferstel's** last work. The Madonna Altar has Vienna's oldest votive picture of the Virgin. Lying in the tomb chapel, which was converted into a crypt in 1960, are the founder of the church, Henry II Jasomirgott, his consort Theodora, his daughter Agnes, Count Rüdiger von Starhemberg († 1701) and the Baroque painter Paul Troger († 1762).

The Schottenstift, connected to the Schottenkirche by the Schottenhof, has a famous secondary school and an important picture gallery that has been open to the public since 1994. The Foundation Bull dates from 1161, and the abbey was turned over to the German Benedictines in 1418. The buildings date from the 12th century, but were extensively renovated in the 17th century and enlarged in the 18th century. In 1832, they were rebuilt by Josef Kornhäusl in Classical style. Pupils who attended the school included the poets Bauernfeld and Nestroy, the Waltz King, Johann Strauss (son), and the painter, Moritz von Schwind. The abbey's **painting collection** has been in existence for more than 250 years and not only displays works from the 16th to the 19th century in the chapter house, but also 19 pictures from its famous late Gothic winged altar (1469 – 1475). It was painted by two »Scottish masters« and originally stood in the Schottenkirche. The oldest surviving views of Vienna can be seen in the backgrounds of these pictures. Opening hours: Thu – Sat 11am – 5pm, tours: Sat 2.30pm.

Schottenstift (Benedictine Abbey of Our Dear Lady to the Scots)

An interior open to the public: shopping arcade in the Palais Ferstel

The Kinsky Palais with its handsome façade and magnificent staircase was built between 1713 and 1726, to a design by Johann Lukas von Hildebrandt. It was commissioned by Count Daun, the father of the commander in the Seven Years War against Frederick II of Prussia.

The palace with an Italian air about it was built by Heinrich Ferstel, concurrently architect of the Votivkirche and the University and, from 1856 – 1860, for the National Bank (1878 – 1923 Austrian-Hungarian Bank). The Stock Exchange was located here until 1877. In 1925, the National Bank acquired its present building on Otto-Wagner-Platz no. 3. The fountain of the Danube nymphs (Donaunixenbrunnen) by Anton Fernkorn stands in the central courtyard that links the three entrances of the magnificent shopping arcades.

✱
Palais Ferstel

Palais Mollard-Clary	Palais Mollard-Clary is located south of Palais Ferstel in Herrengasse 9. The palace, built at the close of the 17th century, was restored for the Austrian National Library's music collection, the Globe Museum and the Esperanto Museum, and was opened mid-2005.
Music Collection ▶	Austria's largest music archive includes priceless manuscripts and original scores, including Mozart's Requiem, Beethoven's Violin Concerto, Haydn's Imperial Anthem, Franz Schubert's autograph, some items left by Anton Bruckner and the score of Richard Strauss' *Rosenkavalier*. Moreover, there are the personal papers and bequests of Alban Berg, Hans Pfitzner and numerous Austrian composers of the 20th century, as well as close to 20,000 recordings. Opening hours: July – Sept Mon – Fri 9am – 1pm, Oct – June Mon – Wed 9am – 4pm, Thu noon – 7pm, Fri 9am – 1pm.
Globe Museum ▶	The Globe Museum with its 350 exhibits is the only one of its kind worldwide. Globes of the world and the heavens are shown, as well as pre-1850 armillary spheres or spherical astrolabes. Particularly worth seeing are two Mercator globes dating from around 1550, Austria's oldest globe from the first half of the 16th century, and a vibrantly colourful celestial globe (1750) by Eimmart. Opening times: Tue – Sun 10am – 6pm, Thu until 9pm.
Esperanto-Museum ▶	The International Esperanto Museum is a document centre rich in materials about constructed and auxiliary languages. The nucleus of the collection consists of the printed works and museum collections of the »International Esperanto Museum of Vienna« founded in 1927, which was taken over by the National Library in 1928. Today, the special collection is composed of more than 17,000 volumes, and 260 periodicals are being evaluated and archived, including gazettes from China and Korea. As well as textbooks, autographs, posters and articles written in Esperanto, the museum also exhibits translations of the Bible, Dante's *Divine Comedy*, and works by Goethe and Heine (opening times: same as Globe Museum).

Graben

Location: 1st District   **Underground:** Stephansplatz (U1, U3)

The hub of Vienna is the wide Graben, half street and half square, where the city's first fluorescent lighting was installed in 1950. It became Vienna's first pedestrian zone in 1971, and soon afterwards the former thoroughfare was taken over by attractive summer street cafes.

The Graben was once the defensive moat encircling the Roman camp; later it became the flour and vegetable market and, from the 17th century onwards, it was the scene of glittering court festivities.

Half square, half thoroughfare: view of the evening hustle and bustle on the Graben

The Joseph Fountain and the Leopold Fountain were both altered many times, and in 1804 lead figures by Johann Martin Fischer were added. Of the many Baroque buildings that used to surround the Graben in the 18th century, only the **Palais Bartolotti-Partenfeld** (No. 11) remains, believed to have been designed by Johann Lukas von Hildebrandt in around 1720. The shop façade of the jeweller Caesar, designed by **Hans Hollein**, has long been attracting architecture fans. Dominated by a polished granite slab and an ensemble of metal pipes, it is reminiscent of the jewellery fashions of the early 1970s. Next to it are the shops of other renowned firms and boutiques that make a shopping tour well worthwhile.

In the middle of the square stands the famous 21m/69ft high Plague Column, also called the Trinity Column, which owes its existence to a vow made by Emperor Leopold I. He swore that when the plague raging in Vienna in 1679 passed, he would have a pillar built reaching up to heaven. (Estimates of the number of plague victims vary between 30,000 and 75,000). The first temporary plague column went up that same year, but construction of the final Plague Column was begun in 1681, by **Matthias Rauchmiller**. After his death in 1686, **Johann Bernhard Fischer von Erlach** continued the work, which was completed by Lodovico Burnacini in 1693. The figure of the kneeling emperor was created by **Paul Strudel** and the *Holy Trinity* by **Johann Kilian** of Augsburg.

✱
Plague Column

Tuchlauben Lane branches off to the right, at the upper end of the Graben. It was here that the wealthy cloth merchant Michael Menschein had the great hall on the first floor of his Gothic house at

Neidhart Frescoes

🕑 Opening hours:
Tue 10am – 1pm,
2pm – 6pm, Fri –
Sun 2pm – 6pm

no. 19 decorated with frescoes depicting Neidhart's poetry in around 1400. When the house was remodelled in the Baroque style around 1715, most of the paintings were destroyed and the rest disappeared under a thick layer of plaster. The original wall decorations were discovered by accident during renovation work in 1979 and it took three years of laborious restoration before they could be opened to the public under the aegis of the Historical Museum. The oldest secular wall paintings in the Danube capital bear eloquent witness to popular art in the late Middle Ages, depicting typical scenes from Neidhart's songs. The cycle of the four seasons illustrates entertaining comic tales and legendary childish pranks from the Minnesongs of Neidhart von Reuental, who was in the service of the court until 1240.

! **Baedeker TIP**

Sanitary style

A curious sight worth seeing on the Graben are the underground Art Nouveau toilets (1905) designed by Adolf Loos. After a complete renovation, they offer a noble setting for taking care of »urgent business«.

✱ Grinzing

E 1

Location: 19th District

Underground/Bus: U 4 to final station Heiligenstadt, then Bus 38

With its old houses and lanes nestled in gardens and vineyards, Grinzing still evokes thoughts of the classic Viennese *Heuriger* worldwide – that blissfully delicious wine made from the final harvest and drunk in taverns with a similar name (»Heurigen«) just as soon as pine branches hanging over entrances announce the new wine's arrival.

The first recorded mention of the tradition-rich, picturesque **little wine village of Grinzing** was in 1114. It was destroyed by the Turks in 1529, and three more times after that, though never as effectively as now, by the construction of buildings on the vineyards and by pollutants emitted from the solid line of cars heading for Lower Austria, which has recently provoked repeated protest campaigns by Grinzing's vintners. In order to counter this overdevelopment of the tranquil wine village, it has become possible for anyone to purchase 1sq m/3.3sq ft of land, complete with all rights to its vines. Prominent owners of such Grinzing vines, with a certificate of citizenship, include the Dalai Lama, the Swedish king Carl Gustav, Helmut Kohl, Jimmy Carter and Sophia Loren.

Genuine Grinzing *Heurigen* only serve their own wine and are open between three weeks and six months a year, whereas the *Heurigen* restaurants have year round concessions. Their wines, however, often

Striking out to Grinzing: the genuine Heurigen are to be found in selected Viennese suburbs

come from Lower Austria. It is above all in the evenings that Heurigen fans descend on Grinzing. A glass of wine in one of the many wine gardens is a wonderful way to end an evening, while what's left of the lovely countryside here and around Kahlenberg and Leopoldsberg makes for very enjoyable strolling.

Heeresgeschichtliches Museum
(Museum of Military History)

J 9

Location: 3, Arsenalstraße, Objekt 18
Bus: 13 A, 69 A,
Tram: 3, 18

Underground: Südtiroler Platz (U1)
S-Bahn (suburban train): Südbahnhof
(S1, S2, S3, S7, S15, S60, S80)

Vienna's oldest purpose-built museum holds extensive collections of military and historical items pertaining to Austria's military history from the outbreak of the Thirty Years' War up to the year 1945.

Emperor Franz Joseph I commissioned the construction and from 1850–1857 Ludwig Förster and Theophil Hansen built a palace complex inspired by Moorish-Byzantine architecture. The museum concept was not based on a critical historical examination of Austrian military history, but rather presents the exhibit pieces in a simplified, heroic manner.

Opening hours:
daily 9am–5pm

Ground floor On entering the ground floor visitors initially find themselves in the **Feldherrnhalle (General's Hall)** with 36 life-size marble statues of Austria's military commanders and rulers. The **Marinesaal (Navy Hall)** exhibition room on the left-hand side contains an extensive collection of ship models documenting the Imperial Navy (later known as the Imperial and Royal Navy). On display opposite, in the Kaiser Franz-Joseph Hall, are state portraits, the House Order, flags and uniforms from the reign of the emperor. Standing in the room adjacent is the unlucky automobile in which the heir to the throne Archduke Franz Ferdinand and his wife were assassinated in Sarajevo on 28 June 1914. Also included are the blood-stained uniform of the heir to the throne, and various pictures and documents that recall the event that ignited the First World War. Towering above the monarchy's heaviest artillery used between 1859–1916 in the **Artillery Room** is an M 16 38cm / 15in motorized howitzer from 1916. The world's largest collection of artillery is in the **Artillery Halls** (2, 17) flanking the entrance hall. Most of the pieces date from the 16th and 19th centuries.

Glorification of past deeds in the Hall of Fame: fresco of a battle against the Turks

The theme of the fresco decorating the cupola of the **Ruhmeshalle** **First Floor**
(Hall of Fame) on the first floor is the important military events in
Austrian history. The **Radetzky Hall** is dedicated to the Biedermeier
period, from 1815 until the March 1848 revolution, and to the field
marshall himself. There are also mementos of Napoleon's son, the
duke of Reichstadt, displayed in a showcase. The days of Napoleon
are remembered in the **Erzherzog Karl Saal (Room of the French**
Wars) with a captured French hot air balloon (Montgolfière) and the
Russian general Schuwalow's coat, which Napoleon is said to have
worn when he was exiled to Elba. The **Prinz Eugen Hall** holds weapons and armour from the time of the Thirty Years' War and the
Turkish Wars, as well as a cuirass, staffs of command, and Prince Eugene's funeral pall. Subjects covered in the **Maria Theresia Hall** include the War of the Spanish Succession and the last Turkish Wars.
The Turkish state tent on display was probably captured in 1716 at
the Battle of Petrovaradin. The mortar played a decisive role in the
storming of Belgrade in 1717, and the creation of the Military Order
of Maria Theresa after the Battle of Kolin in 1757, is documented in
the centre display case.

Heiligenstadt

G 1

Location: 19th District   **Underground:** Heiligenstadt (U4)

Its narrow winding streets and lack of parking have helped to
keep the oldest winegrowing village free from too much commo-
tion and congestion.

The historic image of urbanized vineyards and Empire and Biedermeier houses has been best preserved in the area around the Probusgasse and Armbrustergasse. The first documented mention of the **St**
Jakobs Kirche on Pfarrplatz, where a statute of the saint stands, was
in the 13th century. It was built in the Romanesque period on a Roman foundation, and was repeatedly destroyed, rebuilt and altered.
Ludwig van Beethoven stayed in Heiligenstadt on several occasions,
which at the time was far beyond the city walls. He was living here
in the autumn of 1802, when he was working on his second symphony. Probusgasse 6, administered by the Vienna Historical Museum as the **»House of the Heiligenstadt Testament«** is where he supposedly wrote the »Heiligenstadt Testament« in 1802 – actually a letter to his brothers Carl and Johann, which he never sent. Opening
hours: Tue – Sun 9am – 12.15pm, 1pm – 4.30pm. Beethoven also
stayed in Heiligenstadt in 1817, this time at Pfarrplatz in house
no. 2, a building completed at the close of the 17th century with an
impressive courtyard, where he composed his »Pastorale« (6th
Symphony).

✶ ✶ Hofburg

G/H 6

Location: 1, Michaelerplatz 1, Burgring
Tram: 1, 2, 3
Internet: www.hofburg-wien.at

Underground: Stephansplatz (U1, U2, U4), Herrengasse (U3)
Bus: 57 A

The Hofburg continues to be the seat of the Austrian head of state and the Federal President of Austria exercises his office and performs state functions in the same magnificent rooms once belonging to Maria Theresa and Joseph II. The palace is comprised of 18 buildings and has an architectural history of no less than 700 years.

The Imperial Castle in the inner city was the residence of the rulers of Austria for more than six centuries, from where the Habsburgs ruled their multinational state, whose existence ceased at the end of the First World War, in 1918. European history was written in this seat of power, and it was here that the Emperor of the Holy Roman Empire had his seat for two and a half centuries, until 1806. Nearly every Austrian ruler since the Middle Ages made additions or alterations to the palace. Thus architectural elements from Gothic, Renaissance, Baroque, Rococo, Classicism and the early 1870s can be seen in the Hofburg, and together with its squares and gardens, the entire Hofburg complex occupies an area of some 240,000sq m/59 acres. The »city in a city« has 18 wings, 54 flights of stairs, 19 courtyards

Hofburg Plan

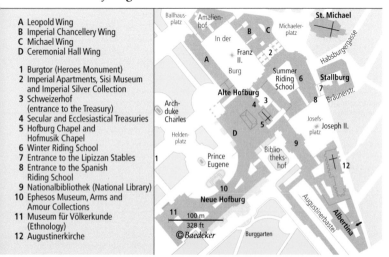

A Leopold Wing
B Imperial Chancellery Wing
C Michael Wing
D Ceremonial Hall Wing

1 Burgtor (Heroes Monument)
2 Imperial Apartments, Sisi Museum and Imperial Silver Collection
3 Schweizerhof (entrance to the Treasury)
4 Secular and Ecclesiastical Treasuries
5 Hofburg Chapel and Hofmusik Chapel
6 Winter Riding School
7 Entrance to the Lipizzan Stables
8 Entrance to the Spanish Riding School
9 Nationalbibliothek (National Library)
10 Ephesos Museum, Arms and Amour Collections
11 Museum für Völkerkunde (Ethnology)
12 Augustinerkirche

St. Michael
Ballhaus-platz   Amalien-hof   Michaeler-platz
In der
B   C
Habsburgergasse
Franz   2
A   II.
Burg
Summer Riding   6   Stallburg
School   7
Alte Hofburg   Bräunerstr.
4   3   8
Arch-duke   5   Josefs-
Charles   D   platz   Joseph II.
Helden-platz
Biblio-theks-   9
Prince   hof
Eugene   12
Augustinerbastei
10
Neue Hofburg
11   100 m
328 ft
© *Baedeker*   Burggarten   Albertina

and 2,600 rooms in which some 5,000 people are employed. A devastating fire in 1992 damaged a whole wing of the former imperial palace, destroying the great 18th century Redoutensaal (Masquerade Hall) – once the scene of frequent glittering balls – and leaving nothing but the shell. The frescoes in the Reading Room of the National Library suffered water damage from the fire fighting efforts, and the Riding School was also affected.

Castle Grounds

The Alte Burg is known as the Schweizerhof or Swiss Wing, recalling the Swiss Guard who once stood watch here. Documented evidence for this oldest part of the Hofburg dates back to 1279. Ferdinand I had the buildings remodelled into a Renaissance castle somewhere between 1547 and 1552, and the massive Schweizertor (Swiss Gate) was also fashioned at that time. From then onwards until 1916, all the emperors resided in the palatial chambers here.

Alte Hofburg (Old Castle)

The present castle chapel at the Hofburg was built by order of Emperor Ferdinand III between 1447 and 1449. The famous Vienna Boys' Choir developed out of the **Hofmusikkapelle** (court musicians) associated with the Burgkapelle, (► Baedeker Special p.168). Opening hours: Mon – Thu 11am–3pm, Fri 11am–1pm.

Burgkapelle (Chapel)

Emperor Maximilian II used the **inner Burghof** as a racecourse as early as 1545; later it became a venue for tournaments, festivities and public executions. Engraved on the base of the statue of Emperor Franz II erected in 1846, is a sentence from his majesty's testament: »My love to my nations«.

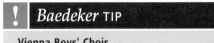

! Baedeker TIP

Vienna Boys' Choir
The performances of the Vienna Boys' Choir in the Hofmusikkapelle during mass on Sundays and religious holidays are very popular (9.15am, except July, Aug), making reservations necessary (at fax no. 533 99 27 75).

In 1558, Emperor Ferdinand I had a Renaissance on Maximilian, which is now one of the most important buildings of that period in Vienna. When his son ascended to the throne and moved into the Hofburg in 1565, so-called Maximilianburg was converted into the imperial stables. The stables for the Spanish Riding School's Lipizzaner stallions (► see below) have been here since Karl VI's time and, since 1997, so has the Lipizzaner Museum (► see below).

Stallburg

Emperor Maximilian II also built a palace for his son. Constructed between 1575 and 1577, and initially known as the Rudolfsburg after his son Rudolf, it was renamed Amalienburg in the 18th century, when the Empress Wilhelmina Amalia decided to live there after she was widowed. The upper floor was added and the tower remodelled

Amalienburg

in the 17th century. The rooms later used by the Empress Elizabeth and Czar Alexander I can be viewed as part of the Imperial Apartments (▶see below).

Leopoldinischer Trakt (Leopold Wing)

The Baroque building connecting the Schweizerhof (Swiss Court) and Amalienburg was commissioned by Leopold I, the grandfather of Maria Theresa, who lived in the wing with Francis Stephen of Lorraine from 1660–1680. Maria Theresa's apartments and those opposite Joseph II's are today part of the Presidential Chancellery.

Reichskanzleitrakt (Imperial Chancellery Wing)

The north-east wing connecting the Schweizerhof and Amalienburg was begun in 1723 by Johann Lukas von Hildebrandt and completed by Joseph Emanuel Fischer in 1730, who added the Baroque façade. Some of its rooms were furnished as imperial apartments.

Winterreitschule (Winter Riding School)

The Baroque hall where the Spanish Riding School performs was the scene of numerous glittering events, especially during the Congress of Vienna, from 1814–1815 (▶see below). J. E. Fischer von Erlach designed and built the beautiful white hall by order of Emperor Charles VI on the site of the »old Paradeisgartl« (park), from 1729 to 1735. The coffered ceiling is suspended 17m/55ft above the riding area.

Michaelertrakt (Michael Wing)

The Hofburg Theatre stood here until 1888. After its demolition, Emperor Franz Joseph I revived old plans drawn up by J. E. Fischer von Erlach for buildings linking the Reichskanzleitrakt and the Winterreitschule, and had them built between 1889 and 1893. The imposing **Michaelertor** (Michael Gate) flanked by figures of Hercules leads into the domed hall. The figures in the niches symbolize the mottoes of various rulers: Charles VI's »Constantia et fortitudine« (Perseverance and Bravery); Maria Theresa's »Justitia et clementia« (Justice and Mercy); Joseph II's »Virtute et exemplo« (Virtue and Example); and Franz Joseph I's »Viribus unitis« (United Strength). The stairs up to the Silver Chamber (▶see below) and to the Imperial Apartments (▶see below) are here.

Hoftafel- und Festsaaltrakt (Ceremonial Hall Wing)

Franz I had a 1,000sq m/10,764 sq ft ceremonial hall in Classical style added to the oldest part of the Hofburg in 1804, whose magnificent coffered ceiling is supported by 24 marble Corinthian columns. It served as throne room and ballroom and was also the setting for

Michaelertor leads directly to the magnificent Kuppelsaal (Dome Hall)

declarations renouncing throne rights by any Habsburger who entered into a morganatic marriage (i.e. a marriage below their status). Today, the hall is part of the Hofburg Congress Centre and on New Year's Eve each year, it provides a suitably formal setting for the famous Imperial Ball.

Heldenplatz (Heroes' Square)

The area west of the old Hofburg was originally known as Paradeplatz, but it became known as Heldenplatz after the statues of the conqueror of the Turks, Prince Eugene of Savoy, and the victor at Aspern, Archduke Karl, were set up to flank the square. Both equestrian statues are the work of Anton Fernkorn. On the square, »Fiakers« await passengers wishing to take a tour of Vienna in a typical horse-drawn carriage.

Outer Gate

The outer castle gate designed by Peter Nobile was built exclusively by soldiers. It was inaugurated in 1824, on the anniversary of the Battle of the Nations at Leipzig; the modification into a memorial to heroes took place in 1933. A metal cross next to the gate commemorates the visit of Pope John Paul II in 1983.

Neue Hofburg

The architects **Karl Hasenauer** and **Gottfried Semper** drew up the plans for a vast Imperial Forum and a monumental new palace. Emperor Franz Joseph I, however, only gave his approval for the con-

Impressive backdrop: the Neue Burg by night

struction of a new wing so that the over-all plan was never carried out. Work on the interior of the new Hofburg lasted until 1926. It has been the scene of a historic event on only one occasion, when Hitler proclaimed the annexation of Austria on the 15 March 1938, while Austrian resistance fighters were being rounded up for the first transportation to German concentration camps. Today, the Museum für Völkerkunde (►see below), the Ephesus Museum (►see below), the Sammlung alter Musikinstrumente (Collection of Ancient Musical Instruments ► see below), the Waffensammlung (Weapons Collection ►see below) and the new Reading Room of the Austrian National Library (►see below) are all located here.

✴ ✴ Silberkammer (Imperial Silver Collection)

Entrance beneath the Michaelerkuppel (Michael Dome)

The **ceremonial and everyday tableware of the Imperial Court** is displayed very effectively in the rooms of the Imperial Silver Collection, where restoration and remodelling work continued until 1995. The collections of imperial silver and tableware have only been on display to the public since 1923, because they were constantly in use until the end of the monarchy (1918). Up to the end of the 18th century, silver tableware was used exclusively at the imperial tables; porcelain was only used to decorate the table. Among the treasures in the collection are 18th century East Asian porcelain; the formal dinner service from the time of Emperor Franz Joseph, still used today

Opening hours: daily 9am – 5.30pm July, Aug until 6pm

for State receptions; a silver travelling service (Paris 1717/1718) for Empress Elizabeth Christine, and three elegant 18th century dinner services of Sèvres porcelain which were a gift from the French Court to Maria Theresa, on the occasion of the pact of 1756. Other outstanding items include the famous Milanese table centrepiece, nearly 10m/33ft long, made of meticulously engraved and gilded bronze; the Meissen service (c1775); the Viennese Empire service (early 19th century); and the superb Grand Vermeil Dinner Service with settings for 140 guests. It was fashioned by a Parisian goldsmith in the early 19th century and once belonged to Napoleon. There are also smaller glass services (c1850); 19th century tableware, including vases decorated with historical scenes; and the »English service«, presents from Queen Victoria to the Emperor Franz Joseph as was a Romantic period service in Neo-Gothic style (Vienna 1821-24).

★ ★ Kaiserappartements (Imperial Apartments)

The Imperial Apartments in the Hofburg are comprised of the Franz Joseph Apartments in the Reichskanzleitrakt together with Elisabeth and Alexander's apartments in the Amalienburg. Six rooms have been set aside especially for the »Sisi Museum« and are dedicated to the legend of the beautiful empress. The living quarters and ceremonial apartments of Empress Maria Theresa and those of her son, Emperor Joseph II (the Leopold Wing) are closed to public view because they are the official residence of the Austrian President. The furnishings of most of the rooms are almost entirely original.

Entrance under the Michael dome
🕐
Opening hours: Same as Imperial Silver Collection

Imperial Apartments and Sisi Museum Orientation

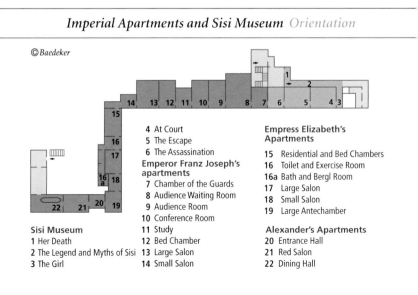

© Baedeker

4 At Court
5 The Escape
6 The Assassination

Emperor Franz Joseph's apartments
7 Chamber of the Guards
8 Audience Waiting Room
9 Audience Room
10 Conference Room
11 Study
12 Bed Chamber
13 Large Salon
14 Small Salon

Empress Elizabeth's Apartments
15 Residential and Bed Chambers
16 Toilet and Exercise Room
16a Bath and Bergl Room
17 Large Salon
18 Small Salon
19 Large Antechamber

Alexander's Apartments
20 Entrance Hall
21 Red Salon
22 Dining Hall

Sisi Museum
1 Her Death
2 The Legend and Myths of Sisi
3 The Girl

★ ★ **Schatzkammer (Treasury)**

Entrance at
Schweizerhof

🕐
Opening hours:
Wed – Mon
10am – 6pm, mid-
May – Nov daily
10am – 6pm

The 21 rooms of the Treasury hold the imperial jewellery and relics of the Holy Roman Empire, coronation and chivalric insignias, badges of rank, secular and sacred treasures, as well as gems, ornaments and mementos of inestimable artistic, historic and monetary value, formerly owned by the Habsburgs. The origins of the Treasury date back to Ferdinand I's »Kunstkammer« (art collection). The Austrian emperors brought their treasures here and stored them in various rooms of the Hofburg from the 16th century. During Karl VI's reign, the treasury was moved to the ground floor of the »Alte Burg«, where the iron door at the entrance bears the date 1712 and the Emperor's monogram. After room 8, the visitor to the Secular Treasury reaches the five rooms of the Ecclesiastical Treasury through the Paraments Corridor, after which the tour of the Secular Treasury continues from room 9.

The Secular
Treasury
Room 1 ▶

Room 2 ▶

Room 3 ▶

Room 4 ▶

Room 5 ▶

The Secular Treasury is housed in 16 rooms, with the collections organized according to themes. The Insignia of the Austrian Hereditary Homage applied to the Habsburg monarchs who, as rulers of Austria, had the rank of Archduke until 1804, whereas during the Holy Roman Empire they ruled as Emperors and Kings. The Imperial orb (second half of the 15th century) was borne by Emperor Matthias, the sceptre (mid-14th century) belonged to Charles VI, and the sword of investiture belonged to Maximilian I.Duke Albrecht V (1397 – 1439) became German king in 1438, after he had inherited the kingdoms of Hungary and Bohemia following the death of his father-in-law, Emperor Sigismund. The highest title in the German Empire remained with the Habsburgs until 1806, the end of the Holy Roman Empire. Since the insignia of the Empire was kept in Nuremberg after 1424, they had their own private Habsburg insignia created that represented this title. The insignia set is comprised of Emperor Rudolf II's (private) crown dating from 1598 – 1602 and fashioned by the court jeweller, and the imperial orb and sceptre dating from 1612 – 1615, both made in the Prague workshop.

In 1804, when the end of the Holy Roman Empire became imminent with the rise of Napoleon, Emperor Franz II proclaimed the hereditary Austrian Empire. He now reigned as Emperor Franz I of Austria. On display is the gold-embroidered mantel with ermine collar which he wore in 1830 when his son was crowned King of Hungary. Also on view are medals for civilian achievements; the Hungarian Order of St Stephen (1764), the Austrian Order of Leopold (1808) and the Order of the Iron Crown (1815). The Congress of Vienna (1814/1815) awarded Austria the Lombardo-Venetian kingdom. The coronation robes, mantle and baldric belonging to the insignia and coronation vestments of this kingdom are on display. Among the possessions of Mary Louise, daughter of Franz I and consort of Napoleon I, are a silver jewel box; a silver-gilt trivet, a present from the City of

Milan on the birth of her son, the King of Rome and Duke of Reichstadt; and a silver-gilt cradle from the city of Paris for the same occasion. In addition, mementos of the Emperor Maximilian of Mexico
can be seen. On display are a christening set composed of christening   ◄ Room 6
gown, blanket and pillow given by Maria Theresa, who, it is said, did
some of the embroidery work herself. There is also a golden baptismal ewer and basin (1571) and a small watering can from the Prague
Court workshop. Only very little of the Imperial jewellery has sur-   ◄ Room 7
vived. On 1 November 1918, on the orders of Charles I, the senior
Chamberlain, Count Berchtold, took the Habsburgs' private jewellery
out of the country. On view are the Colombian Emerald (2,680 car-
ats), cut and hollowed out to form a salt cellar in 1641, and the 416
carat hyacinth »la bella«, set as a double eagle in enamel, flanked by
an opal and an amethyst. A small genealogical tree presents 16 portraits of the Habsburgs in chalcedony cameos, and there are also sets
of jewellery from the 19th century and insignia. There is also the
Golden Rose, a Papal decoration presented in 1819 to Carolina Au-
gusta, fourth wife of Franz I, two Turkish sabres used by Charles VI
and Maria Theresa at the Hungarian coronation and the crown of
Stephen Bocskay, who was chosen king of Hungary in 1605 by the
Hungarian aristocracy. Two personal items of King Ferdinand I were   ◄ Room 8
considered so valuable in 1564 that the Habsburgs elevated them to
the status of »inalienable heirlooms«. They are a fourth century agate
bowl, the largest of its kind, once considered to be the vessel of the

Treasury in the Hofburg *Plan*

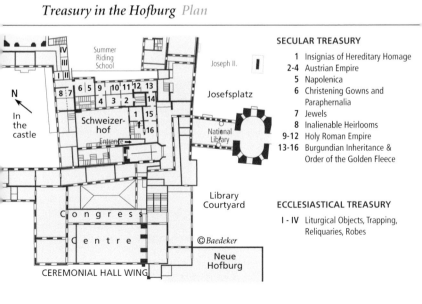

SECULAR TREASURY

1. Insignias of Hereditary Homage
2-4. Austrian Empire
5. Napoleonica
6. Christening Gowns and Paraphernalia
7. Jewels
8. Inalienable Heirlooms
9-12. Holy Roman Empire
13-16. Burgundian Inheritance & Order of the Golden Fleece

ECCLESIASTICAL TREASURY

I - IV. Liturgical Objects, Trapping, Reliquaries, Robes

© Baedeker

Holy Grail, and the 243cm/96in long »Ainkhürn«, actually a nar-whal's tusk, believed in the Middle Ages to be the horn of the legendary unicorn.

Ecclesiastical Treasury

The next five rooms house the Ecclesiastical Treasury with liturgical objects, reliquaries and robes once used at the Imperial Court.

Room 9 ▶

The regalia of the Electoral Prince of Bohemia are part of the collection because, beginning in the 14th century, the elected king was at the same time the King of Bohemia and, therefore, the duties of the electoral office at the coronation festivities were delegated to a deputy. Included are pictures and writings documenting the coronation of Joseph II (1764) and other events in the Holy Roman Empire.

Room 10 ▶

Robes, which formed part of the Imperial regalia since the 13th century, came into the possession of the Hohenstaufens and were presumably used at the coronation of Frederick II (1220). They include the coronation mantle made for King Roger II in 1133-34, a white robe from 1181, which corresponded to the outer garment of the Byzantine emperors, and red silk stockings of the last Norman king, William II.

Room 11 ▶

Among the Imperial Jewels and Coronation Insignia of the Holy Roman Empire are the world's oldest Imperial Crown (second half of 10th century), the Sacred Lance, the Processional Cross and the Imperial Cross (1024-25); in addition, there are also the Orb (end of 12th century), the Gothic Sceptre, the Aspergillum used to sprinkle holy water on the altar and the Imperial Cross that was reworked around 1200. Each new ruler took the oath on the Imperial Gospel, a Carolingian purple codex (end of 8th century), and the sword (first half of 10th century), formerly considered to be a relic of Charles the Great, was girded about the kings at their coronation.

Room 12 ▶

The holy relics belonging to the Imperial Treasury are displayed in this room.

Rooms 13–16 ▶

The Burgundian Inheritance is comprised of the treasures of the Order of the Golden Fleece founded in 1430, and the inheritance of Maria of Burgundy, who married the future Emperor Maximilian I in 1477. Besides the robes and tabards of the Order of the Golden Fleece, the order's liturgical vestments, fashioned between 1425 and 1475, its Cross of Oath (c. 1400), and the Burgundian Court Goblet of Philip the Good (c1453–1467) are on display.

★ ★ Spanish Riding School

Josefsplatz 1
Information:
tel. 53 39 03 10,
www.srs.at ▶

The Lipizzaner stallions which have been bred for centuries are a legacy and final remaining relic of the pomp and regal festiveness of the Austro-Hungarian monarchy. The institution was first documented in the time of Emperor Maximilian II, who introduced the breeding of Spanish horses to Austria in 1562. Numerous historical etchings and descriptions confirm that equestrian ballet and mounted carousel choreography had been among the glittering highlights of the court since the 16th century. Classic equestrian skills, which were

The perfection of court equestrian skills

popular at all the courts of Europe after the rediscovery of Greek equestrianism in Humanism, have only survived in the Spanish Riding School in Vienna. The famous equestrian performances have been presented in the Baroque Winter Riding School which was completed in the Hofburg by **Joseph Emanuel Fischer von Erlach** in 1735, since the time of Charles VI. The magnificent hall, designed for riding competitions among the nobility, was later used for a variety of other purposes but, since 1894, it has been used exclusively for the Lipizzaner equestrian shows that were only opened to the public after 1918.

The horses are a cross between Berber and other Arabian breeds with Spanish and Italian horses. The foals are born with a brown to mouse grey colouring and only turn white after 4 – 10 years. **Lipizzaner horses** are suited more than any other breed of horses to the difficult courtly dressage. Their compact build makes grouping easier; their high-held, strong necks provide the required erect posture. Their powerful hind quarters provide sufficient bounce in performing difficult flying changes, trotting in time in place (piaffes), pirouettes and sideway gaits like travers, renvers and shoulder-ins. The high knee action enables the Lipizzaner to demonstrate the special »Spanish step« whereby the legs appear to bend effortlessly, as if in slow motion. The »silver stallions« were bred in Lipizza until 1918,

Lipizzaner Riding Shows

when the stud farm was transferred to Piber in Styria. The studs had to be moved to Hostau in Bohemia in 1941. Their spectacular rescue in the last days of the war in 1945 was thanks to Colonel Podhajsky, then head of the riding school, and the American general and horse lover, George Patton. Their **training** begins at about the age of seven, when they learn the ground exercises, including high speed gait changes, piaffes, passages and pirouettes, which only very few animals in Vienna and Lipizza are capable of performing. The crowning achievement is their training in the aerial exercises, including pesades, levades, courbettes and caprioles. As always, the performances are in **historical costume**. The riders wear white buckskin breeches, high black boots, a brown riding jacket and a bicorn hat trimmed in gold. Deerskin saddles sit on gold embroidered red and blue caparisons. At the beginning and end of each show, the riders **silently salute** the portrait of Charles VI, who commissioned the building.

Tickets

Aside from the fairly frequent days when the school is closed, the Lipizzaner can be seen either during the two-hour **morning exercises** that begin regularly around 10am, or at various 80-minute gala performances (11am and 7pm). Tickets are available Tue – Sat 9am – 4pm at the visitors centre, Michaelerplatz 1, under the dome, as well as at Josefsplatz, gate 2 on the days of the morning exercises at 9am – 12pm. Tickets for the **gala performances** should be ordered several months in advance because of the enormous demand. Address: Spanische Reitschule, Michaelerplatz 1, A-1010 Vienna or by tel. 0043/1/533 90 31, fax 0043/1/533 90 32, www.srs.at.

Lipizzaner Museum

Opening hours: daily 9am – 6pm

The Lipizzaner Museum was opened at the end of 1997 in the rooms of the old Imperial Court (Reitschulgasse 2) next to the Imperial Stables. The view into the Imperial Stables, where the horses can be seen being fed or harnessed, is a highlight and is made possible by a special mirror to ensure the horses are not disturbed.

✷ ✷ Österreichische Nationalbibliothek (Austrian National Library)

Josefsplatz 1

Opening hours: Tue – Sun 10am – 6pm, Thu until 9pm

The imposing Baroque building of the National Library on Josefsplatz was built during the reign of Charles VI to plans by Fischer von Erlach, father and son, between 1723 and 1726. Nikolaus Pacassi made some alterations in 1763-69. The high Baroque palatial building was originally detached, but it was connected to the Hofburg by the Redouten Wing completed in 1760 (which was seriously damaged by fire in 1992, after which it was rebuilt). The massive middle risalt is crowned by a group of statues depicting the goddess Minerva on a quadriga that Mattielli designed in 1725. The National Library, formerly the Court Library, passed into state ownership in 1920 and is now one of the world's most important libraries.

The Library's extensive collections date as far back as the 14th century. The collections were stored in the upper storey of the Riding School during the 17th century, but a new location had to be provided because there was no longer enough space a century later. Today, the total collection amounts to some 3 million pieces of printed matter. The National Library has the following special collections: prints, manuscripts and incunabula, maps and globes, picture archives, music and theatrical collections and an Esperanto museum. Lack of space long ago led to expansion into the south wing on Josefsplatz and into the Neue Burg. Alte Burg (entrance Josefsplatz): State Hall, Department of Manuscripts, Map Department and Globe Museum, and Old Reading Room.
Neue Burg (entrance Heldenplatz): New Reading Room and Catalogue.

The Library's Collections

Fischer von Erlach, father and son, created one of the most magnificent rooms of High Baroque. The hall, 78m/256ft long and 14m/46ft wide, is 20m/66ft high and stretches up two floors; it is crowned by a massive dome with ceiling frescoes in praise of Charles VI (1730) by Daniel Gran, which were restored by **Maulbertsch** in 1769. The life-size statue of the emperor was fashioned by **Paul and Peter Stru-**

State Hall

15,000 gold-embossed volumes once belonging to Prince Eugene of Savoy, flanked by statues of emperors

del around 1700. In the centre of the State Hall are the 15,000 priceless gold-embossed volumes from the former library of Prince Eugene of Savoy. The hall is used today for changing exhibits and, in addition, four Coronelli globes from the 17th century are on display here.

The historic **Augustinersaal** was decorated with breath-taking frescoes by Johann Bergl in 1773.

Manuscript Collection

Close to 43,000 manuscripts dating as far back as the 4th century, 8,000 incunabula and some 240,000 autographs are preserved on the second floor. Among the most impressive manuscripts are the *Vienna Dioscurides*, a Byzantine medicinal herb book, written and illustrated about 512; the 6th century *Vienna Genesis*, a St Peter's antiphonary crafted around 1160, the *Wenzel Bible* from Prague (1390/95), the beautifully illustrated *Livre du couer d'amour espris* by Duke René d'Anjou (c1465), the *Black Prayer Book* of Duke Galeazzo Maria Sforza of Milan (c1470), one of the most valuable creations of Flemish illumination, the Ambras Book of Heroes (16th century) and a Gutenberg Bible from Mainz (15th century).

Map Department

The Map Department on the third floor currently holds about 260,000 maps and 240,000 geographical and topographical views. The most valuable items are a copy of a 4th century Roman map for travellers, the 46-volume *Atlas Blaeu* dating from the second half of the 17th century, and a map of the world prepared for Charles V in 1551.

Collection of Printed Material

About 2.5 million volumes housed in the Neue Burg have been catalogued and an open shelf collection of about 56,000 volumes is freely accessible at the Austrian National Library

Picture Archive

The Picture Archive (Neue Burg) includes over 1.5 million items and 120,000 volumes of technical literature. It is the largest and most important scientific institution for the cultural history of picture documentation in Austria, and contains the dual collection of negatives, photographs of various types and techniques, and graphics.

✳ Ephesus Museum

⏱ Opening hours:
Wed – Mon
10am – 6pm

Around the turn of the century, Austrian archaeologists working at Ephesus, on the coast of Asia Minor, excavated high-quality statues, reliefs and a considerable amount of bronzes in the ancient trading city that found their way to Vienna as a gift from the sultan to the emperor, where they have been on display in the Ephesus Museum in Neue Burg since 1978. Among the treasures of the sculpture collection is the 2m/6.6ft-high **bronze statue of an athlete** that had been pieced together from 234 fragments (2nd half of the 4th century BC); it is a Roman copy of a Greek original. The approx. 40m /

Archaeological finds from the Aegean island of Samothrace in the Ephesus Museum

131ft long **Parthian Monument frieze** with life-size figures in relief was part of the much longer monument for Lucius Verus († 169), the co-regent and adoptied brother of Emperor Marcus Aurelius,; it was erected after the victorious conclusion of the Parthian Wars (161–165). Also noteworthy are **Hercules and the Centaur** and the **Child with a Goose**, a Roman copy of a Hellenic original. Outstanding among the architectural fragments are the pieces of an altar from a shrine to Artemis (4th century BC), an octagonal gravestone of a young woman flanked by two columns (second half of 1st century AD), parts of a so-called round house (second half of 1st century AD) and fragments of the Great Theatre (mid 1st century AD) with reliefs of cupids and a frieze with masks. An 8x4m/26ftx13ft model provides an imposing impression of the size and grandeur of ancient Ephesus, which was recreated with countless layers of wood. The Archaeological Institute excavated a considerable number of finds on the Aegean island of Samothrace in 1873 and 1875, which augment the collection. Among the exhibit pieces are victory figures, Hellenic pediment sculptures from the Hieron, Ionic capitals from the Ptolemaion and a frieze of lotus fronds from the Arsinoeion of the island.

✽ Collection of Ancient Musical Instruments

The imperial family and the Society of the Friends of Music in Vienna collected all the precious instruments that are housed in the middle section of the Neuer Burg. The valuable collection, whose focus is on the Vienna Classic, possesses some unique Renaissance pieces and an extensive collection of keyboard instruments, from 16th century clavichords and cembalos down to modern pianos. Visitors are provided with headphones for the tour so that they can listen recordings of music being played on the instruments on display in the individual rooms.

Heldenplatz
🕐
Opening hours:
same as Ephesus
Museum

✱ Collection of Arms and Armour

Heldenplatz
🕐
Opening hours:
same as Ephesus
Museum

The first collectors were Archduke Ernst of Styria in the 15th century and Archduke Ferdinand of Tyrol in the 16th century. It first became the major collection of its type in 1889 when all of the Habsburg armouries were combined. Among the valuable exhibits are medieval helmets, the armour of Frederick I of the Palatinate, Frederick III's ceremonial sword, late Gothic suits of armour and swords, Louis XII's crossbow, Maximilian I's tournament armour, jousting equipment, most of it from the Innsbruck court workshops, Charles V's high Renaissance ceremonial weapons with two suits of boy's armour, and the parade armour of Charles V, Philipp II, King Ferdinand I and Francis I, as well as some of the first pistols.

Museum für Völkerkunde (Museum of Ethnology)

Heldenplatz
🕐
Opening hours:
Same as Ephesus
Museum

The Museum of Ethnology developed out of the Anthropological-Ethnographic Department of the Naturhistorisches Museum. The collection is maintained in the former Corps de Logis of the Neue Burg and is comprised of more than 200,000 ethnographic artefacts, primarily from societies that did not use writing, as well as about 25,000 photographs and 136,000 printed works on the history and culture of non-European peoples.

Burggarten

Napoleon had the castle fortifications blown up in 1809 – to the joy of the people at court, because now there was finally room for an imperial garden, which became known as the »promenade«. Later, the Neue Burg was laid out on a section of the park grounds. Three statues of famous men stand in the park. The statue of **Mozart** erected in 1896, is a masterly work in marble by Viktor Tilgner. Its base is decorated with the Mozart family playing music and two reliefs of themes from the opera *Don Giovanni*. The **equestrian statue of Emperor Franz I** that Balthasar Ferdinand Moll created was unveiled in 1781. The statue of Emperor **Franz Joseph I** was first set up in 1957 in a surprise action that took place without political fanfare – to the general amazement of the Viennese.

The **Schmetterlingshaus (Butterfly House)**, a lovely Art Nouveau glass house, contains a tropical rainforest with hundreds of free-flying butterflies.

🕐
Opening hours:
April – Oct
Mon – Fri
10am – 4.45pm,
Sat, Sun until
6.15pm; Nov –
March daily
10am – 3.45pm

Volksgarten

This park was also created on the site of the former castle bastions demolished by the French. The **Temple of Theseus**, modelled on the Theseion in Athens, was built between 1820 and 1823 by Peter Nobile for the statue of Theseus by Antonio Canova. Napoleon I had originally commissioned the statue during his stay in Vienna, but for obvious political reasons was no longer able to take delivery. Franz I leaped into the breach. The statue was removed from the temple in 1890 and placed in the stairwell of the Kunsthistorisches Museum. Notable statues in the park include the **Grillparzer Memorial** by Karl Hasenauer, Karl Kundmann and Rudolf Weyr unveiled in 1889, with reliefs portraying scenes from six of the poet's plays, and the memorial to **Empress Elizabeth** that Hans Bitterlich and Friedrich Ohmann created in 1907.

★ Hoher Markt

H 6

Location: 1st District
Tram: 1, 2

Underground: Stephansplatz (U1, U3), Schwedenplatz (U1, U4)

Vienna's oldest square, on the edge of the textile district that the Viennese also call the »Fetzenviertel« (Rag District), is alive with memories that reach back to the very beginnings of the city's history.

The palace of the commander of the Roman fortress of Vindobona stood here on the »forum altum« and it was probably here that Emperor Marcus Aurelius died. During the Middle Ages, it was the scene of executions, as well as the location for the Babenberg Reuthof, the fish market and for cloth trading. Almost all of the houses around Hoher Markt had to be rebuilt after the destruction of 1945. The focal point of the square is the **Nuptial Fountain or Joseph Fountain** donated by Leopold I. The figures decorating the fountain by Antonio Corradini portray the wedding of Mary and Joseph. **Johann Bernhard Fischer von Erlach** originally erected a wooden fountain; his son made a new version in white marble in 1792.

Anker Clock in Art Nouveau

The **Anker Insurance Company's clock** is impossible to miss on the east side of the square on the arch spanning over Rotgasse. Dedicated to the Viennese people, this animated clock built by Franz von Matsch at the beginning of the First World War parades historical figures every hour: in order of appearance, they are Emperor Marcus Aurelius, Charlemagne, Duke Leopold IV and Theodore of Byzantium, Walter von der Vogelweide, King Rudolf I with his wife Anna of Hohenburg, Master Hans Puchsbaum, Emperor Maximilian I, Mayor Johann Andreas of Liebenberg, Count Rüdiger of Starhemberg, Prince Eugene, Maria Theresa with Emperor Franz I and Joseph Haydn. At noon, all of the figures parade accompanied by music.

Roman Ruins
🕐
Opening hours:
Tue – Sun
9am –6pm

Steps near house no. 3 on the south side of the square lead down to the subterranean excavation of Roman ruins, which were turned into the Roman Museum. The remains of the walls of officers' houses of the barracks district of Vindobona (2nd to 3rd century AD) can be viewed. There are also the remains of a 4th century Germanic house.

✳ Josefsplatz

Location: 1 District
Tram: 1, 2

Underground: Herrengasse (U3)
Bus: 57 A

The uniformly late Baroque buildings framing Josefsplatz are the Austrian National Library, the Winter Riding School (▶ Hofburg), the Palais Pálffy and the Palais Pallavicini.

In the middle of the square is a **monument** created by Franz Anton Zauner between 1795 and 1806, in memory of **Joseph II**, son of Maria Theresa. The dedicated reformer is depicted dressed as a Roman imperator blessing his people. The reliefs on the monument depict

Joseph's services to Austrian trade and recall the numerous trips the monarch took abroad »in order to report to his people of the good in the world«. The monument was a gathering place for those loyal to the emperor in Vienna during the revolution of 1848, where they paid homage to an emperor that had already been dead for half a century.

The **Palais Pallavicini** (no. 5) is a Classical building with a magnificent portal with caryatid columns and figures on the entablature that Zauner created in 1786. The Palais itself was built by **Ferdinand von Hohenberg** in 1783-84. An exhibi-

The monument of Joseph II dressed as a Roman imperator gave the square its name

tion of hand-signed Salvador Dalí dry-point etchings and litho-graphs, as well as sculptures, is on display in the palais. Some of the works are offered for sale by the Gala-Salvador Dalí Foundation

⊙
Opening hours:
daily 10am – 6pm

The former Palais Pálffy, with its modern interior and wonderful Renaissance façade and Classical doorway is now called »Österreich-haus« and is available for cultural events. Around 1500, the Imperial Austrian Chancellery stood on this site. It was converted into a nobleman's palace at the end of the 16th century, and partially re-built following a major fire in the 18th century. Mozart presented the debut performance of his *Marriage of Figaro* to a group of friends in the Figarosaal.

Palais Pálffy/ Österreichhaus

Josephinum

G 5

Location: 9, Währinger Straße 25/1   **Underground:** Schottentor (U2)
Tram: 37, 38, 40, 41, 42, 43, 44

The Late Baroque Josephinum was designed by Isidore Canevale as a place for training military physicians; it was built between 1783 and 1785. It was remodelled in 1822.

The palatial building was elevated to the status of a military academy for surgical medicine in 1854. The **Collection of the Medical University of Vienna** and the Pharmacognostic Institute of Medicine have been located in the building since 1918. The **Hygieia Fountain** with a lead statue by J. M. Fischer has decorated the forecourt since 1787. Included in the museum's comprehensive collection are artistically fashioned anatomical and obstetric wax models (anatomia plastica) commissioned by Joseph II from Tuscan sculptors for anatomy in-struction. The pharmaceutical objects' collection, which is under a preservation order, and the larger Drug Collection, are the educa-tional pharmacy's two historic collections. Included among the dis-plays in the Department of History of Medicine are a microscope by Theodor Billroth, dissection magnifying glasses by Carl Zeiss, old surgical instruments, and a phantom baby for demonstrating birth-ing techniques in Ignaz Philipp Semmelweis's time, as well as letters from Sigmund Freud and first editions of Ignaz Philipp Semmelweis' und Franz Anton Mesmer's books.

⊙
Opening hours:
Mon, Tue
9am – 4pm, Thu –
Sun 10am – 6pm;
tours Thu 11am

The **Old General Hospital** in Spitalgasse 2 (entrance: Van-Swieten-Gasse) is a sprawling complex that Joseph II had modelled on the Paris Hôtel Dieu. It was used as a university campus after the con-struction of the new general hospital. A special feature is the **Narren-turm**, the so-called madhouse tower, built in 1784. The five-storied, circular construction by **Isidore Canevale** served as a psychiatric hos-

Pathologisch-an-atomisches Bun-desmuseum (Federal Patholo-gic-anatomical Museum)

Opening hours:
Wed 3pm – 6pm,
Thu 8am – 11am,
1st Sat of the month
10am – 1pm

pital until 1860. Today it is home to the Federal Pathologic-Anatomical Museum, whose close to 50,000 exhibition pieces make it the oldest and largest collection of its kind. The replicas of bodily deformities, malformed foetuses and lungs eaten away by nicotine, however, are not everyone's cup of tea.

Judenplatz

H 6

Location: 1st District   **Tram:** 1, 2
Underground: Schwedenplatz (U1, U4)

Judenplatz was the centre of Vienna's medieval Jewish quarter from the late 13th century onwards. Here stood the rabbi's house, the hospital, school and synagogue, and it was here that Jewish merchants, bankers and scholars went about their daily business.

In 1420, jealousy and hate unleashed a pogrom known as the »Wiener Geserah« (Viennese Evil Decree), and the 800 inhabitants of the quarter were either driven out or murdered. At the close of the 16th century, a Jewish community developed in Vienna once more, which Ferdinand II resettled in Leopoldstadt in 1624.

No fear of contact: taking a break in front of Rachel Whiteread's Holocaust Memorial

The 15th century »Zum großen Jordan« house (no. 2) recalls the cruelty of the pogrom during which 210 Jews were burned to death on the Gänseheide (Goose Pasture) in 1420. The building's Late Gothic relief of the baptism of Christ has an infamous inscription: »By baptism in the river Jordan, bodies are cleansed from all evils. And even secret sinfulness flees. In the year 1421, a thirst for vengeance raged through the city, purging the terrible crimes of the Hebrew dogs. As the world was once purged by the flood, this time guilt was purged by the flame«. A descendant of Jörg Jordan, the original owner, sold the house to the Jesuits, but it has been in private ownership since 1684.

Zum großen Jordan House

Rachel Whiteread's holocaust memorial of 1999 commemorates the murder of 65,000 Austrian Jews by the Nazis. It symbolizes the obliteration of the »people of the book« and the names of the places where the Jews were murdered during the Third Reich are on floor tiles around the monument.

Holocaust Memorial

The »Museum Judenplatz«, a branch of the Jewish Museum, is housed in the adjacent building. The remains of the first synagogue, which were discovered during the construction of the Holocaust monument, can be seen in the cellar (opening hours: Sun – Thu 10am – 6pm, Fri until 2pm).

Jewish Museum

Sights worth seeing are the Lessing statue by Siegfried Charoux, which was reproduced by artists in 1968, the original having been melted down in 1935, and the Tailors' Guild House (no. 8).

Additional sights

★ Jüdisches Museum (Jewish Museum)

H 6

Location: 1, Dorotheergasse 11
Internet:: www.jmw.at

Underground: Stephansplatz (U1, U3)

The Vienna Jewish Museum regularly presents changing exhibitions of Jewish Vienna, Eastern Judaism and the Viennese salon culture.

The museum is located in a historic Classical palace with a Baroque structural core. Its history dates back to the 11th century, when it was separated from the neighbouring Dorotheerstift, an Augustine monastery. The Dorotheum has owned the Palais Eskeles since 1936. It served for decades as an exhibition hall for art auctions, before it was made permanently available to the Jewish Museum to better inform the visitor about the history of the relationship between Jews and non-Jews in Austria and Europe, and to provide a place of encounter. A permanent exhibit on Austrian-Jewish history is open to the public, which the museum bases on three existing larger collec-

Opening hours:
Sun – Fri
10am – 6pm;
tours: Sun 2pm,
3pm, 4pm

tions of inestimable worth. It includes the Max Berger collection owned by the City of Vienna which, with its more than 10,000 works of art, covers the whole spectrum of art produced by Ashkenazi Judaism; the collection of the Israeli cultural community that contains the Martin Schlaff collection donated to the Jewish Museum in 1993, with close to 5,000 items on the subject of Anti-Semitism, along with collections comprised of objects of unknown origin from the world's first Jewish museum that was founded in 1896 and closed down by the Nazi authorities in 1938. The exhibition is unique in Europe. Among the items on display in the 21 sections of reminiscence are the spout of a 14th century ritual ewer for washing hands from the first synagogue in Vienna, which was found in 1995; a three dimensional model of the first Jewish ghetto in Unteren Werd; Thora scrolls and Kiddush cups; as well as memorabilia of Mendelssohn, Theodor Herzl and Sigmund Freud, including glasses of the satirist Karl Kraus and the inkwell of the lyric poet Peter Altenberg.

✴ Kahlenberg

north E 1

Location: 19th District
Tram/Bus: 3 (12.-Februar-Platz), then Bus 38A

Underground/Bus: Heiligenstadt (U4), then Bus 38A

Vienna's very own mountain rising up in the north-east of the city is the 484m/1.588ft high Kahlenberg. Poets and composers have sung the praises of the mountain again and again. It was originally called Sauberg (sow mountain), undoubtedly because of the many wild boar roaming the dense oak woods.

Opening hours:
Sun 9am –6pm

Grillparzer wrote: »If you have seen the land all around from the top of Kahlenberg, you will understand what I have written and what I am«.

There is a magnificent view, weather permitting, from the well-known Heurigen restaurant and from the panorama terrace of the popular recreation area to Grinzing and Nussdorf, the Vienna Basin, the hills of the Vienna Woods and the Danube Valley beyond, to Marchfeld, the Little Carpathians, and all the way to the Schneeberg region.

Standing on the summit of the Kahlenberg are the television tower and the **Stephanie Observation Tower**. The 22m/72ft high observation tower was donated in the 1880s by Stephanie of Belgium, the widow of Crown Prince Rudolf; it was designed by the Ringstrasse and theatre architects Ferdinand Fellner and Hermann Helmer. In 1683, the Polish Prince Sobieski brought a relief army to rescue the city under siege for the second time by the Turks, which is commemorated by the Sobieski Chapel in the little Baroque Church of St Joseph.

★ Kaisergruft (Imperial Vault)

H 6

Location: 1, Neuer Markt   **Underground:** Stephansplatz (U1, U3)

Members of the Habsburg ruling family and their relations rest in 138 metal coffins. They have been buried here since the 17th century and the funeral of Austria's last empress took place here with a great deal of ceremony in 1989.

The mortal remains of the Habsburgs resting here are not complete; only the embalmed bodies lie in the coffins. Their hearts are in the Augustinerkirche, while their viscera are preserved in the catacombs below the Stephansdom.

Opening hours:
Daily 10am – 6pm

The entrance is on the right, next to the Kapuzinerkirche (►see below). With very few exceptions, all of the Austrian emperors since 1633 have been buried here – Ferdinand II was buried at Graz, Frederick III in the Stephansdom, and the last Emperor, Charles I, was laid to rest in Funchal on Madeira, where he was in exile. The nine vaults are arranged in chronological order, making it easy to trace the evolution of styles in the art of the individual eras. The corrosive damage (tin pest) threatening the tin alloy coffins of the 17th and 18th centuries necessitates extremely expensive conservation work.

Emperor Matthias († 1619) and his consort Anna († 1618), who are considered the founders of the family vault, were originally buried in the chapel of St Dorothea and were the first to be transferred to the Imperial Vault in 1633. **Leopold's Vault** is also called the Angel Vault because 12 of the 16 sarcophagi here are children's coffins. Ferdinand III († 1657) is also buried here. **Balthasar Ferdinand Moll's** casket for Eleanor of Palatine of Neuburg († 1720) made such a good impression on the Emperor that afterwards Moll, a professor at the Academy for Fine Arts, spent half his time producing nothing but sarcophagi. **Johann Lukas von Hildebrandt** designed the sarcophagi for Leopold I († 1705) and Joseph I († 1711). Moll designed the magnificent sarcophagus for Karl VI († 1740) with the coat of arms of the Holy Roman Empire, Bohemia, Hungary and Castile, resting on four lions. Jean Nicolas Jadot de Ville Issey is responsi-

Eerily beautiful to look at: Karl VI's tomb in the Capuchin Crypt

Imperial Vault Plan

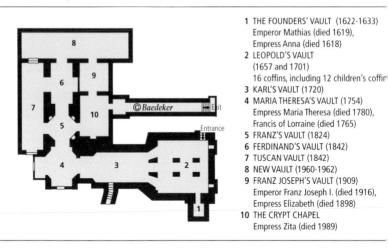

1 THE FOUNDERS' VAULT (1622-1633)
  Emperor Mathias (died 1619),
  Empress Anna (died 1618)
2 LEOPOLD'S VAULT
  (1657 and 1701)
  16 coffins, including 12 children's coffins
3 KARL'S VAULT (1720)
4 MARIA THERESA'S VAULT (1754)
  Empress Maria Theresa (died 1780),
  Francis of Lorraine (died 1765)
5 FRANZ'S VAULT (1824)
6 FERDINAND'S VAULT (1842)
7 TUSCAN VAULT (1842)
8 NEW VAULT (1960-1962)
9 FRANZ JOSEPH'S VAULT (1909)
  Emperor Franz Joseph I. (died 1916),
  Empress Elizabeth (died 1898)
10 THE CRYPT CHAPEL
  Empress Zita (died 1989)

ble for the **dome chamber** dominated by Moll's double sarcophagus in the Rococo style for Maria Theresa († 1780) and for Franz I († 1765). The sarcophagus is fashioned in the form of a bed of state; at the head of the half upright-sitting imperial couple, an angelic herald with trumpet and a crown of stars proclaims the triumph of faith. Numerous reliefs along the sides depict scenes from Maria Theresa's life. It is further adorned with four mourning figures and the crowns of Austria, Hungary, Bohemia and Jerusalem. Moll also fashioned several Rococo sarcophagi for the children of the Imperial couple, not, however, the plain copper coffin for Emperor Joseph II († 1790), who died in 1790. In a niche in the **Maria Theresa Vault** is the coffin of Countess Karoline Fuchs-Mollart († 1754), Maria Theresa's governess and the only person buried here who was not a member of the Imperial House. The last emperor of the Holy Roman Empire, Franz II († 1835), rests in the company of his four wives in a Classical copper casket by Peter Nobile.

Ferdinand I († 1875) – his sarcophagus is standing on a pedestal – shares the room with 37 other Habsburgs in the wall niches. The **Toskanagruft (Tuscan Vault)** holds the Tuscan branch of the Habsburg Family. Among those resting in the **New Vault**, consecrated in 1960 – 1962, are Emperor Maximilian of Mexico (executed in 1867) and Marie Louise († 1847), Napoleon's wife. Emperor Franz Joseph I († 1916), Crown Prince Rudolf, who took his life in 1889 in the Mayerling Hunting Lodge and Empress Elizabeth (Sisi), who was murdered in Geneva in 1898, found their final resting place in the Franz Joseph Vault constructed in 1909. A bust of Emperor Karl I († 1922) in the chapel is in memory of the last Austrian emperor, who died in exile on Madeira and was canonized in 2004.

You would not know it to look at it, because the Capuchin Church (St. Mary of the Angels) appears modest, sober and almost totally lacking in ornamentation – in keeping with the vows of a mendicant order – but it was sponsored by a female monarch, Empress Anna, in 1618. Her death, and her husband's, as well as the uncertain times (Thirty Years' War) delayed the building, and it was not dedicated until 1632. The most valuable piece of art in the church is a pieta group near the altar, in the right-hand transept, by Peter von Strudel, the founder of the Academy of Fine Arts.

Kapuzinerkirche (Capuchin Church)

Neuer Markt (New Market)

Despite its name, the **Neuer Markt** served as a flour market, herb market, tournament site and arena for the Viennese equivalent of »Punch« (Hanswurst) from 1220 onwards, and it was also where the court and aristocracy went sledging. The oldest houses still standing, like »Herrenhuterhaus« (no. 27), date back to the 18th century. Joseph Haydn lived in the house where no. 2 now stands in 1795/96, and wrote the Austrian imperial anthem there. The west side of the square is dominated by the Kapuzinerkirche.

Maria Theresa was offended and had the figures of the river gods removed from the Donner Fountain

Commissioned by the city, **Georg Raphael Donner** created the Providentia Fountain between 1737 and 1739, better known in Vienna as the »Donner Fountain«. The city fathers wished the central figure of Providentia to reflect the »caring and wise government« of the city, so Donner decorated its plinth with four graceful naked cherubs. The sensuous figures on the sides of the fountain's basin symbolize the Rivers Enns (an old man), Traun (a youth), Ybbs and March (both in female form), but Empress Maria Theresa was offended by so much nakedness and had the figures removed. It was not until the reign of Franz II, in 1801, that they were returned to their original places. The too delicate lead figures were replaced by bronze replicas in 1873, and the originals are now on display in the Baroque Museum at the Lower Belvedere (►Belvedere).

★
◄ Donner-Brunnen (Donner Fountain)

Karl Marx Hof

Location: 19, Heiligenstädter Straße 82 - 92   **Underground:** Heiligenstadt (U4)
Tram: 3

The more than 1km/0.6mi long Karl Marx Hof is symbolic of the 398 council houses that »Red Vienna« – as the city governed by social democrats was called between 1919 and 1934 – had constructed between the two world wars to combat the overwhelming misery caused by housing shortages at that time.

A total of 64,000 dwellings were constructed through the social building program, mainly in the outlying Vienna districts. They were financed by drastic luxury taxes on champagne, maids and automobiles, and a steeply graduated tax on housing construction. The rent the tenants paid for an average 40m²/430ft² living unit, on the other hand, was affordable, amounting to only 5%-8% of their wages. Gas and electricity rates were low and there was no charge for the basic ration of water. Added to that, were exemplary community facilities, such as baths, laundries, community rooms, restaurants, shops and

Very desirable in the 1920s: today a piece of architectural history

libraries, plus nursery schools and wading pools. There were also many green areas, which made living in these »welfare palaces« extremely attractive. **Karl Ehn** was responsible for the planning of Karl Marx Hof, which was built between 1927 and 1930, and contains 1,382 flats grouped around several inner garden courtyards. Only about 18% of the grounds are built-up. In February 1934, when the »red« workers fought against the Austro-fascists, Karl Marx Hof became the centre of worker resistance. The uprising collapsed after three days of shelling with heavy artillery by the government. Today, Karl Marx Hof is a historic monument. It had an overall renovation in the 1990s and many flats were joined together so that now there are 1,252. There are even tenants still living in Karl Marx Hof who moved in right after it was first completed.

✶✶ Karlsplatz

H 7

Location: 1st District
Bus: 4 A, 59 A

Underground: Karlsplatz (U1, U2, U4)
Tram: 1, 62

Although Karlsplatz is intersected by roads with heavy traffic and there is little that encourages pedestrians to tarry, there is one highlight: the Karlskirche which dominates the busy square is a masterpiece of Baroque by J. B. Fischer von Erlach and son and rises above all on the southern side.

The north side is lined by the Handelsakademie (business school), the Künstlerhaus and the Musikverein building, while on the south side stand the Karlskirche and the Technical University (erected 1816–1818 with a floor added later). The east side is taken up by the Wien Museum. Statues of Johannes Brahms (1908), the inventor of the ship screw Josef Ressel (1862) and the inventor of the sewing machine Josef Madersperger (1933) stand in the park on the southern end of Karlsplatz.
Karlsplatz is crossed by important tram and Underground lines of Vienna's inner city. The square was given a fundamental redesigning when the Underground was constructed. Sven Ingvar Andersson planned the square; the striking light railway (Stadtbahn) station building by Otto Wagner was also reconstructed.

! *Baedeker* TIP

Party on Karlsplatz

Obliquely opposite to the Secession on the Karlsplatz, where a yellow exhibition container regularly used to cause sensation, there now stands a stylish glass cube. It is called »Project space« and is a flexible and experimental branch of the Kunsthalle that has moved to the Museum Quarter. The programme includes lectures, live concerts, DJ line-ups and individual events, and the café with its large terrace has become a second home for Vienna's »in crowd«.

One of Wagner's 1901 pavilions, decorated expensively with marble and gold leaf, now serves as an entrance to the Underground station and also for minor temporary exhibitions of the Historical Museum; the other one is now a cafe, a popular meeting place during the summer months.

✱ ◄ Otto Wagner Pavilions

✱ ✱ Karlskirche (St Charles' Church)

The father and son Fischer von Erlach team designed Vienna's most outstanding Baroque ecclesiastical building, which was sponsored by Emperor Charles VI during the year of the plague, in 1713.
The church was dedicated to St Charles Borromeo in 1737, given over to the Knights of Malta in 1738, and declared an imperial prebend church in 1783. All crown lands were forced to help finance the building and even the city of Hamburg contributed to the total amount by means of a fine imposed for the wanton destruction of the Austrian embassy chapel in the Hanseatic city.

Opening hours:
Mon – Sat
9am – 12.30pm,
1pm – 6pm, Sun
noon – 5.45pm

The façade has a kind of Greek **temple portico** superimposed on it, whose form was influenced by Palladio. The relief on the pediment depicts the end of the plague – the devastating epidemic that had claimed more than 8,000 lives. The Latin inscription records the words of Emperor Charles VI, »I fulfil my vow in the presence of those who fear the Lord«. The two 33m/108 ft high **triumphal columns** were based on the Trajan column in Rome. An eagle and imperial crown as emblems of state are above the louvers, and spiralling bands in bas-relief depict scenes from the life of St Charles Borromeo. The building is crowned by a 72m/ 236 ft high dome. The portico is flanked by two bell towers inspired by Bernini und Maderna. An interesting modern synthesis of Classical architecture was created in the Karlskirche through the integration of Greek and Roman architectural forms, which nevertheless fulfilled the requirements for buildings to appear suitably imperial.

Exterior

> **!** *Baedeker* TIP
>
> **Baroque art up close**
> A glass panorama lift was installed in the course of the present renovation of the Baroque frescoes on the dome. The lift goes up to a 32m/105ft high terrace, from where there is a close up view of Johann Michael Rottmayr's magnificent pictures, as well as a fabulous panoramic view of Vienna.

Johann Michael Rottmayr's dome frescoes dominate the bright interior – an elongated ellipsoid with a high tambour, dome and lantern dating back to 1725 and 1730. They depict the glory of St Charles and the plea of deliverance from the plague that afflicted Milan in 1576. An angel on the left with a torch is setting fire to Luther's Bible that has fallen to the ground.

Interior

← *Greek, Roman, Baroque: Johann Bernhard Fischer von Erlach made use of many architectural styles to create the Karlskirche*

Karlskirche Plan

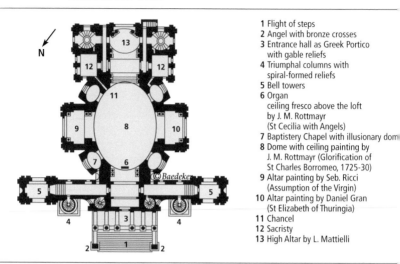

N

1 Flight of steps
2 Angel with bronze crosses
3 Entrance hall as Greek Portico
with gable reliefs
4 Triumphal columns with
spiral-formed reliefs
5 Bell towers
6 Organ
ceiling fresco above the loft
by J. M. Rottmayr
(St Cecilia with Angels)
7 Baptistery Chapel with illusionary dom
8 Dome with ceiling painting by
J. M. Rottmayr (Glorification of
St Charles Borromeo, 1725-30)
9 Altar painting by Seb. Ricci
(Assumption of the Virgin)
10 Altar painting by Daniel Gran
(St Elizabeth of Thuringia)
11 Chancel
12 Sacristy
13 High Altar by L. Mattielli

©Baedeker

Rottmayr is also responsible for the **frescoes above the organ loft** portraying St Cecilia with music-playing angels. St Charles Borromeo being taken up to heaven is the subject of the magnificent **high altar**. The sculptured decoration of clouds in the background as he floats upwards was based on a sketch by Johann Bernhard Fischer von Erlach, carried out by Camesina.

The altar paintings, *Jesus with the Roman Captain* and *The Healing of a Man Sick of the Palsy* were painted by Daniel Gran, *The Raising of the Youth of Nain* was done by Martin Altomonte, and the *Saint Luke* by van Schuppen. The painting of the *Assumption of the Virgin* on the main altar to the left was produced by Sebastiano Ricci, and the *St Elizabeth of Thuringia* opposite on the right is also by Gran.

✶ Wien Museum Karlsplatz

Opening hours:
Tue – Sun
9am – 6pm

The Historisches Museum (Museum of History) was founded in 1888 and first housed in the new Rathaus. Then it was moved to its present home on Karlsplatz designed by Oswald Haerdtl in 1959, where it is today called Wien Museum Karlsplatz. The vivid and clear exhibitions present historically significant personages and outstanding events, as well as everyday life in Vienna during various eras.

Ground floor | **The beginnings of the city's history** are documented by finds from the Stone, Bronze and Iron Ages, as well as from the Roman period and the time of the Great Migration. The most important items on display are a Sequani gravestone (2nd century AD), Roman ex-voto altars, reliefs and face urns from Vindobona, and a hoard of ancient coins. On display from the **Middle Ages** are historic views of the city and maps of its historic development, including the »Albertine Plan« from 1421/1422, held to be the oldest map of Vienna. There are fragments and valuable pieces of architecture from the Stephansdom that were removed during restoration work, including an early Gothic Anna Selbdritt (c1320), three over-sized princely couples (c1360/ 1365), Gothic glass windows from the Herzogskapelle and the remains of a carved wooden alter (14th century). Included in the collection of arms and armour taken from arsenals and armouries are the oldest Italian horse armour and Frederick III's funeral arms.

The exhibits displayed on the first floor cover the **Modern Age up to the early 19th century**. Weapons can be seen from the war-torn 16th century, gold-etched armour of the imperial princes, banner flags, orders, large-sized paintings of battles and battle reports from besieged Vienna. Impressive portraits, etchings, medallions, coats-of-arms and copperplate engravings provide a look at urban life during the 17th century from the Counter-Reformation to the Great War against the Turks. Wallenstein's game board, a memento of the Thirty Years' War, the so-called Turkish plunder captured during the **Turkish siege**, Turkish flags and Franz Geffels' painting, *Battle near Vienna* can all be seen. The Baroque to Classical era, and city history up to the start of the 19th century, are evoked by Deisenbach's panoramas of Vienna, guild chests, old house and tradesmen signs, paintings and engravings, including a picture of the Free Mason's lodge »Crowned Hope« with Schikaneder and Mozart, and a large model of the inner city from 1854.

First Floor

The second floor, dedicated to the 19th and 20th centuries, begins with the **Napoleonic era** and coins from the reign of Franz II. The gold and white empire style Pompeian Salon that the Geymüller banking family had furnished around 1800 in Palais Caprara gives an impression of the lifestyle of the nobility of the period. All of the Viennese Biedermeier painters, like Fendi, Danhauser, Reiter, Waldmüller and Amerling, are represented among the multitude of paintings here. Fashion and the fashionable are shown – including Klimt's fashion-conscious wife, Emilie Flöge – fine glass and porcelain, a survey of social games in Vienna during the Biedermeier period, Lanner's giraffe piano and the butterfly wings of the idolized dancer Fanny Elßler. Graphics and paintings, as well as the weapons of the National Guard, can be seen from the **time of the revolution**. Franz Grillparzer's flat was removed when the house in Spiegelgasse 2 was demolished in 1872, and faithfully reconstructed again in the museum. The Founder's era is documented in portraits, busts and inventions in craftwork. A look is given into the theatrical life of Raimund and Nestroy. The living room of the architect Loos, from Bösendorfer Straße 3 (1903), provides a striking example of Viennese

Second Floor

interior decorating at the beginning of the 20th century. Counted among the Art Nouveau works are pictures by Klimt and Schiele, and designs by Kolo Moser.

Moreover, works by Fritz Wotruba, Oskar Kokoschka and Albert Paris Gütersloh can be admired. Included among the additional picture material are portraits of important personages and illustrations of the municipal housing projects between the second world wars.

✳ Musikvereinsgebäude (Music Society Building)

The »Society of the Friends of Music«, founded in 1812 and known simply as the Musikverein (Karlsplatz 6), commissioned **Theophil Hansen**, who later built the Parliament, to design a concert hall in 1867. The terracotta statues on the sienna red neo-Renaissance building are for the most part by Franz Melnizki. Prominent musicians give guest performances in the Golden Hall and it is the home of the **Vienna Philharmonic**, founded in 1842, whose legendary New Year Concert is broadcast all over the world from here. Gustav Mahler and Hugo Wolf once taught here, and illustrious conductors like Furtwängler, Böhm, Karajan, Bernstein and Claudio Abbado have thrilled audiences here. The **Golden Hall**, decorated with 36 gold car-

 DID YOU KNOW ...?

■ ...that in addition to the world famous Gold Hall and the smaller halls named after Johannes Brahms and Gottfried von Einem, the Musikverein building has four new halls since 2004? They are all underground and enjoy outstanding modern technical facilities and excellent acoustics. The Glass, Metal, Wood and Stone Hall are used for concerts, as well as for receptions and conferences.

The Gold Hall is one of the world's best concert halls

yatids, is dominated by a magnificent coffered ceiling suspended from a steel construction. The hall seats an audience of 2,000 and provides space for 400 musicians and thanks to excellent resonance, it enjoys one of the world's best acoustics among concert halls. The organ installed in 1968 has 100 registers and 7,500 pipes. The Friends of Music also possess a comprehensive collection relating to the history of music and an outstanding archive of musical scores with over 300,000 compositions.

Künstlerhaus (House of Artists)

The stately Künstlerhaus (no. 5) on the north side of Karlsplatz is the venue of important exhibitions, cultural events and popular art festivals, also including the famous »Gschnasfeste« during carnival. This **neo-Renaissance building** was constructed by **August Weber** from 1865 to 1868, for the Vienna Artists Society founded in 1861. Later, a side wing was added that is now used by the Theatre in the Künstlerhaus and as a cinema. The marble statues standing by the entrance represent Diego Velásquez, Raphael Santi, Leonardo da Vinci, Michelangelo Buonarotti, Albrecht Dürer, Titian, Bramante and Peter Paul Rubens.

Kärntner Strasse

Location: 1st District
Tram: 1, 2, 3, 62

Underground: Stephansplatz (U1, U3), Karlsplatz (U1, U2, U4)

Vienna's main artery and most important shopping mile leads from Stephansplatz to the Staatsoper on the Ring and ends at Karlsplatz.

It has been a pedestrian zone to Walfischgasse since 1974, with linden trees, cafés, shops rich in tradition, elegant boutiques and busy shopping arcades. Below the intersection with Kärntner Ring is the Opernpassage, Vienna's first subterranean shopping zone opened in 1955. In contrast with the surrounding side streets, Kärtner Strasse, first documented in 1257 as »Strata Carinthianorum« and widened in the early 1970s, has very few historic buildings. Most of these date from the 18th century, including nos. 4, 6 and 17 with interesting façades. The oldest building is the **Palais Esterházy** (no. 41) dating from 1698, which is home to Vienna's gaming casino and the Adlmüller fashion house. Famous designers like Jil Sander, Dior and Pierre Cardin are represented in Kärntner Strasse; everything can be found here, from local folk costumes to fabulous evening wear. The major chains with young fashion are also to be found on Vienna's elegant shopping boulevard. The Lobmeyr china and glass house

! *Baedeker* TIP

Fine Things for the Home

Quality products are offered in the Österreichische Werkstätten (Austrian Arts and Handicraft, Kärntner Str. 6): from beautiful Art Déco jewellery to exquisite silk accessories and high quality items for the home made of pewter.

(no. 26), founded in 1823, has a glass museum worth a visit on the upper floor. Only the **Maltese church** (no. 37), built in the 14th century and consecrated to St John the Baptist, still exhibits a few architectural elements dating back to 1265. The Classical façade was completed in 1808. Inside there are numerous coats of arms of the Knights of Malta to be seen, as well as the 1806 stucco monument flanked by Turkish figures in memory of Grand Master Jean de la Valette, the defender of Malta against the Turks.

Kirche am Steinhof (Church am Steinhof)

A 6

Location: 14, Baumgartner Höhe 1   **Bus :** 47 A, 48 A

Otto Wagner's church building is considered one of the major works of Viennese Art Nouveau. It was built between 1904 and 1907 on the grounds of the former Lower Austrian State Psychiatric Institute –

Emphasis on the religious was in keeping with the times:
Otto Wagner's slim angels encourage contemplation

today the Vienna Psychiatric Hospital. Built on the highest point on the grounds, the church and its dome flanked by two towers can be seen for some distance; inside the institute's church, however, there is only flat vaulting. The church interior is simple and bright; the floors and walls are tiled in keeping with Wagner's goal of »making hygiene real« using light and air, and keeping things functional, even in a church. The glass mosaics in the windows were designed by Ko-lo Moser.

Opening hours: Tours: reservations required, tel 91 06 01 10 07.

★ Kunst Haus Wien

J 6

Location: 3, Weißgerberstraße 13   **Tram:** N, O
Internet:: www.kunsthauswien.com

»Kunst Haus Wien. Museum Hundertwasser« opened its doors in 1991, a double monument to the architect and painter **Friedensreich Hundertwasser**. The museum building itself is as much a display of the rebel architect's multi-faceted oeuvre as the exhibition inside. The house, re-designed by Hundertwasser and Peter Pelikan in the style of the nearby Hundertwasserhaus (▶ see below), was used by the **Thonet** brothers as a workshop for their world famous bow wood furniture from 1892, and there are over 100 different Thonet chairs to try out in the **museum café**, which also has a lovely garden. Spread over two floors inside Kunst Haus Wien, there are around 300 paintings, graphics, tapestries and models of Hundertwasser's environmentally friendly architectural projects, both completed and planned, and two further floors are reserved for changing exhibitions of works by internationally renowned artists. This fascinating building of one architect's creative dream – rich in colours and form – is decorated by a bright ceramic façade, whose lively chess board patterning contains various window designs. Inside, an uneven floor intended to mimic nature and to put a spring in the visitor's step, leads the way to a magical museum journey into the land of creativity.

Opening hours: daily 10am – 7pm; tours: Sun noon, 3pm and by appointment, tel. 7 12 04 95

Hundertwasserhaus

Not far from Kunst Haus Wien, the painter Friedensreich Hundertwasseralready gave full reign to his tremendous imagination when he designed the »nature and people-friendly« house on the corner of Löwengasse and Kegelstrasse in 1977. The city administration had it built from 1983 to 1985, as part of its social housing programme, though the rents are not exactly charitable. Artists and intellectuals mostly live in the small flats, which in turn pleased Hundertwasser, who claimed that if »privileged people move in here, then it is proof to me that the house is good«. In consideration of the residents, the colourful apartments can only be seen from the outside. In keeping with the artist's **economic principles**, only brick and wood were used in the complex, no synthetic materials. There are 50 one and two-floor flats of various sizes, with or without a garden, either flooded with sunlight or a bit shadier, with views of the street or of the courtyard. A terrace café, a doctor's surgery and a health food store were also integrated. In general, Hundertwasser followed his principle of »tolerance of irregularity«, so that all corners are rounded and the windows are all different sizes, widths and heights. The front and back façades of the complex are fashioned like those of the old patrician buildings and the Venetian palaces on the Grand Canal. In addition, a section of the old house was recreated in the façade so that the »spirits of the old house can resettle into the new one« and place it under their protection. Two golden **onion towers** decorate the building which, according to Hundertwasser, »raises the inhabitant to the status of a king«. Some of the elements that give life to the building are the colourful, sometimes crooked pillars, the fountain, and the figural decoration based on the old original.

? DID YOU KNOW ...?

■ ...that right next to the colourfully fanciful Hunderwasserhaus there is an icon of 1920's functionalistic architecture? The Wittgensteinhaus, an avant-garde building of perfect simplicity, was designed with the help of the famous philosopher of the same name (entrance Parkgasse).

Village Gallery
🕐
Opening hours:
daily 9am – 7pm

Opposite the Hundertwasserhaus, Peter Pelikan and Hundertwasser converted a turn-of-the-century house in Kegelgasse with the imaginative design typical of Hundertwasser into an irregularly-shaped shopping arcade in 1990 – 1991.

★★ Kunsthistorisches Museum

(Art History Museum)

G 6/7

Location: 1, Maria-Theresien-Platz	**Underground:** Volkstheater (U2, U3)
Tram: 1, 2, 3	**Bus:** 57 A
Internet: www.khm.at	

The Kunsthistorisches Museum contains one of the most significant art collections in the world. The centuries of collecting by the Habsburg dynasty formed the basic stock for this museum in neo-Renaissance style, and the picture gallery on the first floor is particularly noteworthy.

Gottfried Semper erected the building during the reign of Emperor Franz Josef I between 1871 and 1891. An imperial forum was planned in the course of developing the Ringstrasse together with

Maria Theresa casts her eye over the Kunsthistorisches Museum by Gottfried Semper

the Naturhistorisches Museum on the opposite side of Maria Theresien Platz and the Neue Burg, but it was never completed. Despite the state having recently withstood a bankruptcy, planners were not forced to economize, and were able to use expensive materials and entrust prominent artists with the interior decoration. Thus the vestibule is dominated by **Canova's** marble group *Theseus fights the Centaurs*, while the ceiling painting *Apotheosis of the Arts* in the colourfully marbled stairway was created by the Hungarian **Michael Munkácsy**, and the neighbouring lunette pictures and spandrel allegories were produced by **Hans Makart**, the brothers **Ernst** and **Gustav Klimt**, as well as **Franz Matsch**.

The works of art exhibited in the Kunsthistorisches Museum and its branches span art history ranging from the ancient Egyptians to Greco-Roman Antiquity, and from the Middle Ages to the particularly diversely represented Renaissance and Baroque periods.

The displays in the Kunsthistorisches Museum are divided into eight collections. The main building holds the Egyptian and Near East

⏲ Opening hours:
Tue, Wed, Fri – Sun
10am – 6pm, Thu
10am – 9pm

Collections

Collection, the Collection of Greek and Roman Antiquities, the Collection of Sculpture and Decorative Arts, the Painting Gallery and the Coin Cabinet. Located elsewhere are the Treasury in the Hofburg, the Collection of Ancient Musical Instruments, the Ephesus Museum and the Collection of Arms and Armour in the Neue Burg (all ▶Hofburg), the exhibition rooms in Palais Harrach (▶Freyung) and the Wagenburg in ▶ Schönbrunn Palace. There are 51 rooms alone in the main building on Maria Theresien Platz, whose core is the Painting Gallery.

The Egyptian and Near East Collection

Room I Room I is dedicated to the Egyptian death cult. Among the things to see are sarcophagi and coffins (1100 – 100 BC), mummies, viscera vessels (canopes), ushebti (workers for the next life) and other burial inventory.

Room II Vessels and jewellery from Egypt's prehistoric and early periods (5000 – 2635 BC) are displayed. Moreover, the foreign rule of the Hyksos in Egypt (1650 – 1550 B.C) is illustrated.

Rooms III, IV The animal cult is presented in room III by, for example, sacred animal mummie. In the following room is the development of ancient Egyptian writing.

Room VI The chamber of Prince Kaninisut of Gizeh (5th Dynasty, c2400 BC) dates back to the Old Kingdom.

Room VII Outstanding among the sculpture works in room VII are the sitting figures of King **Horemheb** and the falcon-headed **Horus** (18th Dynasty, c1320 BC), wearing the double crowns of Upper and Lower Egypt; the upper part of the statue of King Thuthmosis III (18th Dynasty, c1460 BC) with a head cloth, an Egyptian cobra and a wide, ritual beard; a large commemorative stela from Elephantine of Amenhotep II (1439 – 1413 BC) with an inscription extolling the war and a relief reproduction of the king being led by the goddess of the cataract, Ankhet, to the right, and the state god Amun, the Lord of Elephantine, to the left; the head of a sphinx of **Sesostris III** (12th Dynasty, c1850 BC) with realistic, serious facial expressions as part of the figure of a sphinx. An official of the granary, **Si-ese** (19th Dynasty, c1220 BC), appears in formal costume, carrying a sacred staff

✔ DON'T MISS

- *The Peasant Dance* and *The Peasant Wedding*: Breughel's best
- Giuseppe Arcimboldo: Mannerist symbolic work *Summer*
- Parmigianino: Self-portrait in a convex mirror
- Raphael: *Madonna in Green* – pure poetry
- Titian: *Madonna of the Cherries* – grandiose Renaissance

Stone witnesses to the past

and crowned by the jackal head of the god Wepwawet. Among the rarities is also a **hippopotamus** (11th/12th Dynasties, 2000 BC), a burial object made of glazed faïence painted with swamp thickets meant to recall that hunting hippopotami was a privilege bestowed on private citizens by the king.

Particularly worth noting among the exhibits on the Old Kingdom (2635 – 2155 BC) is the bust of a young man finely worked in limestone (c2550 BC), the so-called reserve head, assumed to be the seat of the soul of the dead when the mummification technology had not yet been perfected.

Room VIII

Collection of Greek and Roman Antiquities

Standing out among the Bronze Age finds from Cyprus is a handmade lidded box with simple scratched patterns (2000 – 1800 BC). Also to be seen are tomb reliefs from Palmyra and a highly stylized, archaic votive statue of a priest (c500 BC)

Room IX

The Greco-Roman sculpture collection presents the bronze figure of the youth from Magdalensberg, a Renaissance copy of the missing Roman original of the 1st century BC; also a small, **marble head of the goddess of the hunt, Artemis** (2nd century BC), the marble portrait bust of the philosopher Aristotle, the Roman Mithraic relief

Rooms X – XII

(2nd half of the 2nd century AD) with the Persian god of light killing the bull; furthermore, a multi-figured hunting sarcophagus (2nd half of the 3rd century AD) and a mosaic with Theseus and the Minotaur in the labyrinth (4th century AD).

The following pieces among the small Greek bronzes are worth seeing: the geometric votive horse, the archaic laughing youth, the powerfully modelled forepart of a centaur (170 – 160 BC) and the face of Jupiter framed in curls.

Room XIII A figured urn, an engraved bronze mirror and the clay statute of Athena of Rocca d'Aspromonte represent Etruscan culture (5th – 2nd century BC).

Room XIV The small **Ptolemaic Royal Couple Cameo** (278 – 269 BC), cut in eleven layers of onyx with the profile portraits of Ptolemy II Philadelphos wearing an Attican helmet and his sister and wife Arsinoë II, under a crown-like headdress, is a masterpiece.

Room XV The Roman emperors from Augustus to Trajan and Commodus are presented in the form of portrait busts, while fine glasswork, pottery and a silver cup demonstrate Roman tableware. The cameo collection is world-class, from the simple eagle and lion cameos of onyx to the fascinating **Gemma Augustea** (after AD 10) with Augustus posed and dressed as Jupiter in the company of Roma, the patron of the city. Next to Roma stands Augustus' great nephew, Germanicus, and Tiberius as crown prince descending from a war chariot. The lower scene shows Roman soldiers erecting a victory monument commemorating the Roman suppression of the revolt of the Dalmatians (AD 10). The five-layered onyx cut of the **Gemma Claudia** (c AD 49) is unique. Out of two cornucopias sprout the profile portraits of Emperor Claudius and his spouse Agrippina the Younger and, opposite them, Germanicus and his wife Agrippina the Elder, the emperor's parents-in-law.

Gemma Augustea

Room XVII Alongside textiles from Egypt and early Christian handicraft, there are the priceless 23 gold vessels comprising the late Avar-Hungarian-Bulgarian hoard of gold from Nagyszentmiklós.

Kunstkammer
(Collection of Sculpture and Decorative Arts)

Room XXXVI Among the precious objects of Romanesque metal art are the partially gilt silver **communion chalice** (c1160/1170) with Old and New Testament scenes executed in niello technique from Wilten Abbey, the gilt bronze Griffin Ewer (Aquamanile) (1st third of the 12th century) and the bronze Püsterich »fire-blower« (1st half of the 12th century). Also noteworthy are the jug and goblet of rock crystal (13th/14th century), the Carolingian ivory tablet with St Gregory

Museum of Art History *Plan*

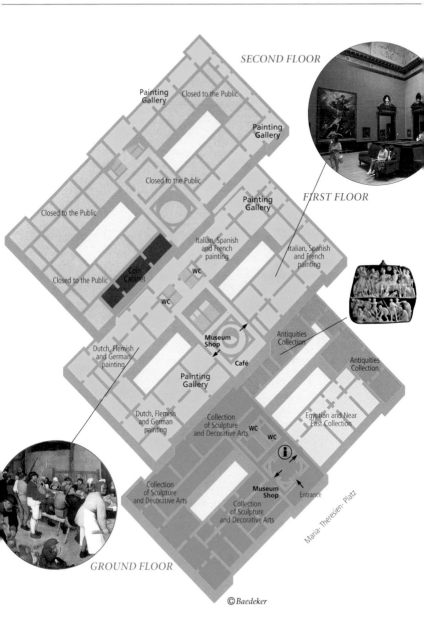

SECOND FLOOR

Painting Gallery

Closed to the Public

Painting Gallery

FIRST FLOOR

Closed to the Public

Closed to the Public

Closed to the Public

Italian, Spanish and French painting

Italian, Spanish and French painting

Coin Cabinet

WC

WC

Closed to the Public

Museum Shop

Café

Antiquities Collection

Antiquities Collection

Dutch, Flemish and German painting

Painting Gallery

Dutch, Flemish and German painting

Collection of Sculpture and Decorative Arts

WC

WC

Egyptian and Near East Collection

Collection of Sculpture and Decorative Arts

Museum Shop

Entrance

Collection of Sculpture and Decorative Arts

Maria-Theresien-Platz

GROUND FLOOR

© Baedeker

with the Scribes (c870), as well as the late Gothic silver gilt **Adders' (dragon) Tongues** (c1450), a table decoration with fossilized sharks' teeth.

Rooms XXXVII, XXXV Interesting in the collection of automatons, scientific instruments and clocks from the 16th and 17th centuries are a rock crystal clock by Jost Burgi, the **crystal globe** by Georg Roll from 1584 for Emperor Rudolf II and a mechanical doll playing the cittern from Spain.

Room XXXIV Masterpieces of German metal sculpture of the Late Middle Ages and Renaissance are the silver gilt **lidded goblet** from Nuremberg, the so-called Dürer goblet and the so-called Maximilian goblet (c1500–1510). Worth noting in addition are the silverpoint drawings in the **Viennese Sample book** (1st quarter of the 15th century) as model for the workshops and wandering artists, as well as the sets of coloured game cards »Ambraser Hofjagdspiel« (Ambras court hunting game) and »Hofämterspiel« (court office game).

Also outstanding is the **Krumau Madonna** (1390–1400), fashioned in »soft style« in sandstone and originally painted in two colours: blue and white. This is one of the delicate »beautiful Madonnas«, figures of Mary that are distinguished by a special grace and loveliness in their expression. The fullness of the drapery with its deep hollows is typical of the soft style. This Madonna comes from southern Bohemia, but in the style and artistic technique of the court art of Prague. The »Virgin and Child« (c1495) is an early work by **Tilman Riemenschneider**. He gave Mary's face a middle class character. The nude »Adam« dating from 1510 was conceived as part of a group; his pose is clearly orientated towards Eve as a complimentary figure. On the whole, the figure remains bound to the Late Gothic canon of figures.

> **!**
> ## Baedeker TIP
>
> ### Relaxing between Masterpieces
> Take a break for coffee and cake in the Kunsthistorisches Museum's magnificent and stylish Cupola Hall – a setting to match the glorious masterpieces.

Room XXXII Standing out among the numerous works of the Florentine early Renaissance are the portrait busts from Donatello's and della Robbia's workshops. The »Laughing Boy« by **Desiderio da Settignano** expresses his childlike nature both spontaneously and genuinely and was probably conceived to be displayed in the private chapel of the person who commissioned it. This marble bust, dated around 1464, was more than likely the last work by Settignano, who died young.

Francesco Laurana is also considered to be one of the great Renaissance artists. During his stay in Naples, he created the bust of a young woman that probably portrayed Laura, the mistress of Petrarch. The marble bust's lifelike quality was achieved by an application of coloured wax.

The busts, plaques and small bronzes of northern Italy's Renaissance art are best represented by **Antico** with *Venus felix*, a free variation of the antique marble sculpture. Antico frequently worked in Rome as a restorer of antique figures. **Moderno** is represented with *Sacra Conversazione* and Riccio with the *Resting Woodcutter* in painted terra cotta, which is fascinating in its extreme naturalism.

Room XXX

The elegant Italian vessels of rock crystal, lapis lazuli, jasper and prase, the preciously set cameos of the 16th century and the elaborate Spanish gold work are impressive.

Room XXIX

German Renaissance sculpture is well represented with figures by Conrad Meit, Christoph Weiditz, Peter Flötner and Hans Daucher. The priceless **Tricktrack Board** (1537) of oak, walnut, briarwood, mahogany and rosewood was fashioned to play backgammon by Hans Kels the Elder. The exterior is dedicated to the glorification of Charles V and Ferdinand I; the latter, probably the owner of the game board, is depicted mounted on a horse in the middle.

Room XXVIII

Benvenuto Cellini's golden saltcellar (1540–1543), called the »Saliera«, the highlight of the Kunstkammer, was stolen in 2003 in Austria's most sensational art heist and recovered almost undamaged in 2006. The Italian bronze figures by Giambologna are also noteworthy: the arresting dual-figured Raptus Group (c1580) in the form of a figura serpentinata was intended to show figures in extreme motion, and shows that for this artist, drama was more important than subject.

Room XXVII

French Mannerism of the 16th century is well represented by an excellent gold enamelled **onyx jug** with precious stones by Richard Toutain the Younger, as well as a copper bowl, enamelled on both sides, with the triumphal procession of Diana by Pierre Reymond.

Room XXVI

Archduke Ferdinand II's Mannerist art and curiosity cabinet dating from the 16th century is comprised of rare glass jewellery from Venice, humorous vessels of Tyrolean Hafner pottery and little coloured wax pictures. Elaborately worked intaglio vessels, Florentine mosaics of semi-precious stones (pietra dura) and magnificent sets of gold and silver, including the **Sumptuous Vessel** (c1605) by Christoph Jamnitzer are all from the art collection of Rudolf II.

Rooms XXIV, XXV

High Baroque and Rococo art is represented by small sculptures, ivory statuettes, bronze busts and figural reliefs, as well as wood and ivory works by the Austrians Matthias Steinle, Ignaz Elhafen, Jacob Auer, Johann Ignaz Bendl and Ch. Maucher; also by a marble bust of Marie Antoinette by Jean-Baptiste Lemoyne, a gold **breakfast service** once belonging to Maria Theresa and by the gold toilette set of her husband, Emperor Franz I.

Rooms XXII, XX

Room XIX   The 17th century carvings in rock crystal and smoky quartz are fascinating, as is the **rock crystal pyramid** carved from a single stone by Dionisio Miseroni for Emperor Ferdinand III, the only work that the artist signed and dated.

Picture Gallery

Cabinets 1 – 4   Italian Renaissance painting is outstandingly represented by **Andrea Mantegna's** *St Sebastian* (1457 – 1459) in a realistic portrayal of space and figures. **Antonello da Messina** used the new Franco-Flemish technique of oil painting, unknown in Italy until then, to model three-dimensional forms and give subtle colouring to materials and objects in his *Madonna with the Saints Nicholas of Bari, Anastasia, Ursula and Dominic* (1475 – 1476).

Raphael's triangular composition of the *Madonna in the Meadow* (1505 to 1506), with John and Christ as children in a tranquil landscape, represents the painting of the high Renaissance, as does **Giorgione** with his *Three Philosophers* (c1508 – 1509) in an atmospheric space of colour and light. **Lorenzo Lotto** endows his *Portrait of a Youth Against a White Curtain* (c1508) with an air of mystery, with the oil lamp visible on the side behind the curtain, whereas **Correggio's** *The Rape of Ganymed* (c1530) is a brilliant play of motion and already anticipates Baroque.

A stylish setting to enjoy paintings

The observer can trace the development of **Titian's** painting from the powerful harmony of colours in his early work, the *Gypsy Madonna* (c1510), to the reality intensifying light-dark contrasts in the semi-nude *Girl in a Fur* (1535) to the choreographed, multi-figured group viewed as if on a stage in the Ecce-Homo depiction (1543), which combines events from Roman times with contemporary references indicated by a large shield with the Habsburg double eagle. The use of colour and form in the late work, *Nymph and Shepard* (1570 – 1575), only achieves a fleeting sensation by comparison. **Veronese**, actually Paolo Caliari, offers large format, for the most part solemnly staged versions of *The Anointing of David* (c1555 – 1560) and the *Raising of the Youth of Nain* (c1565 – 1570). In comparison, *Lucretia* (c1580 – 1583) and *Judith with the Head of Holofernes* (1583 – 1585) are painted more intimately and are sensually decorative. **Tintoretto**, actually Jacopo Robusti, produced impressive official three-quarter profile portraits that enhanced the dignity and splendour of his subjects such as city councillor *Lorenzo Soranzo* (1553) or Admiral *Sebastiano Vernier* (1572), under whose supreme command the Turkish maritime supremacy of the Mediterranean was broken in 1571 at Lepanto. Extreme proximity and distance in landscape permeate each other in the painting *Susanna at her Bath* (c1555), whose sensuous beauty is lustfully eyed by two ugly men.

Room I – III

Michelangelo Merisi da **Caravaggio** launched the Baroque period. The strong physical presence is achieved through bright and dark contrasts shown in his *Madonna of the Rosary* (1606 – 1607), in which the enthroned Mother of God instructs St Dominic to distribute rosaries to the people thronging around him. The Bolognese **Il Guercino** stages the parable of the *Return of the Prodigal Son* (c1619) in an ever-changing play of light and shadow with the dark coloured figures overlapping each other in their movements. **Guido Renis'** *St Jerome* (c1635) is a marked diagonal composition set in subtle colouring. In a dramatic move, **Luca Giordano** has *St Michael* hurling the rebellious angels into the depths (c1655). **Francesco Solimena** painted the *Descent from the Cross* (1730 to 1731) as a triangular composition full of figures in a visionary atmosphere bathed in light. **Bernardo Bellotto** devoted himself to landscapes done as vedute with a view of the city exact in its topographic detail. *View of Vienna from the Belvedere* and *Freyung in Vienna, View of the South-east* (both 1758 – 1761) are excellent examples.

Rooms V – VII

The child portraits of *Margarita Theresa* in a pink dress and in a blue dress, and of *Philipp Prosper* in matchlessly appealing colours and a relaxed style of painting are among the outstanding achievements of the Spanish court painter **Velázquez** (1599 – 1660).

Cabinet 10

Early Dutch painting was already marked by unforgiving realism in the 15th century, as seen in the traces of age in the portrait of

Cabinet 14

In the midst of things: this painting earned the artist the name Peasant Breughel

Cardinal *Nicolo Albergati* (c1435) by **Jan van Eyck** and the body shaken by pain at the foot of the cross (Crucifixion triptych, c1440) by **Rogier van der Weyden**, and the faces distorted by hate in the mob shown in *Christ Carrying the Cross* (1480 to 1490) by **Hieronymus Bosch**.

The solemn and contemplative staging of the Madonna with the donors in the presence of John the Baptist and John the Evangelist in **Hans Memling's** *Triptych of John* (c1490–1494) is continued in the architectural and landscape background of the *Winged Altar* (c1530) by **Joos van Cleve** with the Holy Family and St George and St Catherine recommending the sponsor to the picture of the Mother of God.

Room X The world's largest collection of paintings by **Pieter Breughel the Elder** (c1525–1569) includes the multi-figured *Peasant Wedding*, as well as the cheerful *Peasant Dance* and the equally enigmatic as entertaining *Fight Between Carnival and Lent*. The *Hunters in the Snow* with great visual depth and an icy atmosphere is a landscape similarly impressive as the *Gloomy Day* with typical peasant activities like gathering wood and cutting willow rods. The *Tower of Babel*, in contrast, becomes a symbol of the failure of rational thought because Breughel puts the tower into the painting as an inconsistent, unstable construction.

Cabinets 16–19 The **Albrecht Dürer** collection includes the charming *Portrait of a Young Woman* (1505), the shifty face of *Johann Kleberger* (1526), the portrait of *Emperor Maximilian* (1519) with a pomegranate as a symbol of power and wealth, the powerful *Virgin and Child with Half a Pear* and the dramatic *Martyrdom of the 10,000* (1508). The highlight of the collection is the *Adoration of the Trinity* dated 1511. The picture was commissioned by the Nuremburg patrician Landauer for the Zwölfbrüderhaus, an asylum for tradesmen, and is based on St Augustine's concept of a City of God following Judgement Day when the earthly community of Christians with popes, emperors and the donors of the altar gather together to worship the Holy Trinity together with the heavenly hosts led by Mary and John the Baptist, while Dürer depicts himself on bare earth in the sunriseof a new era. The *Stag Hunt of the Elector Frederick the Wise* (1529) by **Lucas Cranach the Elder** is a picture recalling a hunt experienced by Frederick the Wise of Saxony together with Emperor Maximilian I, whereas *Judith with the Head of Holofernes* (c1530) is the portrait of a noble lady of the Saxon court combined with the Old Testament heroine. The paintings by Bartholomeus Spranger – *Minerva Victorious over Ignorance* (c1591), full of movement and figures – and the profile busts by **Giuseppe Arcimboldo** of symbolic objects used to render elements like *Fire* (1566) or seasons were influenced by Mannerism.

Noble attitude, colour glaze and empathy are typical of the portraits by **Anthonis van Dyck** (1599 – 1641) as seen in the young military commander in parade armour, Prince Rupert, Count Palatinate, and the English court musician, Nicholas Lanier. Van Dyck painted *Samson and Delilah* showing Samson's betrayal by his lover Delilah full of both drama and melancholy.

Rooms XII – XIV

The collection of paintings by **Peter Paul Rubens** is of the highest rank. Among the religious paintings are *The Ascension of Mary* (1611 – 1614) in a geometric composition of circles and triangles and the *Mourning of Christ* (1614) combining idealism and illusion in tangible reality. The *Ildefonso Altar* (1630 – 1632) for the brotherhood of the same name in Brussels, is a masterpiece in which the atmospheric colour shifts from contemplative stillness to frenetic visionary drama. The *Festival of Venus* (c1636 – 1637) presents the omnipotence of love in a turbulent, orgiastic play of figures before a landscape backdrop imitating classical forms, whereas the *Stormy Landscape with Philemon und Baucis* (1620 – 1625) takes the elementary natural catastrophe as its subject. Ruben's self-portrait (1638 – 1640) shows him in a proud pose and noble dress, while his wife Helene Fourment reveals erotic temptation in *The Fur* (1635 – 1640).

The art of portrait painting flourished in 17th century Dutch painting with enigmatic self-portraits by **Rembrandt** that probed his state of being at the time, and realistic likenesses by **Frans Hals**, who captured his fellow townsmen in fleeting situations with casual brush strokes. The figure painter **Jan Vermeer** created for the Delft painters guild a colouristic masterpiece in *The Art of Painting* (also: The Ar-

Room XV, Cabinets 21 – 24

tist's Studio, 1654–1666) with dot-like patches of luminous light and colour. It is an ambiguous allegory in which Clio, the muse of history, inspires the painter and the fame of Dutch painting is immortalized through the large map of the historical Seventeen United Provinces of the Netherlands.

Coin Cabinet

Room I The development of monetary systems from primitive money to modern forms of cashless transaction is documented, including primitive money from Asia, Africa and America, stone money from Yap Island (Micronesia), money in the form of bars and rings, minted currencies and rare old issues of paper money.

The regent points the way: Maria Theresa and her ministers

Particularly worth noting is the presentation of the history of medallions from Roman times to the present (room II).

Medals, badges of honour, and contemporary medallion art are shown in room III.

✷ Maria Theresien Platz

One of Vienna's most impressive monuments is the one dedicated to Maria Theresa. The imposing figure of the empress dominates the square named after her. The square itself is laid out as a formal Baroque garden and is flanked by the Kunsthistorisches Museum and the Naturhistorisches Museum. Franz Joseph I commissioned **Kaspar von Zumbusch** with the monument, which was unveiled in 1887. It shows the monarch sitting on her throne, holding the Pragmatic Sanction of 1713 in her left hand. She is surrounded by the most important men of her time. The standing figures are State Chancellor Kaunitz, Prince Liechtenstein, Count Haugwitz and her physician, van Swieten; on horseback are Generals Daun, Laudon, Traun and Khevenhüller. The high reliefs in the lunettes depict illustrious personages of politics, business and art, including Haydn, Gluck and Mozart. Museumsplatz, on the southwest side of the park, leads into the ▶Museum Quarter.

Leopoldstadt

Location: 2nd District **Underground:** U1, U2 (Praterstern)

Leopoldstadt was once the centre of Jewish life in Vienna (►Bae-deker Special p.248) and, in the first half of the 19th century, it was also at the heart of entertainment for the city, containing two of the largest and most elegant dance halls.

But the economic significance of the district lay in trade and finance – Vienna's first savings and loan bank opened here in 1819. Leopoldstadt (2nd District) forms together with Brigittenau (20th District) an island running in a north-western to south-easterly direction between the Danube Canal and the river. This was where the terminal stations were, the gateways for most of the immigrants streaming out of Bohemia, Moravia and East Galicia from the 19th century onwards. Now almost 60% of the old suburb has been taken over by **green spaces and lakes**. With the harbour, exhibition grounds, sports centre and ► Prater established here, Leopoldstadt has assumed a central function once again, and today houses one of the most diverse communities among Viennese districts.

The Vienna Criminal Museum presents the history of crime in Vienna from the late Middle Ages to the present in 20 rooms in one of the oldest buildings in Leopoldstadt : the »Seifensiederhaus« (Soap Boiler's House - first recorded mention in 1685) located at Grosse Sperlgasse 24. The exhibits cover the judicial system, criminal law reforms and public executions, the assassination attempt on Emperor Franz Joseph in 1853, spectacular police operations and infamous criminals such as the poisoner Hofrichter and the poetic killer of servant girls, Hugo Schenk. Gruesome curiosities include a wheel on which the offender's bones were broken before they were executed, pieces of equipment from a 19th century sado-masochist salon, and items from a secret brothel at the turn of the 20th century.

Criminal Museum
🕐
Opening hours:
Tue – Sun
10am – 5pm
www.kriminal
museum.at

Liechtenstein Museum

Location: 9, Fürstengasse 1 **Underground:** U4 (Rossauer Lände)
Tram: 3 (Bauernfeldplatz) **Bus :** 40 A (Bauernfeldplatz)
Internet: www.liechtensteinmuseum.at

The Liechtenstein Museum presents diverse facets of early 18th century art in »A World of Baroque Pleasures«.

Magnificent ceiling fresco by Andrea Pozzo in the Hercules Hall

🕐 Opening hours:
Fri – Tue
10am – 5pm

The Liechtenstein garden palace was erected in the Viennese district of Rossau during the reign of Prince Johann Adam Andreas I of Liechtenstein (1657 – 1712). With his castles and palaces in Moravia and Vienna, he was one of the greatest builders of his day. He first entrusted **Johann Bernhard Fischer von Erlach** with the design of the Garden Palace, then **Domenico Egidio Rossi**, who had been trained in Bologna. Beginning in 1692, Rossi's design was developed further by**Domenico Martinelli**, an architect from Lucca, who finalized the prince's vision of a mighty Roman palace. The Bolognese artist Marcantonio Franceschini, was responsible for the paintings in the palace. The stucco work throughout the entire garden palace was done by Santino Bussi and is a rare example of Baroque stucco decor in Vienna, which remained historically unaltered in the late 19th century. **Johann Michael Rottmayr** was charged in 1705 with painting the fresco cycles in the Sala Terrena and in the two stairways. The centrepiece of the decorations was the monumental ceiling fresco in the Hercules Hall created in 1704 by the grand master of the Roman Baroque, **Andrea Pozzo**.

Another major object of the prince's creative interest was the **garden**. The original Baroque gardens were the most important example of Baroque horticultural art in Vienna alongside the Belvedere Palace garden. With the sculptures by Giovanni Giuliani and its diverse array of ornamental flowerbeds, it formed a cosmos in itself. In the 18th century, the gardens were redesigned into an extensive English landscape garden. Until the end of the 1990s, the collection of Modern Art of the Ludwig Trust Vienna was on loan in the Garden Palace; it has now found a permanent home in the Museum Quarter (► Museum Quarter). Subsequently, the prince's descendants paid 20 million Euros from their own funds to have the whole complex thoroughly renovated.

The paintings, statues, furniture and other works of art that had once graced palaces in Vienna and today's Czech Republic are now reunited. Only about 15% of the collected pieces that were evacuated to the principality of Vaduz in 1938 are on display – including large numbers of paintings by Peter Paul Rubens, Raphael, van Dyck, Hals and Rembrandt, as well as sculptures by Andrea Mantegna and Adrian de Fries. The **library**, a magnificent example of neo-Classical library architecture holding 100,000 volumes, is open to the public for the first time. The large garden has been for the most part returned to its original Baroque state.

✔ DON'T MISS

- The Sala Terrena with the Rottmayr frescoes
- The Hercules Hall with the ceiling fresco by Andrea Pozzo
- The Classical library
- The colossal painting of the Decius Mus Cycle by Peter Paul Rubens
- The Garden where concerts and matinees are often held
- And finally: culinary delights in Rubens' Brasserie and in the Rubens' Palais restaurant.

Mecharistenkloster

(The Mechitharist Congregation Monastery)

F/G 6

Location: 7, Mechitharistengasse 4
Bus: 48 A

Underground: Volkstheater (U 2, U 3)

Hidden behind the nondescript monastery walls of the Mechitharists between the Neustiftgasse und Lerchenfelder Strasse lie precious treasures of Armenian art and culture.

Mechithar founded this Armenian order in 1701, in Constantinople; it was soon confirmed by Pope Clement XI and adopted the vows of St Benedict – it therefore became known as the »Armenian Order of St Benedict«. Driven out of Trieste by the Napoleonic wars, a group of brothers of the order came to Vienna in 1810, where they were granted asylum by Emperor Franz I and given a deserted monastery on the street that was subsequently named after them: the Mechi-

🕐
Opening hours:
by appointment, tel.
523 64 17

MORE BAD THAN GOOD – JEWISH LIFE IN VIENNA

Throughout their history, the Viennese Jews, who settled for the most part in Leopoldstadt, were repeatedly driven out and murdered. A systematic persecution and extermination of the Jews was carried out in the time of the Nazis.

The story of the Jews in Vienna is closely tied to **Leopoldstadt**. It was here that most of the Jews settled. More than half of Vienna's some 180,000 Jews lived here prior to the Second World War. Today there are hardly 8,000 Jewish Viennese in the city, and not many of them still live in the former Jewish working class quarter, which is as much a part of Old Vienna as the brilliant culture in the salons of Jewish high finance. The comparatively peaceful period which the medieval Jewish quarter at the foot of the ducal castle experienced up to the beginning of the 14th century,

was followed by a gradual worsening through **anti-Jewish regulations**. These were passed as early as 1215 at the Fourth Council of the Lateran, and subsequently also made their appearance in the metropolis on the Danube. Viennese Jews were increasingly at the mercy of the king's erratic good will.

Jews as Scapegoats

Archduke Albert V finally made the Jews the scapegoat for his political and military misery in 1420, whereupon all the inhabitants of Judenplatz were either **driven out or murdered**.

Numerous lanes and squares still recall the Golden Age of Jewish Vienna.

Jewish charity board dated 1857

In the course of the 16th century, Jewish families once again settled in Vienna. **Ferdinand II** offered the Jewish community certain advantages, and though they were forbidden from minting coins, Jewish merchants were closely associated with the Austrian Mint as suppliers of precious metals.

Setting up a Ghetto

In 1624, the emperor gave the order to establish a Jewish Ghetto on the north bank of the Danube. By 1660, it had **three synagogues**, each with a school, a large hospital, a community hall and Vienna's very first refuse collection service. Among the immigrants to the Leopoldstadt ghetto were many families from the Polish Ukraine who had fled from the **Cossack pogroms**. They soon gave Vienna a mediatory function between Eastern and Western Judaism that it retained right up to the 19th and 20th centuries. The pendulum swung in

the other direction again with Leopold I, who expelled almost 3,000 Jewish citizens in 1670, on the insistence of his bigoted wife and Bishop Leopold Kollonitsch.

Edict of Toleration

The Jewish Vienna that flourished from the late 18th century to the early 20th century began in 1782 with **Joseph II's Edict of Tolerance**, which precipitated a great wave of immigration, primarily from Eastern Europe. Whoever wanted to break out of the confines of the »Shtetl« was drawn to enlightened Vienna. As Jews were only allowed to purchase land to build factories, Jewish high finance soon acquired a dominating position in the credit market in the imperial city through their **accumulation of capital**. Beginning in 1796, leading bankers were elevated to peerages, among them Salomon Baron von Rothschild – Austria's second most

A heated political debate raged on the Memorial against War and Fascism, on the square in front of the Albertina – not least on where it should finally be located. The Austrian Alfred Hrdlicka created a four-part work. »Orpheus enters Hades« (in the picture's foreground) refers to the bomb victims in the air raid shelters of Philipphof (an apartment block opposite the Albertina) that stood on this spot. The hopeless situation of the street-scrubbing Jews is made apparent through barbed wire. Other parts include the Gateway to Violence and a stone with the Austrian declaration of independence.

powerful man prior to the 1840s, after Prince Metternich – and Joseph von Wertheimer, one of the leading voices of Viennese Liberal Judaism in the mid-19th century. At the same time, a bustling commercial centre developed in the city centre around Rotenturmstrasse, the Graben and Tuchlauben. Soon the construction of worthy Jewish cultural premises and religious schools followed.

Freedom of Religion

The Austro-Hungarian Compromise of 1867 brought complete **freedom of religion** per decree for both halves of the empire. After this granting of equal rights under Emperor Franz Joseph I, »His Apostolic Majesty the King of Jerusalem«, who felt a sincere sympathy for the Jews, the Jewish population exploded from around 2% (6,200) in 1857 to almost 11% (72,400) in 1880. About a third were in Leopoldstadt, where small merchants and craftsmen, labourers, students and artists lived, and where most of the new arrivals from Galicia, Hungary and the Sudetenland looking for a new homeland arrived. They had little in common with the world of the up and coming, well-off, assimilated Jews, who primarily settled in the 1st and 9th districts, though the autonomous Jewish Religious Community encompassed the whole of the Jewish population.

Increasing Hate

The closing decades of the 19th century was marked by renewed anti-Semitic hate campaigns influenced by men like Karl Lueger, Georg Ritter von Schönerer and Ernst Schneider, while at the same time racial fanaticism spread. The hate slogans published in the racially motivated »Ostara« magazine between 1906 and 1911, found an impressionable reader in the young

Adolf Hitler, who's later »Final Solution to the Jewish Question« was the horrifying continuation of the ideology expressed there. The Zionist idea developed at this time and was realized through **Theodor Herzl**, leading to the return of the Jews to Jerusalem. The pressure grew on the Jewish community after the First World War and was expressed in increasing acts of violence, despite the committed efforts of upstanding Viennese like Cardinal Theodor Innitzer.

Holocaust

With the annexation of Austria to Hitler Germany in 1938, the Jews were once and for all abandoned to the brutal arbitrary terror of the Nazis. Arrests and seizures of property followed; synagogues and educational facilities were destroyed. Attacks on Jews were an everyday occurrence.

Adolf Eichmann was made the notorious head of the Vienna »Central Office for Jewish Emigration«, which was responsible for almost 225,000 Jews being forced to flee the city in exchange for a horrendous ransom by the end of 1939, while at the same time the first deportation transports to the concentration camps in occupied Poland were carried out. When emigration was finally banned in 1941, the **death trains** began rolling systematically from Vienna to Theresienstadt and Auschwitz. By 1945, almost 40,000 Viennese Jews had fallen victim to the Holocaust. «Matzos Island« remained deserted for a long time after the Second World War. Today, the quarter around Taborstrasse is a residential area like many others, in which only a few Jewish schools, prayer houses and kosher restaurants survive to recall the lost world of Jewish Vienna.

tharistengasse. Here, true to the order's principles of pursuing religion, education and science, the fathers began to produce a wealth of spiritual and scientific papers in their own printing shop, soon making the monastery an important home of Armenian culture. The church integrated in the monastery complex was designed by **Camillo Sitte** in 1874, and **Theophil Hansen**, builder of the Viennese Parliament, was responsible for the side altar dedicated to St Gregory. The library and museum impressively illuminates Armenian history and literature with 2,600 manuscripts, the oldest of which dates from the 9th century, some 170,000 volumes, an extensive coin collection, as well as rare items of religious and popular art. The herb liqueur (»Mechitharine«) that has been produced in the monastery according to an old recipe dating back to 1680 is very popular with visitors.

★ Michaelerplatz

G/H 6

Location: 1st District   **Underground:** Herrengasse (U3)

Michaelerplatz was begun with the plans of Johann Bernhard Fischers von Erlach, but Adolf Loos was responsible for finishing it. The foundations of a Roman settlement and remains of the walls of the »Paradeisgartl« (Garden of Paradise) were discovered during archaeological excavations.

The Viennese architect and designer Hans Hollen had a stone framework put around the **excavations** in 1991, to provide a display window to Vienna's history which ensures protection for the historic remains, though it also detracts somewhat from the much acclaimed elegance of the square.

Michaelerkirche (St Michael's Church)
⏱
Opening hours:
Tours: Wed 1pm

The Salvatorian Church of St Michael is the former court parish church of the imperial family. It is also a cultural centre and the church where prominent Austrians are buried. It stands obliquely opposite the Michaeler Wing of the Hofburg, on the east side of the square. The founder of the church may have been the crusader, Archduke Leopold VI, or perhaps Ottokar Premsyl. The Late Romanesque pillar basilica was built in the first half of the 13th century, at the same time as the Alte Burg – its architects belonged to the same group that built the Stephansdom. The basilica was enlarged in the 14th century and restored to Gothic in the 16th century. The Baroque entry narthex was added between 1724 and 1725. The west door with the sculpture of the Fall of the Angels by **Lorenzo Mattielli** and the Classical façade both date from 1792.

Among the oldest treasures of the church are the remains of the once-famous Late Romanesque frescoes in the tower chapel, the »Man of Sorrows« (1430) in the baptistery and the stone figures

(1350) in the Chapel of St Nicholas. The Late Baroque high altar was designed by Jean Baptiste d' Avrange in 1781. The Chapel of St Nicholas, to the right in the chancel, was donated by a duke's chef around 1350, in gratitude for being acquitted in a poisoning case.

The **vaulted crypt** served as a burial place. All of the floors and walls are covered with bones and there are close to 250 coffins of wood, metal and stone.

⏰
Opening hours:
Tours: Wed–Sat
11am, 1.30pm

On the west side of the square stands a piece of scandalous Viennese architectural history, the six-storey Loos-Haus, carefully restored in 1989, where the Raiffeisenbank now has its seat. **Adolf Loos** designed the linear functional building in 1910, for the men's tailors Goldmann & Salatsch, incurring the displeasure of Emperor Franz Joseph, who thought the house looked »like a woman with no eyebrows«. The windows had no frames and the emperor found the house a down-right monstrosity, but Loos was demonstrating against the pompous Ringstrasse style of the Hofburg, and his plain building next to the Michaeler Wing was intended as a counterpoint. Simple elegance is expressed in well-proportioned marble on the façade of the lower double-storey, and the interior is adorned with precious mahogany and an endlessly mirroring brass clock. The reconstructed tailoring rooms are now used for exhibitions.

Michaelerhaus

Wall fountain with fallen giants and sea monsters on the Michaelertrakt (Michael Wing)

Café Griensteidl

Cafe Griensteidl is one of the legendary symbols of old Vienna's coffee house culture. From 1847 to 1897, the former chemist Heinrich Griensteidl ran a popular coffee house here in the Palais Dietrichstein, where writers and artists like Hermann Bahr, Hugo von Hofmannsthal, Arthur Schnitzler, Karl Kraus, Hugo Wolf and Arnold Schönberg liked to meet. After Griensteidl's death, the cafe was forced to move to the Palais Herbertstein. Karl Kraus subsequently ensured it a place of honour in literary history in his satirical, polemical periodical »Die demolirte Litteratur« (Demolished Literature).

★ Museum für Angewandte Kunst (Museum of Applied Art)

J 6

Location: 1, Stubenring 5
Bus: 1A, 74A
Internet: www.mak.at

Underground: Stubentor (U3), Landstraße (U4)
Tram: 2

The collections of the Museum für Angewandte Kunst, MAK for short, present European arts and crafts in an unusual context. Contemporary artists were commissioned to redesign the eleven exhibition halls, creating an interesting interplay of old and new, of the traditional collections and current art.

Opening hours: Tue 10am – midnight, Wed – Sun 10am – 6pm, Sat free admission

The building came into being during the course of the conversion of the old fortifications into state buildings for the Ringstrasse. The building that **Heinrich Ferstel** conceived in Italian Renaissance style was opened on the Stubenring in 1871, and was augmented by **Ludwig Baumann** in 1909, with an extension in Weisskirchnerstrasse. The museum was founded in 1864 as the Austrian Museum for Art and Industry, modelled after the South Kensington Museum in London (now the Victoria & Albert Museum). The underlying concept was to document and promote the current development of arts and crafts through the study of old works of art. A school of applied arts was added in 1868 – now an independent institution, known today as the University of Applied Arts. The school was conceived to offer systematic training in the applied arts for the first time. The museum was reorganized at the turn of the 20th century, and the collections now dealt to an equal extent with both historical and contemporary works. Today, the institute is counted among the most impor-

✔ DON'T MISS

- The bentwood chairs by Thonet in the Jugendstil section
- The valuable collection of oriental rugs
- The Viennese workshop's furniture, vases and tableware
- The study collections of glass and porcelain in the basement

tant museums of applied arts on the Continent. Its mission is the historical documentation of applied arts and to be a centre for the arts. Its rooms are in chronological order. Rather than putting a wide range of objects on display, the museum concentrates on highlights from its collections.

On the **ground floor** is the room designed in ultramarine by **Günther Förg**, dedicated to Romanesque vestments with rich silk embroidery produced around 1260 from the Benedictine Convent of Göss in Styria. It is the only preserved ensemble of liturgical robes from such an early date. Also on display are brightly coloured Renaissance majolica and various pieces of medieval furniture. In the middle of the room realized by **Donald Judd** is a reconstructed furnished room from Palais Dubsky in Brno (Czech Republic), dating back to around 1740. Further ex-

Pompous: the MAK's Italian Renaissance style columned hall by Heinrich Ferstel

amples of the art of furniture-making in the 18th century include Austrian cabinets and small tables, Parisian commodes and southern German tabernacle cupboards with artistic inlay work and gilded bronze fittings. The Viennese centrepiece consisting of 60 groups of porcelain figures and vases was ordered by Zwettl Abbey in 1768, for the golden anniversary of Abbott Rayner I – Joseph Haydn composed his *Applausus* for the occasion; the female voices can be seen as allegorical figures in the centrepiece. Lavish decorative needlework and lace from Venice and Brussels and beautiful Bohemian and Venetian glassware provide examples of craft techniques of the 16th to 18th centuries (room design: **Franz Graf**).

◀ Baroque, Rococo, and Classical

◀ Baroque, Rococo

The Industrial Revolution and its effects in the first half of the 19th century were reflected in the increasing variety of consumer goods produced, ranging from luxury commodities to affordable, mass-produced goods. The wealth of form can be seen in the many different types of furniture and tableware (room design: **Jenny Holzer**).

◀ Empire, Biedermeier

The aesthetic woodwork, innovatively economic in its production, by the successful furniture designer Michael Thonet is exemplary of the late 19th century. The Thonet brother's beech wood furniture won international prizes and became a feature of many Viennese coffee houses (room design: **Barbara Bloom**).

◀ Historicism, Art Nouveau

Museum of Applied Art (MAK) *Plan*

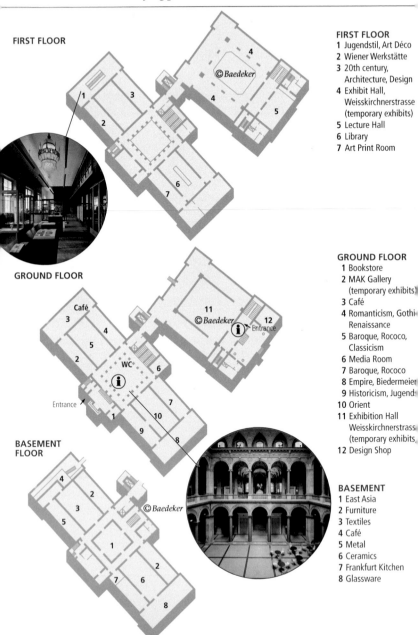

FIRST FLOOR

GROUND FLOOR

BASEMENT FLOOR

© Baedeker

FIRST FLOOR
1 Jugendstil, Art Déco
2 Wiener Werkstätte
3 20th century, Architecture, Design
4 Exhibit Hall, Weisskirchnerstrasse (temporary exhibits)
5 Lecture Hall
6 Library
7 Art Print Room

GROUND FLOOR
1 Bookstore
2 MAK Gallery (temporary exhibits)
3 Café
4 Romanticism, Gothic, Renaissance
5 Baroque, Rococo, Classicism
6 Media Room
7 Baroque, Rococo
8 Empire, Biedermeier
9 Historicism, Jugendstil
10 Orient
11 Exhibition Hall Weisskirchnerstrasse (temporary exhibits)
12 Design Shop

BASEMENT
1 East Asia
2 Furniture
3 Textiles
4 Café
5 Metal
6 Ceramics
7 Frankfurt Kitchen
8 Glassware

The highlight of the valuable collection of oriental rugs is the knotted carpets of the 16th and 17th centuries (room design: **Gang Art**).

◄ Orient

Gustav Klimt's preliminary sketches for the frieze he designed from 1905 to 1909 for the Palais Stoclet, which was executed by the Viennese Workshop and installed in Brussels in 1911, are among the items on display. During the remodelling of the museum, the frieze designed by Margaret Macdonald, the wife of Charles Rennie Mackintosh, was rediscovered. She had designed it in 1911 for Fritz Waerndorfer's villa. Also worth admiring are a writing desk by Koloman Moser, decorative vases by Josef Hoffmann and a rosewater sprinkler by Louis Comfort Tiffany (room design: **Eichinger/ Knechtl**). The exhibits are from the estate of the **Wiener Werkstätte (Viennese Workshop)**, which was set up in 1903 by Josef Hoffmann, Koloman Moser und Fritz Waerndorfer, to create articles for daily use. They were to be in line with the changing tastes and demands of the new era both decorative and functional. Initially strictly geometric in design, ornamental fantasy increasingly played a greater role in the furniture, vases and tableware produced (room design: **Heimo Zobernig**).

First Floor
◄ Art Nouveau, Art Deco

The Architectural Department documents new architectural concepts and idealistic designs, up to and including utopian projects, with plans and models by the Austrians Coop Himmelb(l)au, Günther Domenig, Carl Pruscha and Helmut Richter and the Americans Frank O. Gehry and Lebbeus Woods. The design section displays exemplary furniture by Walter Pichler, Philip Starck and Jasper Morrison (room design: **Manfred Wakolbinger**).

◄ 20th Century

The museum's specialized library grew out of the private library of the museum's first director, Rudolf von Eitelberger (1817 – 1885). It was supplemented by generous donations from the nobility, the imperial family and the emerging manufacturing sector. Today the library contains about 150,000 volumes, including costly manuscripts, incunabula, printed works and treatises from the Renaissance to the 19th century, as well as pattern books for all fields of applied art from the 18th to the 20th century. The collection of art prints encompasses more than 500,000 pieces, including exceptional ornamental prints from the 15th to 18th century, pattern books of the Vienna Porcelain Factory, portions of the archives of the Wiener Werkstätte, Japanese coloured woodcuts and the famous »Hamza-Nama« – a 16th century Moghul romance and a unique marvel of Indo-Persian illumination.

◄ Library

◄ Print Collection

The reading room, newly designed by **Ursula Eichwalder** and **Hermann Strobl**, offers a reference library, periodicals and publications on current architecture.

◄ Reading Room

The collection of contemporary art begun in 1986 has its place in the bright room designed by **Peter Noever** on the second floor. Among the works to be seen are some by Günther Brus, Gregor Ei-

Second Floor
◄ Contemporary Art

chinger, Bruno Gironcoli, Heinz Frank, Donald Judd, Birgit Jürgenssen, Hans Kupelwieser, Helmut Mark, Arnulf Rainer, Eva Schlegel, Rudolf Schwarzkogler, James Turrell, Hans Weigand and Erwin Wurm, as well as architectural designs by Coop Himmelb(l)au, Frank O. Gehry and Lebbeus Woods.

Basement Seating and carcass furniture is shown in a broad spectrum of materials in two rooms, while candlesticks, drinking vessels and pots and jugs are presented in the field of metal. The **study collection** of glass and porcelain in historical order offers an insight into the history of hollow glass and glass-painting from the Middle Ages to the modern era, with the focus of European porcelain being the Viennese Porcelain Factory. The Textile Collection displays liturgical vestments and explains the stylistic and technical developments in textile production from the 13th to the 20th centuries. The East Asian Collection contains Kangxi porcelain from the collection of Augustus the Strong, 14th century Chinese porcelain and burial objects from the Han dynasty (AD 25-220).

Heimo Zobernig's interior design for the estate of the Wiener Werkstätte is strictly geometrical

★ MuseumsQuartier (Museum Quarter)

Location: 7, Museumsplatz 1
Bus : 48 A, 2 A
Internet: www.mqw.at

Underground: Volkstheater (U2, U3)
Museumsquartier (U2)
Tram: 49

The Museum Quarter with its numerous museums has quickly developed into a popular venue for art education. The large number of cafés, independent projects and initiatives have seen to it that the huge complex has become a popular place to frequent, even for those outside the art scene.

The architectural basis was provided primarily by the former **Imperial Stables**, a 360m/1,181ft long building constructed from 1723 to 1725,on plans by **Johann Bernhard Fischer von Erlach** and son, which once housed the coaches and horses of the imperial court. Frequently altered in subsequent years, the building complex then served as an exhibition hall for decades. The architectural firm of **Ortner & Ortner** was responsible for the remodelling done behind the historic listed façade. The special feature of the design lies in the exciting blend of the historical fabric of the building and contemporary architecture, and in its cultural density and diversity. The Museum Quarter spans 20 cultural segments; from the novel children's creative centre to the classic art museum, from the departments for dance, film architecture and theatre to the forum for new media and art theory. Rounding it all off are shops and facilities offering food.

Museum Moderner Kunst Stiftung Ludwig Wien

The Museum of the 20th Century and the Museum of Modern Art, which were once housed in separate buildings, are now combined in the Museum Moderner Kunst Stiftung Ludwig Wien (MUMOK; **Museum of Modern Art Ludwig Foundation Vienna**), which found its home in a new building. This new construction is completely faced with anthracite-coloured lava basalt – a very young stone – that is meant to illustrate the mission of the museum, to address the modern currents of art and to classify them historically. The museum possesses one of the largest European collections of modern and contemporary art. The collections and special exhibits are displayed on eight levels. Rotating exhibits present selected works from the collection, highlighting their thematic and art historical aspects. The museum focuses on classic modern art from the 1960s and 70s, Fluxus objects, Viennese Action Art, Pop Art, New Realism and installation art and Object Art of the recent past, as well as medial works of contemporary art. Important artists are Ernst Ludwig Kirchner, Oskar Kokoschka, Piet Mondrian, Paul Klee, Max Ernst, René Magritte, Pablo Picasso, Roy Lichtenstein, Andy Warhol, Georg Baselitz, Robert

🕐
Opening hours:
daily 10am – 6pm
Thu until 9pm
www.mumok.at

Rauschenberg and Gerhard Richter. Nam June Paik is shown as an important exponent of media art. The museum offers a diverse programme of events for visitors of all ages, ranging from children's afternoons to tours, lectures and discussions.

Leopold Museum

The Austrian state acquired the country's largest private art collection in 1994, from the eye specialist Rudolf Leopold, a passionate art collector. The famous collection, whose focus is on **Austrian art of the 19th century** and the first half of the **20th century**, contains 5,200 objects. The most important artists of Austrian modern art are presented on six floors of the newly constructed Leopold Museum – two subterranean floors, the ground floor and the first, second and third floors. The gem of the museum is **the world's most important collection of works by Egon Schiele**. The new building is faced with Vratza shell limestone and its centre is an atrium, around

Relaxed evening rendezvous in the inner court of the Museum Quarter

which the exhibit halls are grouped in windmill fashion. The ground floor of the museum is devoted to Gustav Klimt and his period, and the Wiener Werkstätte. Paintings by Klimt and Richard Gerstl are combined with furniture and design objects by Koloman Moser, Otto Wagner and Josef Hoffmann. On the second floor, the span of art history reaches from the painter Albin Egger-Lienz to the period between the world wars, and to painting after 1945. The famous Schiele collection (third floor) contains 47 works by the early expressionist. Rudolf Leopold also published an extensive Schiele monograph with a catalogue of works in 1972. Oskar Kokoschka, Ernst Ludwig Kirchner and Lovis Corinth, as well as Austrian artists are also represented here.

The first basement floor covers the 19th century, on the one hand with a graphic collection and, on the other hand, with paintings by Ferdinand G. Waldmüller, Anton Romako, Emil Jakob Schindler and Carl Schuch. The graphics collection is continued in the second basement floor. Displayed here is non-European art from Africa,

Opening hours:
Wed – Mon
10am – 6pm
Thu until 9pm
www.leopold-museum.org

Oceania, China and Japan. The Japanese colour woodcuts are meant to illustrate the connection between modern European art and so-called primitive art. Furthermore, special exhibits from the graphics collection are held on this floor.

Other Museums

The Kunsthalle Wien presents topical trends and currents in contemporary art in **temporary exhibits** and places them in the context of art history. The main focus of the programme is photography, video, film installations and media. The vermilion building conveys the impression of an inordinately large workshop, illustrating the goal of the Kunsthalle, which orients its programme toward contemporary experimental art.

Kunsthalle Wien
Opening hours:
daily 10am – 7pm
Thu until 10pm

The Architekturzentrum is a venue for presenting the international development of architecture. To be seen are a permanent exhibition on 20th century Austrian architecture and a rotating show of works by international architects, architectural history and cultural history, as well as art installations. Along with its varied programme (exhibitions, seminars, symposiums and congresses), the centre has a technical library.

Architektur-zentrum Wien (Architecture Centre Vienna)
Opening hours:
daily 10am – 7pm,
Wed until 9pm

The Tanzquartier has training studios and an information centre with a public library and a video library dealing specifically with dance. International dance performances are held on the stage.

Tanzquartier

MuseumsQuartier Plan

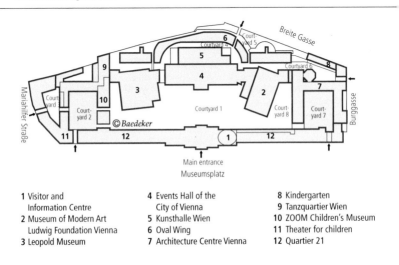

1 Visitor and
   Information Centre
2 Museum of Modern Art
   Ludwig Foundation Vienna
3 Leopold Museum
4 Events Hall of the
   City of Vienna
5 Kunsthalle Wien
6 Oval Wing
7 Architecture Centre Vienna
8 Kindergarten
9 Tanzquartier Wien
10 ZOOM Children's Museum
11 Theater for children
12 Quartier 21

ZOOM Kindermu-seum (Children's Museum)

The Kindermuseum organizes hands-on exhibitions for children up to age 14. Workshops, studios and a multimedia laboratory offer the possibility of engaging in creative activities with artists. Opening hours: Mon – Fri 8.30am – 5pm , Sat, Sun, hols 10am – 5.30pm, for information and reservations call tel. 524 79 08. The theatre **»Dschungel Wien«** opposite shows, among other things, plays and films for children (tel. 522 07 20 20).

quartier 21

Opening hours: daily 10am – 10pm

The quartier 21, designed by artist groups and art offices in the entire Fischer von Erlach Wing and in the Oval Wing, presents a wide spectrum of modern art – electronic music, fashion and video art. Two theme malls were created in the Baroque wing; the »Electric Avenue« with digital art and electronic music and the »transeuropa« where everyday European culture is shown. In addition, artist studios were set up in the Museum Quarter.

Naschmarkt

G 7

Location: 6th District

Underground: Karlsplatz (U1, U2, U4), Kettenbrückengasse (U4)

The Naschmarkt is by far the largest and most interesting market in Vienna with a vast range of fresh food.

Fast food stands and small restaurants round out the food selection. The picturesque **flea market** begins on the southern end of the Naschmarkt (opening hours: Mon – Fri 6am – 6.30pm; Sat 6am – 1pm; flea market: Sat 6.30am – 6pm). While browsing take a look inside the small Naschmarktmuseum, which is located in an unused chapel on the Rechten Wienzeile (opening hours: Sat noon – 2pm).

Linke Wienzeile (Left Vienna Row)

Two Art Nouveau buildings by **Otto Wagner** are worth noting in the adjacent Linke Wienzeile. What catches the eye with these buildings is no longer the piano nobile, but rather the whole ground floor with its shops that are bound together into an independent area through the surrounding balustrades. The medallions between the windows of house no. 38 were created by **Koloman Moser**; the front door in Köstlergasse was designed by **Josef Plecnik**.

The façade of house no. 40 (**Majolikahaus**) was covered with weatherproof majolica sheeting decorated with artistic plant designs in 1899, by Otto Wagner. The only exterior sculpture adornments are the bronze lion heads in the frieze zone.

Theater an der Wien

The Theater an der Wien, built in 1801, has been remodelled frequently. Its »Papageno gate« in Millöckergasse shows the first theatre

There is always something to find at Vienna's famous flea market, especially on Saturdays

director and the librettist of *The Magic Flute*, Emanuel Schikaneder, in the role of Papageno. Theater an der Wien was where Beethoven's *Fidelio* was first performed in 1805, and dramas by Grillparzer, Nestroy and Raimund, as well as numerous operettas by Strauss, Léhar and Franz von Suppé had their premieres here. The Staatsoper temporarily lodged here between 1945 and 1955. In the early 1990s, the venue became a first class musical theatre under the direction of Peter Weck.

★★ Naturhistorisches Museum

(Natural History Museum)

G 6

Location: 1, Burgring 7 (entrance Maria Theresien Platz)
Tram: 1, 2, 3, 46, 49

Underground: Volkstheater (U2, U3)
Internet: www.nhm-wien.ac.at

The Natural History Museum lies directly across from its twin building, the Art History Museum. Both were designed in 1872 by Gottfried Semper and Karl von Hasenauer for the imperial collection and completed by 1881.

The collections that are today counted among the most significant natural science collections in Europe are displayed in 39 exhibition halls and one cupola hall. They were founded as a natural history collection by Emperor Franz I and opened to the public by his wife, Maria Theresa, in 1765. The museum, in its present home since 1889, is constantly being expanded and updated.

Standing amazed between elephants and giraffes; Franz I founded the collection

Collection

🕐 Opening hours:
Mon, Thu – Sun
9am – 6.30pm;
Wed until 9pm

The nucleus of the **Mineralogical – Petrographical Department** (rooms 1 – 5) is made up of the extensive and impressive mineral collection that includes striking examples found in Austria, as well as material for Viennese buildings such as the limestone blocks and Lias limestone columns used in the Burgtheater. Among the minerals from all over the world are a 1m/3.3ft long rock crystal from Madagascar. There are some beautiful pieces in the Precious Stone Room (Room 4), including Maria Theresa's **bouquet of jewels** for her husband Franz I, composed of 2102 diamonds and 761 coloured precious stones and gemstones. The highlights of the Meteorite Collection (room 5) include a 900kg/1,984 lb iron meteorite from Australia and a moonstone, which the crew of Apollo 17 brought back from their flight to the moon in 1972. There is also an artistic orrery (mechanical solar system) on display, which was constructed around 1750 for Emperor Franz I.

Geological and
Palaeontological
Department ▶

Among the fossils shown in the **Geological and Palaeontological Department** (rooms 6 – 10) are numerous finds from the Alps. Especially spectacular is the complete skeleton of a 17 million year old Deinotherium (type of elephant) from Františkovy Lázn in the Czech Republic (room 9). The Dinosaur Room (Room 10) has finds from the Mesozoic period, including a 27m/86ft long impression of a skeleton from California and an Archaeopteryx (type of bird). The **archaeological finds** from Austria range from the Stone Age to the early Middle Ages (rooms 11 – 15). A key exhibit in room 11 is the world famous, barely 11cm/4.3in high limestone figure of **Venus of**

Willendorf, a fertility statue created around 25,000 BC. She was discovered in 1908 during excavations in Willendorf on the Danube. The oldest human sculpture in the world is also here – it is the 32,000 year old statuette of Galgenberg. The Hallstatt culture (800 – 400 BC) is represented with bronzes, burial objects and the remains of Illyrian wood houses.

The **Anthropological Department** (Upper Ground Floor) has a large number of human skeletons from the neo-Palaeolithic period up to the present day. Together with the Somatological Collection, it provides information about the history of the development of mankind (rooms 16, 17).

In the **Children's Room** (room 18), young visitors can leaf through colourful picture books, play in a block house or explore nature for themselves with microscopes and video recorders.

> ✔ **DON'T MISS**
>
> - A bouquet of jewels instead of flowers: Maria Theresa had the unusual present made for her husband Franz I, around 1760.
> - Venus of Willendorf: the 25,000 year-old fertility symbol is only 11cm/ 4.3in high.

First Floor   The latest 3-D projectors, microscopes for use by the public and the Micro Theatre in the **Botanical Exhibition Gallery** (room 21) carry the visitors off into the hidden world of the microscopic.

The **Zoological Department** (rooms 22 – 39) impressively illustrates the various stages of evolution from the single cell to anthropoid apes, and provides detailed information about the various species of vertebrates, insects and invertebrates. Among the museum's rare treasures are the richly detailed coelenterates, polyps and medusas (room 22). The two halves of the giant clam (Tridacna gigas) with a reproduction of its soft body inside can be seen in room 23. In addition, there is a fantastic bird collection as well as an extensive collection of vertebrates.

Maria Theresien Platz   ►Kunsthistorisches Museum

★ Parlament (Parliament)

G 6

Location: 1, Dr.-Karl-Renner-Ring 3   **Underground:** Volkstheater (U3)
Tram: 1, 2, 3

Both houses of the Austrian parliament, the National Council and the Federal Council, have been holding their sessions in the impressive parliament building since 1918. Theophil Hansen created an allusion to the birthplace of democracy by using Greek forms, Corinthian columns and rich decoration on the entablatures and pediments.

🕐 Tours:
mid-Sept – mid-July
Mon – Sat 11am,
2pm, 3pm, 4pm, Fri
also 1pm, Sat also
noon, 1pm, mid-
July – med-Sept
Mon – Sat hourly
11am – 4pm

Hansen built the complex between 1873 and 1883 for the newly created house of lords and house of deputies as prescribed by the new imperial constitution, known as the »February patents« of 1861. Up until the First Republic was declared on 12 November 1918, the deputies of the »kingdoms and nations represented in the Council of the Empire« of the Austrian half of the Austro-Hungarian dual monarchy met there. At the time the monarchy stretched from Galicia (today part of Ukraine and Poland) to Dalmatia on the Croatian Adriatic coast.

The bestowal of the constitution on the 17 nations of Austria by Franz Josef I is depicted on the pediment above the portico; the attic is decorated with 76 marble statues and 66 reliefs. Josef Lax's bronze statute, *The Horse Tamers*, keeps watch over the ramp; to the left are the seated figures of Herodotus, Polybius, Thucydides and Xenophon, and to the right are those of Sallust, Caesar, Tacitus and Livy.

Pallas Athena, Goddess of Wisdom, stands guard for democracy

The **Athena Fountain** (Pallas Athene Brunnen) has been standing in front of the portico since 1902. It was originally planned to be the personification of Austria, but a Solomonic compromise changed it to Athena, wearing a golden helmet and armed with a lance. The reclining figures were allowed to remain and symbolize the rivers of Austria, the Danube, Inn, Elbe and Moldau.

The **monument** to the left of the building commemorates the social democrats Jakob Reumann (mayor of Vienna, 1919 until 1923), Viktor Adler (one of the founders and first foreign minister of the First Republic in 1918) and Ferdinand Hanusch (Social Minister, 1918 – 1920).

A statue on the right honours **Dr. Karl Renner**, who led Austria when the Republic was founded in 1918 and again in 1945 and who held the office of Federal President until 1950.

✷ Peterskirche (St Peter's Church)

H 6

Location: 1, Petersplatz   **Underground:** Stephansplatz (U1, U3)

The collegiate and city parish church of St Peter was inspired by St Peter's in Rome. According to tradition, it was originally the site of a late Roman church, and, after 792, of one founded by Charlemagne. The first written mention of a church here, however, was in 1137.

⏲
Opening hours::
Mon – Fri
7am – 8pm, Sat, Sun
9am – 9pm

The church was restored several times, but was replaced at the beginning of the 18th century by the present church, which was begun by **Gabriel Montani** and probably completed by **Lukas von Hildebrandt**. The church, a centrally planned building on an oval ground plan, is vaulted by a massive dome with a fresco by **Johann Michael Rottmayr**. A tour of the church taken in a counter-clockwise direction would start, after entering through Andreas Altomonte's magnificent porch, at St Barbara's Chapel, which holds a painting by Franz Karl Remp (*Decollation of St Barbara*). The side altar to the left is adorned by an altarpiece by Anton Schoonjan's (*Martyrdom of St Sebastian*), and a painting by Altomonte hangs in the Chapel of the Holy Family. Just past the richly carved Baroque pulpit is the choir. Beneath the illusionary dome by Antonio Bibiena stands the high altar, a work by Santino Bussi, with an altarpiece by Altomonte and an *Immaculata* by Kupelwieser. The entrance to the crypt is also in the choir, where every year at Christmas a popular manger display can be seen. On the right side of the church is the Johann von Nepomuk altar with a *Virgin in Glory* attributed to Matthias Steinl. The Chapel of St Michael is decorated with a *Fall of the Angels* by Altomonte. Benedict, a Catacomb-Saint, rests in the glass coffin. Rottmayr is also responsible for the altarpiece of the side altar on the right, whereas the Chapel of St Anthony contains more works by Altomonte (*St Anthony with the Virgin*)) and Kupelwieser (*Heart of the Madonna*).

Piaristenkirche Maria Treu

F 6

Location: 8, Jodok-Fink-Platz   **Underground:** Rathaus (U2)
Bus: 13 A

The Piaristenkirche is a parish church and a church of the order of Patres Scholarum Piarum (Poor Clerics of the Mother of God). The Piarists first built a small chapel when they arrived in Vienna in the 17th century. The present church building is based on plans done by **Johann Lukas von Hildebrandt** in 1716. After a change of plans, the construction was continued up to the middle of the 18th century –

presumably by **Kilian Ignaz Dientzenhofer**. The final consecration took place in 1771. The towers were not completed until between 1858 and 1860. The interior was provided with a particularly fine ceiling fresco by **Franz Anton Maulbertsch** in 1752/1753, the first major fresco done by the master. The oldest of the eight chapels is the Chapel of Sorrows, which is in fact the founder chapel of 1699, with *St Maria da Malta*, an historical painting held to have miraculous powers dating from the first half of the 15th century. The Chapel of the Holy Cross (left of the choir) is the most exceptional of the remaining chapels. The picture of *Christ on the Cross* (1772) is also the work of Maulbertsch. The painting *Maria Treu* on the high altar, also said to have miraculous powers, is only a copy. The original is hanging in Rome.

★ Prater

Location: 2nd District
Tram: O, 5
Internet: www.prater.at

Underground: Praterstern (U1, S7)
Bus: 80 A

The large nature park between the Danube and the right-hand Danube canal is almost a world of its own: lively and enjoyable by day, somewhat disreputable at night.

The park, covering an area of 1287ha/3,180 acres, stretches to the south-east from the Praterstern (where wide paths in the park converge, forming a star) for almost 10km/6.2mi through the former Praterstern meadow to the tip of the Prater. The Wurstelprater or Volksprater lies in the front part with snack bars and restaurants, the giant Ferris wheel, carousels, a roller coaster, spook rides, grotto rides and many more attractions. Almost every **form of sport** is present in the Prater. There are a race track and a number of riding clubs in Freudenau, harness racing is catered to in Krieau, swimming in the Stadium pool. Football is on offer in the roofed Ernst Happel stadium built in 1931, cycling in the Ferry Dusika indoor stadium; and there is tennis and even bowling at the Vienna Athletic Sport Club (WAC) grounds.

DID YOU KNOW …?

■ …that the Danube, where it flows by the Prater at Freudenau, has been dammed to over 8m/26ft high by a run-of-river power station since 1997? The reservoir reaches 27km/16.7mi back through the entire area of the city past Klosterneuburg.

History The Prater was first mentioned in 1403 and Maximilian II had the area fenced off in the 16th century, to use as his personal hunting preserve. It was not opened to the public until 1766. The first sausage

The Prater would be only half as nice without the giant Ferris wheel

stalls were opened in the Wurstlprater in 1767, and the first firework displays shot off in 1771. Blanchard was the first to rise up over the Prater in a Montgolfier hot air balloon in 1791, and Basileo Calafati started operation of the first large merry-go-round in 1840, which has been guarded by the figure of the »Great Chinese« since 1854.

The planetarium, located by the giant Ferris wheel and donated by the Zeiss company of Jena in 1927, was one of the first of its kind in Europe.

The development of the imperial hunting reserve into an amusement park is documented in the **Prater Museum** in the planetarium. The focus of the show is the story of the Wurstelprater, the grand era of Punch and Judy shows, ventriloquists, and the legendary Prater festivals that have always been as much a social event as great fun for everyone. A unique figure also shown here is the so-called »Watschenman« (scapegoat/whipping boy) on which people were able to measure their strength or take out their aggression by slapping the cheek as hard as possible (opening hours: Tue–Fri 9am–12.15pm, 1pm–4.30pm, Sat, Sun 2pm–6.30pm).

When spring arrives, the Volksprater awakes from its hibernation, the Ferris wheel renews its daily rounds, and the chamber of horrors, the rollercoaster and the carousels return to running at full steam. The tumultuous folk festivals also begin, including the colourful family days, children's festivals and the traditional Prater festival on

Planetarium

Opening hours:
Tue, Thu
8.30am–12pm
1pm–2.30pm; Wed
8.30am–12pm,
6pm–8pm; Fri
3pm–8pm; Sat, Sun
2pm–7pm

**Volksprater /
Wurstelprater**

Tour through Vienna's sewers on the trail of »The Third Man«.

HUNT THROUGH THE UNDERWORLD

The Third Man, a film of intrigue and crime written by Graham Greene and set in Vienna, became a world hit and a classic of film history.

Vienna after the Second World War: the city severely damaged by the air raids; hunger and suffering dominate between the dismal ruins on the banks of the Danube; and each of the four victorious Allied Powers have several city districts under their command, except the **First District**, in the heart of the city bounded by the Ringstrasse and the Danube Canal, which is governed jointly. This is the backdrop for Graham Greene's screenplay about the writer Holly Martins, who is searching for his friend, Harry Lime. It is incomprehensible to Martins that Lime, as it seems, was the victim of a **mysterious accident**. At the funeral, Martins learns from a British police officer that Lime was accused of being the head of a penicillin trafficking gang. Martins believes neither the police's strong suspicion nor that it was an accident. The only witness is **murdered** a day later, but Martins learns from him that not two, but three men were at the scene of the crime. He now searches for the assumed murderer of his friend – for the third man, only to find that he is Harry Lime himself, who had faked his death to escape the police.

Rise and Fall

The 1949 black and white film version of *The Third Man* by Carol Reed (starring Orson Welles, Joseph Cotten and Trevor Howard) became a worldwide blockbuster; now there is even a »Third Man Museum« (► p. 122). Fans of the film and book can still follow the trail of Harry Lime today. It was filmed in the nightclub of the Hotel Orient on Tiefen Graben in Bäckerstrasse in Old Vienna, and symbolically ends the friendship of the two men in a cabin stopped at the highest point of the Prater's giant steel Ferris wheel. Thereafter, it goes down hill for Lime in every respect. The story plunges into the Viennese underworld, into the labyrinth-like sewer system under the city. In a desperate attempt to flee, Lime jumps into a sewer shaft under Girardiplatz and is even able to elude his pursuers until Friedrichstrasse; but he is finally the 1st of May. Even though today's Volksprater is dominated by the sheer unlimited possibilities of modern technology, the concessionaires attempt to retain something of the Viennese flair of yesteryear. As in olden days, there is still an abundance of carousels, bumper cars, hippodromes, swings, rides and shooting galleries and, just as before, there are strength-measuring »Watschenmänner«, hurdy-gurdy men, sword swallowers, ventriloquists and ponies to brighten things up.

The highlight, and one of Vienna's most famous landmarks, is the mighty yet elegant giant Ferris wheel. A ride on the wheel up to its dizzying heights provides a grand view of Vienna. The originator and financer of the wheel was Gabor Steiner. He rose to become one of the most versatile and inventive impresarios of amusements at the turn of the 20th century with the theatre and amusement city »Venice in Vienna« which he founded in 1895 in the part of the Prater called »Kaisergarten« at the time. The giant wheel was constructed by the Englishman Walter Basset, who presented similar designs in London and Paris. The monumental iron construction was erected in a record time of eight months and put into operation in 1897. It was spruced up with 5 tonnes of fresh paint for its 100th anniversary in 1997. After being destroyed in the war and then reconstructed, the giant Ferris wheel has been in continuous operation since 1946, albeit with half the number of cabins. The wheel's diameter is 61m/200ft and its speed of rotation is 0.75m/s /2.46ft/s (operating times: Jan, Feb, Nov, Dec 10am – 7.45pm, March, Apr, Oct. 10am – 9.45pm, May – Sept 9am – 23.45pm).

★
◄ Riesenrad

> ! **Baedeker TIP**
>
> **Private Parties on the Giant Ferris Wheel**
>
> The giant Ferris wheel offers a special service: its cabins can be hired for parties. There are two luxury cabins and several extra cabins for up to 12 persons available (Information and reservations, tel. 729 54 30; www.wienerriesenrad.com).

A narrow gauge railway starts next to the giant Ferris wheel. It is partly steam and partly diesel driven. Its 4km/2.48mi long track leads along the major avenue into the meadow area. A sightseeing train that takes a 2km / 1.2mi round trip through the Volksprater also leaves from the giant wheel.

The café-restaurant at the end of Hauptallee has been a country pleasure house or retreat for 400 years. Emperor Joseph II had the two-storey pavilion remodelled in 1783 by Isidor Canevale. The most congested it has ever been here was in 1814, during the Congress of Vienna, when the allied monarchs and generals celebrated the anniversary of the Battle of Leipzig and 18,000 soldiers were served food at tables set up around the house.

◄ Lusthaus (The Pleasure House)

The small pilgrimage church stands on the site of an ancient shrine in the woods. The painting above the high altar (*Maria Grün*) is the object of veneration. A large mass is held annually in the chapel venerating St Hubert.

◄ Maria-Grün-Kapelle

✳ Rathaus (City Hall)

G 6

Location: 1, Rathausplatz
Tram: 1, 3

Underground: Rathaus (U2)
Internet:: www.wien.gv.at

With its open arcades, lancet windows, loggias and decorative elements, the Rathaus is a typical neo-Gothic building. The massive building complex was erected from 1872 to 1883 during the reign of Franz Joseph I by the cathedral architect from Cologne, Friedrich von Schmidt who also conceived the designs for the decorations and furnishings.

🕑
Tours:
Mon – Fri 1pm,
except session days

The impressive Rathaus is the seat of the Vienna city and state parliaments and the main administrative building of the municipality. Symbol of the building is the »Iron Rathausmann«, a statue on the 97.9m/321ft high tower that was a gift donated by the locksmith Ludwig Wilhelm. Including the standard that the figure is holding, the statue is 6m/19ft high and was the work of Alexander Nehr. The Arkadenhof (arcade courtyard) in the centre of the building measuring 81x35m/115ft is the largest of the total of seven courtyards. Originally conceived as a place for assemblies, the courtyard is now used for the popular concerts of the »Wiener Musiksommer«.

A tour of the interior of the Rathaus begins in the Schmidt Hall, the former civic vestibule. Formerly, horse-drawn carriages were able to

Always good as a backdrop for a summer event: the neo Gothic Town Hall

drive up here; today it houses the City Information Centre of the City Council. The two grand staircases lead up to the heritage protected official rooms: the large Festival Hall, two coat of arms halls, the City Senate Chamber, the »Red Salon« and the Mayor's Reception Room. The Council Chamber of Vienna's City Council and Diet extends over two floors. Austria's capital has held the status of a federal province since 1922, so the City Council is also the Provincial Diet. Decorative pieces of the furnishings include the gold-leaf coffered ceiling of precious wood and the Art Nouveau chandelier, also produced from a design by Friedrich von Schmidt.

Ringstrasse

G – J 5 – 7

Location: 1st District
Tram: 1, 3

Underground : Karlsplatz (U 1, U 2, U 4), Schottentor (U 2), Schottenring (U 2, U 4) Schwedenplatz (U 1, U 4), Stubentor (U 3)

Vienna's ornamental Ringstraße enclosing the inner city consists of the sections Stubenring, Parkring, Schubertring, Kärntner Ring, Opernring, Burgring, Dr.-Karl-Renner-Ring, Dr.-Karl-Lueger-Ring and Schottenring. The Franz-Josefs-Kai (quay) is an extension of the Ring on the Danube canal. The demolition of the bastion fortifications during the reign of Emperor Franz Joseph I made the construction of the tree-lined boulevard possible between 1858 and 1865, and many monumental buildings in the grandiose »Ringstrasse style« were erected in the second half of the 19th century. The ceremonial opening of the 4km/2.5mi long and 57m/62yrd wide Ringstrasse took place in 1865. Its day of glory, however, was in 1879, when the painter Hans Makart arranged the parade with 10,000 participants celebrating the silver wedding anniversary of Emperor Franz Joseph I and Empress Elizabeth.

Monumental Boulevard

The following buildings and parks can be seen during a stroll on the Ringstrasse between Stubenring and Schottenring: ▶ Museum für Angewandte Kunst, ▶ Stadtpark, ▶ Staatsoper, ▶ Hofburg, ▶ Kunsthistorisches Museum, ▶ Naturhistorisches Museum, Volksgarten (▶ Hofburg), ▶ Parlament, ▶ Rathaus, ▶ Burgtheater and University (▶ Old University Quarter); see also ▶ Tours, p.144.

> **!** *Baedeker* TIP
>
> **Rainbow Parade (Regenbogenparade)**
> The Regenbogenparade is for all of those who like a flamboyant party with dazzling colours. This gay pride festival celebrating life and tolerance has become a permanent fixture in Vienna's calendar of events over the last few years. More than 100,000 dancers and onlookers, often in saucy, colourful dress, converge at the end of June/beginning of July, when the demonstration parade spends many hours moving along the Ringstrasse to hot rhythms (info: www.hosiwien.at).

Ronacher

H 6

Location: 1, Seilerstätte 9
Tram: 1, 2, 3

Underground: Stephansplatz (U1, U3)

The Wiener Stadt Theater (Vienna City Theatre) built in 1871/1872 by Ferdinand Fellner the Elder was gutted in a major fire in 1884, leaving only the façade intact. In its place, Anton Ronacher had a magnificent variety theatre built in 1886 – 1888, which also incorporated a coffee house. When Ronacher withdrew from the business for financial reasons in 1890, the house was also being used for theatrical performances, operettas and concerts. After the First World War, the building was used as a radio broadcasting centre. After the Second World War, it was used as an alternative stage for the Burgtheater until 1955, and thereafter as a recording studio for television programmes of the Austrian Broadcasting Corporation. Between 1991 and 1993 the Ronacher was renovated and used for international theatre productions. Finally the former »Etablissement Ronacher« was elaborately restructured as a musical theatre.

✶ ✶ Schönbrunn

B-D 8-10

Location: 13, Schönbrunner Schloßstrasse
Tram: 10, 58

Underground: Schönbrunn, Hietzig (U4)
Bus: 10 A
Internet: www.schoenbrunn.at

Schönbrunn Palace, the summer residence of the Habsburgs, is one of the major tourist attractions in Vienna. 40 representative exhibition rooms from among the palace's numerous rooms can be toured on the first floor. The extensive gardens and park are also worth seeing.

Emperor Maximilian II acquired a manorial estate in 1559 that had been converted from a water mill. After victory over the Turks in 1683, Emperor Leopold I commissioned the architect **Johann Bernhard Fischer von Erlach** in 1696 with the design of an imperial château de plaisance on the site of the destroyed Katterburg manor house. Construction on the Baroque Schönbrunn palace began in the same year and, from 1743 to 1749, **Nikolaus Pacassi** arranged the grounds as a summer residence for Maria Theresa. Further remodelling followed from 1816 to 1817. It took until 1952 to repair all the heavy damage it suffered during the Second World War. After Maria Theresa, the palace experienced its most glamorous time during the Congress of Vienna that convened here in 1814/1815. Other historically significant dates associated with the palace were the years

Schönbrunn: Maria Theresa's Baroque residence

1805 and 1809 when Napoleon I, whose armies had occupied Vienna, made his quarters in Maria Theresa's favourite rooms. In 1918 Karl I abdicated the throne, and in 1945 the English high commissioner set up his headquarters in the palace. The former summer residence of the Habsburgs was placed on the list of UNESCO World Cultural Heritage Sites in 1997.

The wrought iron main gate to the **forecourt** of the beautiful Baroque grounds is flanked by two obelisks.

State Rooms

The **Palace Chapel** left of the foyer was installed around 1700, the ceiling fresco, *The Apotheosis of Maria Magdalena* was painted by Daniel Gran in 1744. The high altar painting, *The Marriage of the Virgin*, was done by Paul Troger; the altar itself is the work of Franz Kohl.

The **Billiard Room**(room 2) is the first in a suite of Emperor Franz Joseph's audience chambers. It is named after Franz I's billiard table, as the game was very popular in his time.

The audience chamber (**Walnut Room**, room 3) of Emperor Franz Joseph takes it name from the walnut panelling completed in 1766; the wood-carved chandelier is covered with real gold.

The modest furnishings of the **Study of Emperor Franz Joseph I** (room 4) stand in complete contrast to the sumptuous decoration of the audience chamber. Numerous private pictures and photos, many among them of his wife, Empress Elizabeth, provide a glimpse of Franz Joseph's private life. One of the two large portraits show the Emperor at the age of 33, the other, Empress Elizabeth, who was called Sisi by her family.

Marie Antoinette, daughter of Maria Theresa, had herself painted in hunting costume

Emperor Franz Joseph I died in the simple iron bed in his **Bedroom** (room 5) on November 21, 1916, after reigning for almost 68 years. The **Stairway Cabinet of Empress Elizabeth** (room 7) served as her study in which she wrote letters, diaries and poems. A spiral staircase leads from here to her private Garden Apartment.

In order to keep slim, Elizabeth spent a lot of time on beauty care, exercise and sport. Alone the maintenance of her magnificent head of hair took several hours (Empress Elizabeth's Dressing Room, room 8). The **Marital Bedroom** (room 9) of the imperial couple, who married in 1854, was only used during the first years of marriage. Elisabeth rejected the strict formality of court life from the very beginning and, from the 1870's onwards, she led an independent life of her own, travelling extensively. (► Baedeker Special p.62–65). On the walls of her reception room, **Elizabeth's Salon** (room 10), hang pastel portraits of Maria Theresa's children done by the Genevan painter Jean Etienne Liotard. One picture portrays Marie Antoinette in a hunting costume. She was married at the age of fifteen to the future French king, Louis XVI. The clock in front of the mirror on the window side of the room has a reversed face on the back so that the time can be read in the mirror.

The **Marie Antoinette Room** (room 11) served during Elizabeth's time as the family dining room. The table is laid with the original family dinner service. As soon as the Emperor had finished eating – and he was a fast eater – the meal was over. The white and gold panelled **Nursery** (room 12) is decorated with portraits of Maria Theresa's daughter. A portrait of the Empress Dowager by Anton von Maron is on the easel. The door offers a view into the bathroom that was installed for Empress Zita. The small **Breakfast Cabinet** (room 13) is furnished with delicate pictures of flowers in silk appliqué embroidery done by Elizabeth Christine, the mother of the Empress. The **Yellow Salon** (room 14) owes its name to the yellow damask covering the furniture. The paintings by Jean Etienne Liotard, which very realistically portray children of the bourgeois class, are in stark contrast to the typical court portraits of Maria Theresa's children displayed in the previous and following rooms. The Louis XVI lady's writing secretary belonged to Marie Antoinette.

Ministers took the oath of office in the **Mirror Room** (room 16), which is decked out with crystal mirrors in gilt Rococo frames. Mozart gave a concert here as a six-year-old child prodigy in 1762. His proud father wrote that after performing, »Wolferl leaped onto Her Majesty's lap, threw his arms around her neck and planted kisses on her face«. The former private chambers of Emperor Joseph I have been preserved in the **Rosa Rooms** (rooms 17-19) since the 1760s. They are named after the impressive landscape pictures that Joseph Rosa painted in late Rococo style between 1760 – 1769.

The Great and Small Galleries lie in the centre of the Palace. The crystal mirrors on opposite walls, the lush white and gold decorations and the ceiling painting depicting the glory of the monarchy and the multi-national state combine to make the **Great Gallery** stand out as one of the most magnificent Rococo ceremonial halls.

With such furnishings, the Great Gallery was the ideal setting for glittering balls, state receptions and banquets of their imperial highnesses. The **Small Gallery** (room 22), whose windows open to a wonderful view of the flower parterre of the park, was used for smaller formal imperial family dinners. The ceiling fresco painted by Gregorio Guglielmi in 1761 glorifies the House of Habsburg and its regency. Maria Theresa set up her »conspiratory« conference chamber among the East Asian lac-

> ✔ **DON'T MISS**
>
> - A leisurely stroll through the palace gardens as far as the Gloriette
> - The Millions Room: magnificent Rococo
> - Large and Small Galleries: glorious ceremonial halls in white and gold
> - The Zoo: the oldest zoo in existence in the world
> - Café Residenz: oven-warm apple strudel and cream with an excellent cup of coffee in the side wing

quered screen panels and under a cupola delicately ornamented with stucco (Round Chinese Cabinet, room 23). Her chancellor, Kaunitz, had 24-hour access to the room by way of a secret stairway. **Chinese art** had a great influence in the 18th century on decorative fashions in royal residences.

Important family celebrations, like a baptism, for instance, were held in the **Hall of Ceremonies** (room 26). The monumental gold-framed paintings from van Meyten's workshop depict the marriage of Joseph II with Isabella of Bourbon-Parma in 1760. The hand-printed Far Eastern wallpaper, the blue and white Japanese vases and the light blue silk formed the noble setting for the end of the monarchy: It was in the **Blue Chinese Salon** (room 28) that Karl I signed the renunciation of participation in the affairs of government in 1918, making Austria a republic. East Asian art is combined with Viennese Rococo in the **Vieux-Laque Room**, Maria Theresa's luxurious private chamber (room 29). After the death of her beloved husband, Franz Stephan, it was redecorated as a memorial room. Maria Theresia wore mourning for the rest of her life. Napoleon I lived in Maria Theresa's former bed chamber (**Napoleon Room**, room 30) in 1805 and 1809. The room was decorated with costly Brussels tapestries in 1873. Napoleon's son, who had grown up in Schönbrunnen, died in this room in 1832, at the age of 21. Blue and white lacquered wood garlands deceptively give the impression of a room covered with real **porcelain** (room 31). The 213 blue ink drawings were done by Franz Stephan and some of his artistically gifted children. Maria Theresa's gorgeous private salon is panelled with precious rosewood covered in carved gilt ornamentation. Hence the room is known as the **Millions Room** (room 32). Recessed in the panelling are 261 Indo-Persian miniatures under glass that came to the Vienna court by way of the Netherlands in the mid-18th century. The miniatures were cut up by the imperial family and set together to form new pictures. The walls and the chairs of the **Gobelin Room** are decorated with Brussels tapestries depicting Dutch folk scenes from the 18th century, including the large »harbour and fish market« (room 33).

The Great Gallery is a fitting setting for elegant balls

Schönbrunn Palace Plan

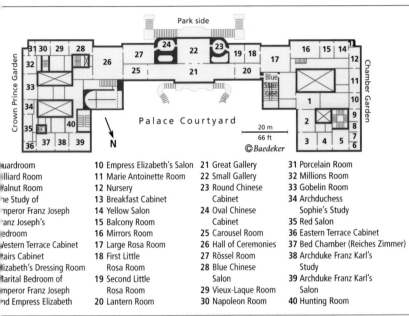

Park side

Palace Courtyard

Crown Prince Garden

Chamber Garden

20 m
66 ft
©Baedeker

N

uardroom
lliard Room
Valnut Room
he Study of
mperor Franz Joseph
ranz Joseph's
edroom
Vestern Terrace Cabinet
tairs Cabinet
lizabeth's Dressing Room
Narital Bedroom of
mperor Franz Joseph
nd Empress Elizabeth

10 Empress Elizabeth's Salon
11 Marie Antoinette Room
12 Nursery
13 Breakfast Cabinet
14 Yellow Salon
15 Balcony Room
16 Mirrors Room
17 Large Rosa Room
18 First Little
   Rosa Room
19 Second Little
   Rosa Room
20 Lantern Room

21 Great Gallery
22 Small Gallery
23 Round Chinese
   Cabinet
24 Oval Chinese
   Cabinet
25 Carousel Room
26 Hall of Ceremonies
27 Rössel Room
28 Blue Chinese
   Salon
29 Vieux-Laque Room
30 Napoleon Room

31 Porcelain Room
32 Millions Room
33 Gobelin Room
34 Archduchess
   Sophie's Study
35 Red Salon
36 Eastern Terrace Cabinet
37 Bed Chamber (Reiches Zimmer)
38 Archduke Franz Karl's
   Study
39 Archduke Franz Karl's
   Salon
40 Hunting Room

The famous painting by Friedrich von Amerling portraying *Emperor Franz I in Toison Regalia with the Order of the Golden Fleece* is in the **Red Salon** (room 35). Franz Joseph was born in the **Reiches Zimmer** (rich room / room 37). In it is a state bed of red velvet with costly gold and silver embroidery, which was originally in Maria Theresa's rooms in the Hofburg. It is the only one of its kind of the Viennese court to survive.

Additional Sights

Vienna's only Baroque theatre still in existence was built by Maria Theresa's favourite architect, Nikolaus Pacassi, in 1747 and remodelled and refurnished in 1767 by the next court architect, Ferdinand Hetzendorf von Hohenberg. The Empress herself took part in stage productions in the »Habsburg House Theatre«. The stage was restored from 1979 to 1980 and is used today by the Max Reinhardt Seminary Drama School.

On display in the former Winter Riding School are more than 60 historical state carriages, sleighs und sedan chairs as well as caparisons and livery of the court dating from 1690 to 1918. The showpiece of the collection is the four tonne, richly decorated imperial

Schlosstheater

Wagenburg
🕐
Opening hours:
Apr – Oct daily
9am – 6pm; Nov –
March Tue – Sun
10am – 4pm

SCHÖNBRUNN PALACE AND PARK

✳ ✳ **The Palace was designed by Johann Bernhard Fischer von Erlach with two long wings, a spacious fore court and a flight of stairs leading to the garden. During Maria Theresa's reign, Schönbrunn became the gleaming focus of the court. Nikolaus Pacassi remodelled the summer residence for her in Baroque and Rococo style. The Palace Garden is also worth seeing with its Palm House and Vienna's zoo, which was founded in 1752.**

🕐 Palace opening hours:
April – June, Sept, Oct daily 8.30am – 5pm
July, August until 6pm, Nov – March until 4.30pm

① Neptune Fountain
The Neptune Fountain designed by Hetzendorf is the crowning element forming the southern boundary of the Garden's Great Parterre. Zauner fashioned the beautiful sculptural group decorating the pool in 1780, using Greek mythological themes for the stone sculpture, including »Thetis entreating Neptune to favour the voyage of her son, Achilles«.

② Maze
In 1998, the laying out of a 49m/160ft x 35m/115ft Maze next to the Neptune Fountain was begun following the historical original. The original Maze was created between 1698 and 1740, and was cleared away in 1892. There is a viewing platform in the centre for the visitors and two energy imparting Feng Shui harmony stones (opening hours: April – Sept 9am – 5.30pm, Oct until 4.30pm, there is an entrance fee for the Maze).

③ Schöner Brunnen (Fair Spring)
The Palace got its name from the old spring, the »Kaiserbrünnl« (Emperor's Spring) and, according to legend, whoever drinks from it will become beautiful. Emperor Matthias (1557-1619) discovered it during a hunt, and Emperor Joseph I had his drinking water fetched from it. It was given a grotto-like pavilion in 1799, in which the water flows from a vase held by the nymph Egeria sculpted by Johann Christian Beyer.

④ Gloriette
Serpentine paths lead from behind the Neptune Fountain up the hill to the Classical colonnaded hall of the Gloriette, which Hetzendorf designed for the spot in 1775 as the crowning conclusion of the park. The Gloriette underwent a complete restoration faithful to the original between 1993 and 1997, with the central hall regaining its former glazing. The former summer dining room of the emperor is crowned by a magnificent domed ceiling.

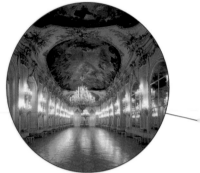

Pacassi moved the great gallery to the courtyard side over a five arched passage leading into the garden. Gregorio Guglielmo is responsible for the ceiling fresco and tells of the income and riches of the Habsburg nations.

Maria Theresa supervised the furnishing of Schönbrunn, demonstrating great artistic sensibility.

Today there is a coffee house in the Gloriette, which affords the visitor a fabulous view of the Palace (open daily; tel.879 13 11).

Maria Theresa in a painting by Martin von Meyten (c1743). She had to find room for her steadily growing family and the court at Schönbrunn. Most of her 16 children stayed in Vienna.

© Baedeker

Black lacquer panels were set into the walnut panelling of the Vieux Lacquer Room. Maria Theresa was a passionate collector of the lacquer panels. Isidore Canevale produced the design for the state room.

A theme from Greek mythology is the basis of the Neptune Fountain.

coach, which, drawn by eight white horses, was used since 1745 for weddings and coronations. The black lacquered hearse drawn by eight black horses was ready when a Habsburg's final ride to the imperial vault was the order of business – the last time was in May 1989 for the funeral of the former Empress Zita, wife of the last Emperor Karl I.. Other displays include Napoleon's Parisian coach for the coronation in Milan, the miniature Parisian coach of the Duke of Reichstadt, Napoleon's son, Empress Caroline's coronation landau, Emperor Franz Joseph's state carriage and the modest coach of Empress Zita.

> ### ! Baedeker TIP
>
> **Classics in the Palace**
>
> The Palace's Orangery provides the unusual setting for classical concerts. Musicians, opera singers and ballet dancers present Mozart's and Johann Strauss' most beautiful melodies daily (information: tel. 812 500 40).

Schlosspark

🕒 Opening hours: April – Oct daily 6am to nightfall, Nov – Mar from 6.30am

The palace park, almost 2 sq km / 0.7 sq mi in size, is one of the most important French Baroque gardens in existence. Jean Trehet laid it out in 1705, following a design by Fischer, and it was given its present appearance between 1765 and 1780, by Adrian von Steckhoven and Ferdinand Hetzendorf von Hohenberg, who created natural elements between geometric flowerbed parterres and attractive architectural accents. 44 mythological figures sculpted in marble dating from around 1773 stand in the avenues on either side of the parterre.

Roman Ruins   The romantic Roman ruins of a half buried palace with Corinthian capitals and a figure frieze were built in 1778. Ferdinand Hetzendorf von Hohenberg wanted to symbolize the might of the Roman Empire through the downfall of the Greek. A few of the decorative elements of the Roman ruins are from the so-called Neugebäude (new building) which is, the half forgotten imperial palace in the present-day suburb of Simmering, which Emperor Maximilian II had constructed for his relaxation and for court festivities. In Maria Theresa's time, the palace served as a powder magazine and, as the magnificent architecture seemed wasted, the Empress ordered it to be »broken up and brought to Schönbrunn«.

Obelisk   Hetzendorf was also responsible for the obelisk at the end of the diagonal axis from 1777. The supporting turtles were formerly gilded and the chiselled scenes depict the Habsburg family saga.

Tiroler Garten   Duke John brought an Alpine touch to Schönbrunn Park when he had two Tyrolean wooden houses and their garden constructed around 1800. The Alpine Garden was removed to the Belvedere in

1865, where it still is today, the oldest of its kind. A café restaurant is now located in the houses.

Tiergarten (Zoo)

The Schönbrunn Tiergarten (Zoo) can be reached directly from Hietzinger Tor. The zoo can be traced back to Emperor Franz I's menagerie of 1752, and is considered to be the oldest zoo in the world. Some 750 species of animals are kept in houses and in the more modern outdoor enclosures that are better adapted to the animals' natural environment. There is an underwater tunnel in the Aquarium-Terrarium House, where fish can be observed close-up. The octagonal Breakfast Pavilion has been standing in the middle of the zoo since 1759. Once the imperial family could look out from the pavilion at the cages with beasts of prey round about. Today it is a café-restaurant.

Opening hours:
Feb daily 9am – 5pm
March, Oct
daily 9am – 5.30pm
April daily
9am – 6pm
May – Sept daily
9am – 6.30pm
Nov – Jan daily
9am – 4pm

Palmenhaus

The Palmenhaus, Europe's largest glass house, is an imposing structure of glass and iron measuring 113m/370 ft in length and 28m/92ft in height, and was built in 1883 by Franz Xaver Segenschmid. It has three different climate-controlled sections featuring exotic plants from all over the world (opening hours: May – Sept daily 9.30am – 6pm, Oct – April daily until 5pm).

Kaiserstöckl

The Kaiserstöckl – the present day post office at Hietzinger Tor – was built by Maria Theresa for her ministers.

Schönlaterngasse

H 6

Location: 1st District

Underground: Stubentor (U3), Schwedenplatz (U1, U4)

The medieval burgher homes and trade houses with Baroque façades that line the old Viennese lane known as the Schönlaterngasse make for romantic strolls, though it is said the legendary basilisk once terrorized the area.

The house »Zur schönen Laterne« dating from 1680, gave the crooked lane in the oldest quarter of the historic city centre its name. The original building is on display in the Historisches Museum and a replica was installed at no.6 in 1971.

Basiliskenhaus

The Basiliskenhaus (no. 7) has been historically documented since 1212. It was formerly also called the »Haus zum rothen Kreuz« (House of the Red Cross). It was restored in the style of 16th century in 1945. A picture on the wall and a sandstone figure in the niche in the second storey of the façade depict the basilisk. According to legend, it was a frightening mythological beast, half rooster, half toad that hatched from an egg and lived in a deep well. It made many people ill with its poisonous breath and could kill with an evil gaze. One day, however, a baker's apprentice, out of love for a beautiful baker's daughter, gathered courage and held a mirror in front of the monster, whereupon the basilisk, horror-stricken at its own appearance, burst and turned to stone.

Alte Schmiede (Old Smithy)
The Alte Schmiede (no. 9) was, until 1974, the blacksmith shop of Master Schmirler, who produced the »beautiful lantern« and donated it to the city. It is possible to tour his workshop. Opening hours: Mon – Fri 2pm – 6pm and by appointment, tel. 5 12 83 29.
In addition, the Alte Schmiede is also a **cultural centre** with an art gallery, café and the Literary Quarter, which organizes readings and lectures.

Heiligen-kreuzerhof
The present monastery complex consists of the abbey courtyard, the prelature, the chapel and the Zinshaus (tenant house) and is situated between Schönlaterngasse and Graßhofgasse. The Heiligenkreuzerhof was built on behalf of the abbots of the Heiligenkreuz monastery in Lower Austria between 1659 und 1676. The grounds gained their present appearance through reconstruction carried out in the 18th century. The **Zinshaus** was added in 1754, and the Baroque painter, Martino Altomonte († 1745) spent his twilight years here. He was responsible for the high altar piece (c1730) in the St Bernhard Chapel next to the prelature. The chapel, consecrated in 1660 and beautifully decorated in Baroque style, is today a popular wedding chapel that offers a magnificent setting for the ceremony.

Secession

G 7

Location: 1, Friedrichstraße 12   **Underground:** Karlsplatz (U1, U2, U4)
Tram: 1, 2, D, J

The dome on the roof of the Secession building is visible from a great distance, a delicate wickerwork of innumerable gilded laurel leaves. The laurel leaves symbolize the dedication to Apollo; after all, the new generation of artists hoped for abundant inspiration from the leader of the muses. Thus the symbolic leaf can be found in other parts of the building as well.

Opening hours: Tue – Sun 10am – 6pm
It did not take long for the Viennese to come up with a nickname for the dome, »Krauthappel« (cabbage head). The epoch defining construction completed by Josef Maria Olbrich in 1898, was the first uniquely Viennese Jugendstil building according to the style of the Secession. The building became necessary in 1892, when the group of young artists led by the painter **Gustav Klimt** broke away from

the conservative Association of Austrian Artists of the Künstlerhaus in 1897. The association that continues to exist to this day, was called the »Secession«, like the artistic style it initiated, and its slogan was »to every age its art – to art its freedom«. Noticeable on the east side of the building is the bronze **Mark Antony Group** by Arthur Strasser. The lion-drawn chariot of the imperator was displayed at the World Exhibition of 1900 in Paris.

Egon Schiele called it »the masterpiece among Gustav Klimt's works«. Klimt created the monumental **Beethoven frieze**, measuring almost 70sq m / 753 sq ft with Ludwig van Beethoven's Ninth Symphony as its subject in 1902, for the 14th Exhibition of

Lovingly called »Cabbage Head« by the Viennese

the Vienna Secession. The state acquired the work from a private collection in 1973. The monumental work's home-coming was celebrated in 1986, in a room specially prepared for it in the basement of the Secession, where it was mounted and can be marvelled at today. The Beethoven frieze symbolizes mankind's longing for happiness.

Spinnerin am Kreuz (Spinner at the Cross)

Location: 10, Triester Straße 52   **Tram:** 1 (Windtenstraße)

The »Spinnerin am Kreuz« is an old Viennese landmark visible for miles. It is a 16m/52ft high Gothic column in the shape of a pinnacle-like tabernacle that was erected by the architect of the cathedral, Hans Puchsbaum, in 1462, to replace an earlier column donated by Leopold III. According to legend, a faithful wife is said to have sat here at her spinning wheel awaiting the return of her husband from the Crusades. Public executions were carried out at »the gallows next the spinner« from 1311 – 1747 and from 1804 – 1868. In 1827, a crowd of 30,000 witnessed the hanging of Severin von Jaroszynski. The Polish aristocrat had committed a robbery that ended in murder in order to fulfill the demanding financial wishes of the popular actress, Therese Krone.

Spittelberg

F/G 6/7

Location: 7, Spittelberggasse and around
Bus: 48 A

Underground: Volkstheater (U2, U3)
Tram: 49

This quarter's charm and atmosphere were rediscovered when the fashion for nostalgia first set in, and the city administration began with its renewal and revitalization programme in the 1970s. Today it is an attractive part of the city offering a great variety of cultural and social activities.

A densely built but architecturally charming district developed during the Baroque period on the hill that once belonged to the public hospital. Turks aimed their canons at the city centre from atop that hill during the Second Turkish Siege in 1683, and Napoleon I's soldiers positioned their artillery on that same hill in 1809. The district deteriorated in time and became a bustling, low class neighbourhood. The Spittelberg was the favoured district for many folk artists, small companies of actors, balladeers and wandering musicians who created the risqué »Spittelberg ballads« some of which have survived to this day. When Emperor Joseph II made an incognito visit to a Spittelberg public house in 1787, he was unceremoniously thrown out by the landlord, who failed to recognise the man who had got into a fight with a notorious whore – an incident that is commemorated in the entrance hall of house no. 13 in the Gutenbergstrasse.

The **Spittelberg Cultural Centre** in the Amerlinghaus (Stiftgasse 8) offers a communal cultural programme of music events, readings, exhibits, children's activities and senior dance evenings, which appeals equally to long-time residents and new arrivals. Alternative shops, boutiques, pubs and galleries have moved into the renovated old buildings round about the Stiftgasse and an arts and crafts and gallery market has also emerged. All these activities combine to make Spittelberg a centre of attraction and a popular place to meet.

Picturesque Biedermeier houses in Spittelberg

✴ ✴ Staatsoper (State Opera House)

Location: 1, Opernring 2
Tram: 1, 2, 3

Underground: Karlsplatz (U1, U2, U4)
Internet: www.wienerstaatsoper.at

The Vienna State Opera House is one of the world's largest and most resplendent music theatres. Since its inception, countless composers and conductors, international soloists and dancers of renown have performed here.

There have been more than 30 directors of the »House of Muses« following Franz Schalk, the first director of the opera; among them Gustav Mahler, Richard Strauss, Herbert von Karajan, Egon Hilbert and Karl Böhm. Right up to Ioan Holender, the latest director following the death of Eberhard Wächter in 1992, all of them have been more or less the target of editorial abuse and admiration. According to law, the republic has charged its most famous opera house with cultivating the entire repertoire of opera and so, for 300 evenings of the year, a different opera or ballet is on the programme daily. The Viennese's obsession with music has its roots deep in Habsburg history. The first verifiable opera performed for the Vienna imperial court was in 1625, on Ferdinand II's birthday; though not in Vienna. It was in the Hradschin, the palace in Prague, where the emperor resided for half a year. Three quarters of a year later, a wooden box-theatre with cleverly designed stage equipment was constructed for the Regensburg Imperial Diet and was torn down after the festivities and stored in the Vienna Arsenal until Leopold I, a great music

⊙
Tours:
daily 10am, 11am,
1pm, 2pm, 3pm
dependent on
rehearsals; often
closed

❗ *Baedeker* TIP

Last Minute Tickets
When tickets are still available for an opera performance, a portion of them are sold at a flat rate of 40 Euros on the day of the performance at the box office from 9am – 2pm, Sat, Sun and Fri from 9am – noon, as well as at the ticket counter in the foyer and at the information centres in the opera arcade. To find out if and how many such tickets are available, call tel. 514 44 29 50.

lover and theatre aficionado, had the delightful little theatre set up on the square in front of the court riding school from 1660 – 1662. After 1668, numerous operas were staged, at first in a splendid wood theatre on the square of what is today the Austrian National Library, later in the Redouten halls and in the old Burgtheater on Michaelerplatz, where Mozart's *Il Seraglio* and his opera *The Marriage of Figaro* and *Così fan tutte* had their premières. After 1710, the leading composers celebrated triumphs with their new works in the Kärntnertor Theatre, and Maria Theresa's theatre reform finally opened up the court stage to the masses. It was here that Carl Maria von Weber's musical drama, *Euryanthe*, was first performed, Beethoven's *Fidelio* started him on his rise to fame in 1814; and a few years later an ab-

An appropriate building for the Viennese music obsession

solute euphoria for Italian opera exploded with the first performances in Vienna of Rossini and Verdi. After the fire in the Ringtheater, the court opera finally moved to its new venue in the Ringstrasse in 1869, which became nationalized in 1918.

Building History   The massive Opera House's clearly delineated forms inspired by the Renaissance were designed by **August von Siccardsburg** and **Eduard van der Null** and constructed between 1861 – 1869. The new opera theatre was opened in 1869, with Mozart's *Don Giovanni*. The two architects of the opera house building did not live to experience it. The criticism and ridicule voiced by the Viennese during the construction drove van der Null to commit suicide; his colleague Siccardsburg died only two months after him of a heart attack, in 1868. The State Opera House was hit by bombs in 1945 and burned to the ground. Its faithful reconstruction as a traditional box theatre lasted until 1955, with the stage area being completely modernized. The second opening of the »House on the Ring« followed in 1955 with Beethoven's *Fidelio*. The new state opera seats 2,211 and provides space for 110 musicians of the Vienna Philharmonic – the resident orchestra since 1842. Some 1,000 employees keep the mammoth theatre running smoothly. Added to that are the troops of the superordinated Austrian Federal Theatre Administration, the extras, the dressers and the brown-liveried ushers who, like the standing-room-only spectators, are never missing at a performance. The main façade of the three part building opens up to the Ringstrasse with a two-storey hall. Inside, a magnificent grand staircase leads up to the first floor. Directly opposite is the Schwind Foyer named after the opera scenes by the painter Moritz von Schwind. The stairs, foyer and the tea salon furnished with valuable tapestries were the only parts of the building that survived unscathed in 1945. The restored former imperial box, the left-side proscenium box, is reserved today for the federal president. The archduke's box opposite is kept for the Austrian chancellor for official purposes.

The annual opera ball on the last Thursday during carnival, a grand gala evening with lilting waltz music, is one of the most famous and elegant balls there is. The rows of seats and the stage in the cream, red and gold hall are brought to the same level by raising the floor (tickets for the ball can only be ordered in writing: Opernballbüro, A-1010 Wien, Goethegasse 1, fax 5 14 44 26 24, e-mail: opernball@ wiener-staatsoper.at).

Opera Ball

Hotel Sacher

The traditional hotel behind the Staatsoper in Philharmonikerstrasse is probably the most famous in Vienna, which even today is still stylish, furnished as it is with costly silk wall coverings, exquisite Biedermeier furniture and valuable paintings. Important state receptions are held as before in the nostalgic marble hall. Eduard Sacher had the house built in 1876, while his cigar-smoking widow, **Anna Sacher**, made it famous. She allowed the offspring of rich parents – so-called »Sacher boys« – unlimited credit until they came into their inheritance, and she also set up those *chambres séparées*, discretely closed off tables, which live on, at least in literature, as **Arthur Schnitzler** ensured in his *A Farewell Dinner*. Nowadays, the little séparées serve as elegant dining rooms. The legendary **Sachertorte** was supposedly created by an ancestor of Eduard Sacher in 1814, on the occasion of the Congress of Vienna, but the origin and authenticity of the recipe has been contested in court for decades with Café Demel. The delicious cake can be bought in all sizes and packaging in a little shop around the corner in Kärntner Strasse.

Hotel with a legendary reputation

Stadtpark (City Park)

H/J 6/7

Location: 1, Parkring
Tram: 2

Underground: Stubentor (U3), Stadtpark (U4)

The Stadtpark (city park), whose two sections are connected by bridges over the Wienfluss (Vienna River), covers an area of 11.4ha/ 28 acres. Franz Joseph I initiated the creation of a garden at the site of the former water glacis in 1857, »to serve as an embellishment for the residence«. Landscape artist Rudolf Siebeck executed the plans drawn up by the landscape painter Josef Szelleny and in 1862 the garden was left to its fate. The Kursalon was opened in 1867, in which primarily waltz concerts are held today. In the part of the park nearest to the inner city there are statues of the painters Hans Canon, Emil Schindler, Hans Makart and Friedrich von Amerling, and of the composers Franz Lehár, Johann Strauß, Franz Schubert, Anton Bruckner and Robert Stolz. The **Donauweibchenbrunnen** (Danube Women Fountain) is a copy – the original is in the Historische Museum.

★ ★ Stephansdom (St Stephen's Cathedral)

H 6

| **Location:** 1, Stephansplatz | **Underground:** Stephansplatz (U1, U3) |

The cathedral and metropolitan church of Stephansdom dominating the skyline of the old city is Vienna's most famous landmark, and Austria's most important Gothic building. The Stephansdom, crowned by a 137m/450ft high tower, has been an archbishopric since 1722.

Generations of architects and master builders have laboured on the church edifice since the 12th century, which today uniquely represents the history of art over a span of eight hundred years. The original Romanesque church made way for a Late Romanesque version in the 13th century, from which the Giant's Door and the Roman towers still survive. The remodelling into a Gothic church was undertaken in the 14th century by Duke **Rudolf IV of Habsburg** – explaining why he was known as »The Founder«. It was in this century that the choir hall, St Eligius Chapel, the Chapel of the Cross (Tirnakapelle) and St Katharine Chapel were finished. The southern tower, the long house and the Barbara Chapel date from the 15th century. The still incomplete north tower was given a temporary cap in the 16th century and improvements and extensions were made from the 17th – 19th centuries. In the last days of the war in 1945, the roof of the cathedral burned down, the vaulting of the middle choir and the choir on the right side collapsed and the towers were gutted. The reconstruction and restoration work that lasted from 1948 – 1962 was a collective project involving all of Austria. The new bell was donated by the province of Upper Austria, the floor by Lower Austria, the pew benches by Vorarlberg, the windows by Tyrol, the chandeliers by Carinthia, the altar rail by Burgenland, the tabernacle by Salzburg, the roof by Vienna and the door by Styria. As is the case with many other historical monuments today, Stephansdom is also threatened by pollutants in the air. In order to arrest the deterioration, it is scrubbed with pure water using soft-bristle brushes. Chemical preservatives and sandblasting were not even considered because they would reduce the stone's ability to breathe and the process of destruction would still continue.

The cathedral is 107m/351ft long and 34m/111ft wide; the height of the middle nave is 28m/92ft. The Roman towers are 66m/216ft high, the southern tower 137m/450ft and the incomplete north tower 68m/223ft. The roof is covered with around 230,000 glazed tiles.

Main Body

Exterior

The late Romanesque Giant's Door dating from about 1230, with its exceptionally rich ornament work, was formerly opened only for festive occasions. During the time of the Babenbergs, justice was administered here. Napoleon's departing proclamation was hung under the frieze of dragons, birds, lions, monks and demonic creatures in 1805. Two iron standard measurement bars are fixed in the wall to the left of the portico. The longer one is the **Viennese normal ell**, the shorter is the Viennese linen ell. It is thought that passion plays were performed in front of the Giant's Door. The stage was erected in the area of the cemetery (▶Stephansplatz).

»Giant's Door«

The Heathen Towers – also known as the Roman Towers – were part of the Romanesque church building first mentioned in 1295. Their name can be traced back to the Roman heathen shrine that is thought to have been located where they now stand. The 66 m / 216ft high towers change from a square outline to an octagonal one above the third floor.

Heathen Towers

The Bishop's Door – a counterpart to the Singer Door – was the entrance for female visitors to the cathedral. Its figural sculpting dates back to the High Gothic period about 1370. The figures of Duke Albrecht III and his wife can be seen next to the shield-bearers.

Bishop's Door

! *Baedeker* TIP

Manner Shop

The pink packaging with the Stephansdom logo is known to sweet-tooths around the globe. The company that produces the famous nougat wafer biscuit known as the »Manner Schnitten« has opened a flagship store (Stephansplatz corner Rotenturmstrasse) within sight of the Stephansdom – a must for visitors to Vienna in search of a sweet souvenir.

STEPHANSDOM

* * The origins of the Stephansdom reach all the way back into the 12th century. The Giant's Door and the Roman Towers date from the 13th century. Duke Rudolf IV of Habsburg, the Founder, instigated its remodelling into a Gothic church with star-ribbed and net vaulting and the 131m/430ft high South Tower. The North Tower remains uncompleted to this day and was given a Renaissance-style cap in 1557.

🕐 Tours:
Mon – Sat 9am – 11.30am 1pm – 4.30pm,
Suni 1pm – 4.30pm

① South Tower
The South Tower is one of the highest church towers in Central Europe. It stands on a square foundation but changes its form into an octagon while continually tapering. The ornament at the top of the spire is a bronze globe fixed with a double eagle.

Only the base of the late Gothic organ by Master Pilgram still exists. The monogram gives 1513 as the date of its origin. The man with the compasses and carpenter's square is Pilgram himself, once again in his famous »Fenster-gucker« (window gawker) pose.

② Madonna of the Servants
The most valuable statue in the cathedral is the Virgin dating back to around 1340. According to legend, when a count's maid was accused of stealing, she appealed to the Madonna. When the real culprit was found, the count's wife donated the figure to the cathedral.

in the church's nave, a masterpiece of Late Gothic sculpture from the workshop of Niclaes Gerhaert van Leyden of Holland.

③ Catacombs
The mortal remains of 15 Habsburgs rest in the catacombs, as well as the viscera of another 56 Habsburgs, who were buried in the Imperial Vault.

⑤ Frederick III's Raised Tomb
The work on the marble sarcophagus covered two generations. The overall design was also by Niclas Gerhaert van Leyden.

④ The Pulpit
The pulpit with the busts of the four church founders is the most magnificent piece of artwork

View from the South Tower

Frederick III donated the winged altar dating from 1447, which was brought from the monastery in the city of Wiener Neustadt to Vienna in 1884. Carved statues of the Virgin and St Catherine can be seen in the lower field of the central shrine of the Wiener Neustädter Altar.

The nave has a net vault with four bays. The figures next to the clustered pillars do not follow any standard iconographic programme.

The Singer Door was the entrance for male visitors. The figures of the founders, the nine Apostles and the legend of St Paul in the tympanum date back to around 1378.

At the foot of the pulpit is the portrait of an unknown artist – presumably Anton Pilgram, who worked on the pulpit – in the familiar pose of the »Fenstergucker«.

© Baedeker

Eagle Door   Master Puchsbaum is considered to be the builder of this part of the church. Frederick III, Maximilian I, Franz Joseph I along with Elizabeth and Maria of Burgund can be seen in the upper row of canopy figures added in the 19th century. The iron roll on the pillar to the left is possibly a medieval sanctuary knocker.

North Tower   The north tower, also known as Eagle Tower, remained incomplete because its builder, Hans Puchsbaum, was said to have sealed a pact with the devil for the quick completion of the tower and was thrown by him into the abyss for uttering a holy name. The new »Pummerin« bell has been hanging in the north tower since 1957. It was cast in 1951, from the remains of the previous bell that had hung there from 1711 until it was destroyed in 1945. The bell weighs 21 tonnes and has a diameter exceeding 3m/10ft. It is rung only on special occasions, such as to ring in the New Year. There is a fast lift up to the bell (admission April – Oct daily 8.30am – 5.30pm, July, Aug until 6pm, Nov – March daily 8.30am – 5pm).

> **! Baedeker TIP**
>
> **Stairway to Heaven**
>
> It is worth taking a tour of the south tower, but it involves climbing 343 steps up to the guard room (admission daily 9am – 5.30pm). The effort of climbing the steps is repaid with a fantastic panoramic view of the city.

South Tower   Construction on the famous south tower, affectionately known as »Steffl«, was begun in 1356. It is 137m/450ft high and is considered – together with the Freiburg Münster tower – to be the most beautiful of German Gothic towers. The statues under the rich baldachin or canopy of state on the second floor represent the benefactors of the church. These are copies. The 14th century originals are in the Vienna Historisches Museum. The portico between the tower's two flying buttresses dates from the 14th century, as do the seated figures of the Evangelists.

Interior

Tirnakapelle (Chapel of the Crosses)   The Chapel of the Crosses, dating back to about 1359, is the burial chapel of Prince Eugene – a grave stone set in the floor commemorates the »Conqueror of the Turks«. The crucifix above the altar dates from the 15th century. Jesus is wearing a beard of real hair and according to legend, it continues to grow.

Stone Baldachin   Hans von Prachatitz probably created this perforated stone altar baldachin around 1437; the Sacred Heart painting below, however, dates from the 18th century.

Nave   The interior is divided by clustered pillars that support the stellar and reticulated vaulting. Life-size statues of stone and clay stand

The pulpit designed by Niclaes Gerhaert van Leyden is one of the most beautiful works of art in the cathedral

next to the pillars. The most valuable of the donated figures is that of St Christoper at the left choir pillar (1470), probably a gift of Emperor Frederick III.

The entrance to the catacombs is in the north tower hall. The catacombs can only be seen during a guided tour. They extend from under the cathedral choir all the way to below Stephansplatz and hold the remains of thousands of Viennese on several levels that are not open to the public. These burial facilities are associated with the cemetery that once surrounded the cathedral, where a stench of decay had spread due to careless burial practices and poor maintenance, necessitating a more effective alternative. So it was decided in 1470 to build a new charnel-house, the catacombs, which reached their greatest extent after the closing down of the Stephansdom cemetery in 1735. By 1783, when Emperor Joseph II had banned further burials in the catacombs, there were still over 10,000 dead interred here.

The highlight of the catacombs is the **Ducal Crypt** that Rudolf IV had ordered in 1363 for the members of the House of Habsburg. Since the construction of the Imperial Vault in the Kapuzinerkirche, it has been customary to keep only the copper urns with the viscera of the members of the ruling house here. The bodies are buried in the Imperial Vault and the hearts in the Herzgruft (Heart Vault) in the Augustinerkirche. There has been a crypt for the archbishop of Vienna in the catacombs since 1953.

Catacombs
Opening hours:
Mon – Sat
10am – 11.30am,
1.30pm – 4.30pm,
Sun
1.30pm – 4.30pm

Barbarakapelle In its basic form, the St Barbara Chapel is much the same as St Katherine Chapel and was also designed by Puchsbaum.

Founder's Sepulchre (Stiftergrabmal) Among the Early Gothic figures dating back before 1340 are an especially beautiful Annunciation Angel and the mantled Virgin Mary the Protector which decorate the so-called women's choir. Among the most important tombs is the empty founder's sepulchre reserved for Rudolf IV.

High Altar **Tobias and Johann Jakob Pock** laboured on the black marble high altar from 1640 – 1660. The statues next to the altarpiece depict the patron saints of the surrounding provinces, St Leopold and St Florian and the plague saints, St Rochus and St Sebastian.
There are Gothic glass paintings to the right and the left behind the high altar that have survived.

South Choir The south choir is dominated by the massive raised red marble tomb of Frederick III – the larger than life figure of the emperor is surrounded by particularly fine coats of arms. It was designed by **Niclas Gerhaert van Leyden** (1467 – 1513), who worked on the cover plate of the Gothic sepulchre himself.

Katharinenkapelle The marble baptismal font dates from 1481, the reliefs of the 14-sided basin depict Christ, John the Baptist and the Twelve Apostles. The Four Evangelists can be seen on the base of the font. The wood carving of the font's cap is particularly beautiful.

Leopold Altar Baldachin The Late Gothic altar baldachin covering the Leopold Altar, donated in 1448, is thought to be the work of **Hans Puchsbaum**.

Maria Pócs Madonna The Maria Pócs icon (Pötscher Madonna) under the Late Gothic altar baldachin has been highly venerated in Austria and Hungary since the Battle of Zenta in 1697. Legend says that tears flowed from the eyes of the Madonna for two weeks during the battle against the Turks.

Eligiuskapelle The chapel of St Eligius is also called the Duke Chapel and its statues are among the most important sculptures of the second half of the 14th century. The »Hausmuttergottes« (Our Lady of the House) originally came from the former Heaven's Gate monastery and had an imperial devotee, Maria Theresa.

✳ Mozarthaus

⏱ Opening hours: daily 9am – 6pm

A must for fans of classical music is a visit to the Mozarthaus in the Schulerstrasse leading away from Stephansplatz (entrance Domgasse 5). **Mozart** lived on the first floor of this typical old Viennese house from 1784 – 1787 with his wife and son, and supposedly spent the happiest years of his life here. It was here that he wrote his opera *The Marriage of Figaro*. Here Beethoven was a student of his for a short time and here he received the appointment to imperial chamber composer. Mozart's rooms in what was then known as the »Camesinahaus« have been furnished as a memorial site. The study, richly adorned with stucco decoration, has pictures and engravings, the original score of *Ave verum* and the first German libretto for *The Marriage of Figaro* on display.

The house in which the brilliant composer died in the nearby Rauhensteingasse no. 8 no longer exists; his grave is in the St Marx cemetery.

Stephansplatz

H 6

Location: 1st District   **Underground:** Stephansplatz (U1, U3)

The square in front of Stephansdom forms the middle point of the Viennese city centre. Stephansplatz and Stock-im-Eisen-Platz merge seamlessly into one another and the Haas Haus is prominently situated opposite the cathedral.

After the damages of war and the construction of the Underground, the spacious open area was redesigned. Of interest around the square are the houses »Zur Weltkugel« (no. 2), Churhaus (no. 3), Domherrenhof (no. 5), Zwettler Hof (no. 6) and the Archbishop's Palais (no. 7). A reminder of the fact that Stephansplatz was a cemetery until

Stephansplatz *Historical Situation*

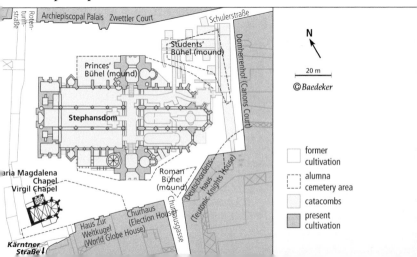

1732 are the gravestones set in the outside walls of the cathedral, and the Late Gothic column in which an eternal flame burned for the dead. A copy can be seen today on the west end of the cathedral's south wall.

Floor plan of the Maria Magdalena Chapel

The floor plan of the Maria Magdalena Chapel is marked with coloured stones to the right of Stephansdom. It once served for confirmation and requiem masses. The funeral chapel, first mentioned in 1378, burned down in 1781 and was removed. Its foundation was unearthed during the construction of the Stephansplatz Underground station, when another discovery was also made: Beneath the chapel's basement floor there was another vault, the Virgilkapelle that was used as a charnel house.

✱ **Virgilkapelle**

This extraordinary witness to the city's medieval past is no longer open to the public for reasons of conservation. Based on architectural comparisons, it was possible to place the construction of the chapel in the 13th century. For example, the zigzag pattern of what is recognizable as a wheel cross, directly beneath the vaulting of the niches, corresponds to the ornamentation of the Giant's Door of the cathedral. Undoubtedly the subterranean niche chamber was planned from the start as a crypt. It was in the possession of the Chrannest family from the beginning of the 14th century, who used the chamber as a **family vault** and decorated it with altars; the most important of them was dedicated to **St Virgil**. The fact that such a monumental crypt was in the hands of a non-aristocratic family raises questions. Quite possibly Frederick the Quarrelsome had the Virgilkapelle built as a crypt for future bishops when Vienna was finally declared a diocese, which he was trying to achieve. The duke's early death prevented the realization of his plan and Vienna did not become an independent diocese until 1469. This would have made it possible for the Chrannest family to acquire the crypt chamber. After the Chrannest family died out, the Virgilkapelle became the seat of the newly founded Brotherhood of Corpus Christi and of a brotherhood of merchants (early 16th century). It was used as a burial site once more in the 16th and 17th centuries. The underground crypt

! **Baedeker TIP**

Culinary Heights

The restaurant »Do & Co« (tel. 535 39 69), on the roof terrace of the Haas House serves, along with its culinary delights, an impressive »eyeball-to-eyeball« view of the Stephansdom and its fantastic Gothic tracery, particularly inspiring in the evening.

was abandoned when the Maria Magdalena Chapel was not rebuilt in 1781. The height of the rectangular Virgilkapelle was about 13m/42ft; today its floor lies 12m/39ft below street level. There are niches in the walls. Access to the crypt was probably through a trapdoor in the floor of the chapel above.

Stock-im-Eisen-Platz

Stock-im-Eisen-Platz merges seamlessly with Stephansplatz and leads into Kärntner Strasse. It received its name from a tree stump studded with masses of nails in the niche of house no. 3/4 (corner Graben and Kärntner Strasse), which was first mentioned in 1533. According to legend, every itinerant locksmith's apprentice passing through Vienna had to hammer a nail into the stump.

Even today, Vienna adheres to an opulent style: Hans Hollein's Haas House

Haas Haus

On the site of no. 6, directly opposite the west door of the Stephansdom is a post modern, futuristic secular building by the prominent Viennese architect Hans Hollein wrapped in a glittering façade. It is an American type shopping mall and one of the many sources of inspiration was the oft-copied Horton Plaza open-air shopping mall in San Diego. Behind the cool and elegant façade of green shimmering quartzite and marble, which is stepped down to the Haas House's massive bow window, is an opulent, eclectic and fanciful collection of exclusive designer boutiques, specialty shops, a large music and video store, an office and a banking floor spread over five floors. And »Do & Co« can be found on the gourmet floor.

Technisches Museum (Technical Museum)

D 8

Location: 14, Mariahilfer Straße 212   **Tram:** 52, 58

Those who want to know how water power was transformed into electricity in the Alpine valleys of 1912, can take a look at the original, reconstructed Ruetz power station with its huge turbines. A guided tour of the mine offers visitors a true-to-life impression of coal mining at the beginning of the 20th century. Emperor Franz Jo-

Opening hours:
Mon – Fri
9am – 6pm Sat, Sun
10am – 6pm

seph laid the cornerstone of the three-storied building in 1909, but it was not opened until 1918, after he had died. The Imperial Physics Collection developed into an Industrial Collection, which later became a Production Collection, out of which eventually emerged the Technology Museum with its Railway, Post and Telegraph Museum. The extensive collection offers a cross-section of the entire development of technology, commerce and industry, with a special focus on Austrian achievements. The palette of exhibits stretches from a **Gothic steam engine (Prick'sche Dampfmaschine)** to virtual robots. The Gallery of Steam Engines possesses a unique collection of steam engines – beginning with the first drive motors of 1790, to Watt's 1825 steam engine and the horizontal steam engine of 1908. In addition, Prick's steam engine (c1872) can be seen in operation. The miniature TMW is a special adventure area for children, that encourages a playful first encounter with technology.

★ Theatermuseum (Theatre Museum)

H 6

Location: 1, Lobkowitzerplatz 2
Tram: 1, 2, 3

Underground: Stephansplatz (U1, U3)
Internet:: www.khm.at

Backdrop in blue and gold

Commissioned by Master of the Horse Count Sigismund Dietrichstein, the monumental **Palais Lobkowitz** was built by **Pietro Tencala** from 1685 to 1687. Between 1709–1711, **Johann Bernhard Fischer von Erlach** added a high Baroque door and a low wall above the entablature of the façade. In 1804, Beethoven conducted the first performance of his Third Symphony and, three years later, his Fourth in the festive Eroica Hall, with its beautiful ceiling frescoes by Jakob van Schuppen. With more than 1.6 million exhibits, the Theatre Musem is the largest of its kind in the world. Along with temporary exhibits and retrospectives on prominent theatre personalities, the permanent collection displays typical items from the museum's rich store of over 1,000 stage models, 600 costumes and props. For example, on display are some of the costumes of the dancer Fanny Elssler and the actress Hedwig Bleib-treu, who wore one of Empress Elizabeth's dresses in her role as Eliz-abeth in *Mary Stuart*, in 1895. There is also a place for the odd and unusual in the museum: for example, the heel of playwright Gerhart Hauptmann's shoe, which he lost in the Burgtheater. Stephan Zweig left his valuable collection of manuscripts to the museum in 1938, before he was forced into exile after the Nazis seized power. At the beginning of the tour, visitors may sit on the imposing »visitors' throne« before moving on to the exciting history of the theatre, and becoming acquainted with the work of the costume and stage design-ers, as well as with that of the sound technicians.

In the nearby **museum department** in Hanuschgasse no. 3, there are a few **commemorative rooms** honouring the actor Hugo Thimig, the director Max Reinhard and the stage designer Caspar Neher, among others.

Opening hours:
Wed – Mon
10am – 6pm

✷ Uhrenmuseum (Clock Museum)

H 6

Location: 1, Schulhof 2   **Underground:** Stephansplatz (U1, U3)
Internet:: www.wienmuseum.at

Vienna's Clock Museum has been located in the »Harfenhaus« since 1921, one of the city's oldest houses. The development of the clock from the 15th century to the present day is shown on three floors.

There are almost 1,200 timepieces to be admired, including basic non-mechanical clocks, roasting jack clocks, tower clocks, table clocks and pocket watches and Austrian Biedermeier lantern clocks. Room 1 has predominantly tower clocks, including a 1699 tower clock from the Stephansdom, and the oldest timepiece in the collec-tion, a 15th century **tower-keeper's clock**.

The show piece among the hand-crafted wall clocks in room 2 is an **astronomical wall clock** dating from 1663.

One of the most valuable pieces in room 4 is the **pendule**, a grandfa-ther clock dating from 1752 by Louis Monet of Paris. The remains of the clock collection of the poet Marie von Ebner-Eschenbach are on display in room 5, including a Swiss gold pendant watch from around 1800, and gold enamel watches. Rare Japanese clocks are dis-played in room 7, among them an unusual pillar clock dating from the 18th century. There is a remarkable decorative astronomical clock from 1863 among the wall clocks in room 12. An especially elaborately carved cuckoo clock from Austria can be found among the Black Forest clocks in room 14.

A night light clock, probably from Switzerland, is one of the rarities in room 15.

Opening hours:
Tue – Sun
10am – 6pm
tours: 1st and 3rd
Sun of the month
10am, 11am

✳ UNO City · Donau City

L 3

Location: 22, Wagramer Straße 5
Bus: 90 A, 91 A, 92 A

Underground: Kaisermühlen/
Vienna International Centre (U1)

UNO City represents a controversial chapter in Viennese architectural history. The modern administration complex has been growing since the 1970s, near Donaupark, with the goal of becoming the third UN city. When plans for a World Expo fell through, the concept for the neighbouring Donau City also ran into trouble.

🕐
Tour:
Mon – Fri
11am, 2pm
(meeting point:
visitors' centre)

After the Danube had been regulated for a second time in the 1970s, **UNO City** and an international conference centre, the **Austria Centre Vienna**, were raised up at the head of the Donaubrücke (bridge) opposite the old city. A 99 year lease was given to the United Nations for the office complex in UNO City for a symbolic rent. Located there, along with smaller sub-organizations, are the United Nations Industrial Development Organization (UNIDO), the Commission on International Trade Law (UNCITRAL), the International Atomic Energy Agency (IAEA) and the office of the High Commissioner for Refugees in Vienna (UNHCR). The complex has been extra-territorial since 1979. Since 1976, the unconventionally curved, 54m to 120m / 177 – 394ft tall **high-rise towers** designed by **Johann Staber** have been setting a new architectural trend in the otherwise metamorphic and unsightly »Transdanubia« quarter, which has remained purely a community of office buildings without gaining any further functions of a city centre. Prominent Austrian artists have been commissioned to adorn interiors and exteriors. For example, a bronze cast by Joannis Avramidis (*Polis*) can be seen on UNO Plaza, and inside are paintings by the likes of Wolfgang Hollegha, Georg Eisler, Karl Korab, Kurt Regschek, Peter Pongratz, Friedensreich Hundertwasser and reliefs by Alfred Hrdlicka and Giselbert Hocke.

Austria Center Vienna

The neighbouring Austria Center Vienna was opened in 1987, a highly modern event and conference centre which can accommodate more than 4,000 participants. Fourteen halls of various sizes are available for concerts, balls, banquets, exhibits, theatre performances and TV shows.

Donau City

The World Expo 1995 that was planned for the area surrounding UNO City, but was cancelled by a referendum, would have facilitated the development of this bridgehead into a second city centre through its multi-functional re-use. Now, in accordance with the will of the city planners, this function will be assumed by UNO City's neighbour, Donau City. Part of it will be erected on the building site that

*Johann Staber designed the curved high rises;
on the left is Holzbauer's Andromeda Tower*

had already been prepared for the World Expo, another part will be on the roofed over motorway, and another on the Handelskai. Donau City is planned not only to provide space for offices and business, but also cultural facilities, and a third is earmarked for housing, making it a living, multi-functional urban centre.

The new part of the city will be in stark contrast to the historic city centre and monumental high-rises on both sides of the Danube will set the trend. The first building completed was the **Andromeda Tower** (110m / 361ft) by Wilhelm Holzbauer in 1998. It is the seat of numerous foreign companies. In the following year, Europe's third largest office tower, the 202m/663ft high **Millennium Tower**, designed by the architectural firm of Peichl/Weber, was built on Handelskai. It is planned that **Tech Gate Vienna**, a science and technology park, and other research facilities and enterprises, will make Donau City Vienna's pre-eminent technological location. The principle of having simply a framework development plan for an entire city district is new. It divides the area of land available into parcels, determines the street routes, heights of the buildings and maximum cubature per parcel. The rest of the architectural shaping of the individual parcels is left for the most part to time and the individual builders. In the meantime, numerous prominent local and foreign architects are involved in the planning and building of the individual projects. The entire Donau City is planned as a pedestrian zone. Motorized traffic will be

Architectural concept

placed below pedestrian level. Some of the offices, flats and shops have already been completed.

✳ Donaupark

Donaupark borders to the north on UN City and is Vienna's second largest park. It was laid out in 1964 for the Vienna International Garden Show. The Donauparkbahn (railway) runs around the park. There is a lake theatre on the artificial Iris Lake that seats 4,000 people. Rising up on the grounds of Donaupark is the **Donauturm** (Donau Tower), at 252m/826ft, it is Vienna's highest structure. The tower was inaugurated as part of the Garden Show. Lifts ride up 150m/492ft to an observation terrace and there are two rotating restaurants, one at an elevation of 160m/525ft and the other at 170m/557ft.

> ### ! *Baedeker* TIP
>
> **Bungee Jumping on the Danube**
> The courageous can plunge into space from the Donau Tower's observation terrace attached only to an elastic cable. Its 152m/499ft jump is a record height in Europe. The season is from July to mid-October. Information and reservations at www.jochen-schweizer.at or tel. 08 20 22 02 11.

Votivkirche (Votive Church)

G 5

Location: 9, Rooseveltplatz   **Underground:** Schottentor (U2)
Tram: 1, 3, 37, 38, 40, 41, 42, 43, 44

The Votivkirche, also called the »Ringstraßendom« was built as a votive gift (thank offering) after a failed assassination attempt of Emperor Franz Joseph I in 1853.

The provost's church »Zum Göttlichen Heiland« (Church of the Divine Savior), was built by Emperor Franz Joseph I in gratitude for having survived a failed assassination attempt on his life in 1853. Archduke Ferdinand Maximilian, later emperor of Mexico and Franz Joseph's brother, took the initiative in raising the necessary funds. **Heinrich Ferstel** built the neo-Gothic church that was consecrated in 1879. It was one of the most successful examples of historically inspired architecture in imitation of French Gothic cathedrals. The Votivkirche possesses two significant works of art: first the elevated Renaissance tomb of Count Nicholas Salm, the commander during the first Turkish Siege in 1529, with the reclining figure of the count on the covering slab and twelve masterly reliefs on the sides produced in the workshops of Loy Hering, in Antwerp (1530–1533) in the baptistery in the south transept; second the Antwerp Altar, a magnificent 15th century carved altar with scenes of the Passion in the side chapel in the south transept. A copy of Our Lady of Guadelupe in a niche in the north transept is a reminder of Emperor Maximilian of Mexico, the first protector of the church.

✷ Zentralfriedhof (Central Cemetery)

beyond the map

Location: 11, Simmeringer Hauptstrasse 234

S-Bahn: Zentralfriedhof (S7)
Tram: 4, 6

Georg Kreisler described it poetically with »Death must be a Viennese« and Helmut Qualtinger commented caustically that »in Vienna, you have to die before they celebrate you, but then you live long.«

Coming to terms with death has always been a major matter of concern in the Danube metropolis. Vienna's cemeteries, with their extraordinarily magnificent tombs and the inviolable funeral ceremony, requisites for a »beautiful funeral«, testify to the exceptional value

The Viennese have an especially intimate relationship with death; funerals are celebrated by huge numbers of mourners and with impassioned eulogies

Zentralfriedhof (Central Cemetery) Orientation Map

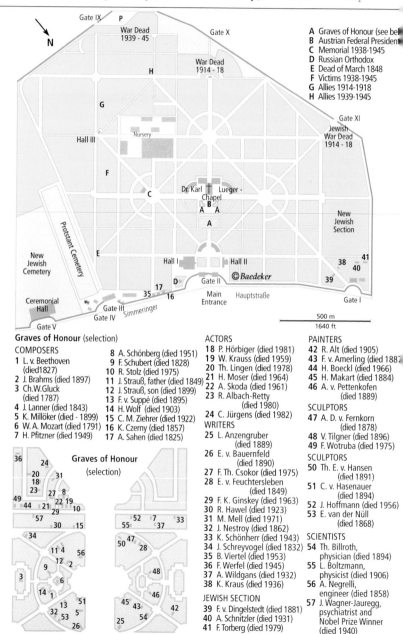

N

Gate IX P
War Dead 1939 - 45
Gate X
War Dead 1914 - 18
H
G
Hall III
Nursery
Gate XI
Jewish War Dead 1914 - 18
F
C
Dr. Karl ✝ Lueger - Chapel
B
A A
A
New Jewish Section
Protestant Cemetery
E
New Jewish Cemetery
Hall I
Hall II
©Baedeker
41
38 40
39
Ceremonial Hall
Hall I
D
35 17
16
Gate II
Main Entrance
Hauptstraße
Gate I
Gate III
Gate IV
Simmeringer
Gate V

500 m
1640 ft

A Graves of Honour (see bel
B Austrian Federal Presiden
C Memorial 1938-1945
D Russian Orthodox
E Dead of March 1848
F Victims 1938-1945
G Allies 1914-1918
H Allies 1939-1945

Graves of Honour (selection)

COMPOSERS

1 L. v. Beethoven (died 1827)
2 J. Brahms (died 1897)
3 Ch.W.Gluck (died 1787)
4 J. Lanner (died 1843)
5 K. Millöker (died - 1899)
6 W. A. Mozart (died 1791)
7 H. Pfitzner (died 1949)
8 A. Schönberg (died 1951)
9 F. Schubert (died 1828)
10 R. Stolz (died 1975)
11 J. Strauß, father (died 1849)
12 J. Strauß, son (died 1899)
13 F. v. Suppé (died 1895)
14 H.Wolf (died 1903)
15 C. M. Ziehrer (died 1922)
16 K. Czerny (died 1857)
17 A. Sahen (died 1825)

ACTORS

18 P. Hörbiger (died 1981)
19 W. Krauss (died 1959)
20 Th. Lingen (died 1978)
21 H. Moser (died 1964)
22 A. Skoda (died 1961)
23 R. Albach-Retty (died 1980)
24 C. Jürgens (died 1982)

WRITERS

25 L. Anzengruber (died 1889)
26 E. v. Bauernfeld (died 1890)
27 F. Th. Csokor (died 1975)
28 E. v. Feuchtersleben (died 1849)
29 F. K. Ginskey (died 1963)
30 R. Hawel (died 1923)
31 M. Mell (died 1971)
32 J. Nestroy (died 1862)
33 K. Schönherr (died 1943)
34 J. Schreyvogel (died 1832)
35 B. Viertel (died 1953)
36 F. Werfel (died 1945)
37 A. Wildgans (died 1932)
38 K. Kraus (died 1936)

JEWISH SECTION

39 F. v. Dingelstedt (died 1881)
40 A. Schnitzler (died 1931)
41 F. Torberg (died 1979)

PAINTERS

42 R. Alt (died 1905)
43 F. v. Amerling (died 1887
44 H. Boeckl (died 1966)
45 H. Makart (died 1884)
46 A. v. Pettenkofen (died 1889)

SCULPTORS

47 A. D. v. Fernkorn (died 1878)
48 V. Tilgner (died 1896)
49 F. Wotruba (died 1975)

SCULPTORS

50 Th. E. v. Hansen (died 1891)
51 C. v. Hasenauer (died 1894)
52 J. Hoffmann (died 1956)
53 E. van der Null (died 1868)

SCIENTISTS

54 Th. Billroth, physician (died 1894)
55 L. Boltzmann, physicist (died 1906)
56 A. Negrelli, engineer (died 1858)
57 J. Wagner-Jauregg, psychiatrist and Nobel Prize Winner (died 1940)

Graves of Honour (selection)

36 24
20 31
18
23
49 8
44 27 22 19
21
29 10
57
30 15
34
11 4 56
12 2
9
3
14 6
1
13 51
32 53
26

52 7 33
55
37
50 47
28
48
46
45 43 42
54
25

placed by the Viennese on the final farewell. The diverse and varied tombs symbolize the transfigured death cult, piety, melancholy and, despite all the mourning, an indestructible love of life. With its 2.5 sq km/0.9 sq mi, the Central Cemetery which opened in 1874, is Austria's largest graveyard. The monumental gate of the main entrance was erected in 1905 and designed by **Max Hegele** (1873 – 1945), the reliefs *Christ Anticipating Age* and *Generations Approaching Him* were created by Georg Leisek and Anselm Zinsler. Hegele also built the **Karl Lueger Kirche** dedicated to Saint Charles Borromeo, from 1907 to 1910, which is the focal point of the cemetery grounds. Its decorative elements of rectangular plates identify Hegele as an Art Nouveau architect. Although the church was inspired by Otto Wagner's ▶Kirche am Steinhof, it represents a clear backward step into the period of Historicism.

An avenue leads from the cemetery's main entrance to the graves of famous people and the vault of the Austrian Federal Presidents. A detailed map of the cemetery and its important graves can be obtained at gate II.

Prominent Graves

Among those resting in the »Ehrengräber« (Graves of Honour) on the right side of the central avenue are the composer Hans Pfitzner, the actor Karl Schönherr, the writers Ludwig Anzengruber and Anton Wildgans, the painters Friedrich von Amerling, Hans Makart and Rudolf Alt, the architect Theophil Hansenas, as well as the scientist Theodor Billroth. In the »Ehrengräber« left of the central avenue lie the composers Ludwig van Beethoven, Johannes Brahms, Christoph Willibald Gluck, Wolfgang Amadeus Mozart (this a memorial; his grave is in St Marx Cemetery, ▶Practicalities, Cemeteries), Arnold Schönberg, Johann Strauss (father and son), Josef Strauss, Karl Millöcker, Hugo Wolf, Franz Schubert, Franz von Suppé and Robert Stolz, the actors Paul Hörbiger, Curt Jürgens, Hans Moser and Theo Lingen, the writers Franz Werfel and Johann Nestroy, the sculptor Fritz Wotruba and the architect Karl Hasenauer.

In the Israelite section by gate I are the final resting places of the critic and writer Karl Kraus and the writers Arthur Schnitzler and Friedrich Torberg.

Crematorium

On the other side of Simmeringer Hauptstrasse, opposite the main gate, stands the crematorium, a very eccentric piece of architecture built by **Clemens Holzmeister** in 1922. It was built on the site of the Neugebäude, the former summer palace of Emperor Maximilian. Three fourths of the former imperial pleasure garden are today covered by the crematorium's urn cemetery.

INDEX

LIST OF MAPS AND ILLUSTRATIONS

PHOTO CREDITS

PUBLISHER'S INFORMATION

Illustrations etc: 167 illustrations, 26 maps and diagrams, one large city plan
Text: Eva-Maria Blattner, Jutta Buness, Helga Cabos, Rainer Eisenschmid, Carmen Galenschovski, Dr. Peter Jordan, Dr. Gerda Rob, Dr. Madeleine Reincke, Reinhard Strüber, Jens Wassermann, Bernhard Wolf
Editing: Baedeker editorial team (Natascha Scott-Stokes)
Translation: David Andersen
Cartography: Franz Huber, Munich; MAIRDUMONT/Falk Verlag, Ostfildern (city plan)
3D illustrations: jangled nerves, Stuttgart
Design: independent Medien-Design, Munich; Kathrin Schemel

Editor-in-chief: Rainer Eisenschmid, Baedeker Ostfildern

Based on Baedeker Allianz Reiseführer Wien, 16. Auflage 2010

2nd edition 2011

Copyright: Karl Baedeker Verlag, Ostfildern
Publication rights: MAIRDUMONT GmbH & Co; Ostfildern

Printed in China

BAEDEKER GUIDE BOOKS AT A GLANCE
Guiding the World since 1827

DEAR READER,

We would like to thank you for choosing this Baedeker travel guide. It will be a reliable companion on your travels and will not disappoint you.
This book describes the major sights, of course, but it also recommends the best pubs and restaurants, as well as hotels in the luxury and budget categories, and includes tips about where to eat or go shopping and much more, helping to make your trip an enjoyable experience. Our authors ensure the quality of this information by making regular journeys to Vienna and putting all their know-how into this book.

Nevertheless, experience shows us that it is impossible to rule out errors and changes made after the book goes to press, for which Baedeker accepts no liability. Please send us your criticisms, corrections and suggestions for improvement: we appreciate your contribution. Contact us by post or e-mail, or phone us:

▶ **Verlag Karl Baedeker GmbH**
Editorial department
Postfach 3162
73751 Ostfildern
Germany
Tel. 49-711-4502-262, fax -343
www.baedeker.com
www.baedeker.co.uk
E-Mail: baedeker@mairdumont.com